30 Days Whole Foods Cookbook

600 Whole Food Everyday Recipes For Your 30-Day Challenge

By Sabella Shaw

Table of Contents

Introduction

You are what you eat, and true enough, many people in our modern, fast-paced world are unhealthy as they tend to overindulge in greasy, processed, calorie-dense foods for the sake of convenience. You can reset your body by accepting a 30 Day Whole Food. In just 30 days, you'll change your habits, learn about proper nutrition, reset your metabolism, and genuinely enjoy what REAL food tastes like.

While some types of carbohydrates are healthy and good for you, there has been a tendency over the last century to consume them in excess. Worse still, an increasing amount of the food we consume is processed and highly refined. It leads to many people's health being impacted negatively, while they remain blissfully unaware and continue eating meals that are making them sick. Adverse effects can include low energy levels, random unexplained aches in the body, weight gain/difficulty losing weight, or even certain conditions, such as skin problems or problems with digestion. These may be explained through your diet, as you may be eating more wrong foods than the appropriate options.

An excellent way to get back on track is to go through a total reboot. Fix your diet by changing it completely, taking away all the unhealthy options and begin eating the right foods, foods that have been proven to provide proper sustenance and aid our body's function, especially when consumed in the appropriate quantities. It is not to say that a person cannot treat themselves now and again, but for now, it will be best to cut as much unhealthy food from your life as possible, to better find out where you are in terms of nutrition and diet.

Chapter 1: Whole Foods 101

The whole foods diet is an approach to reducing the amount of packaged, processed, and premade foods consumed. By replacing these less nutritious ingredients that make up a large portion of most diets with nutrient-rich, colorful, filling, and whole tasty ingredients as detailed in this 30-day plan, you'll see improvements in your overall health and energy levels.

Benefits Of Whole 30

Why should you or anyone else follow a Whole30 diet? Well, there's a massive list of advantages of the Whole30 diet, the significant benefits include the following:

- **Clearer and brighter skin, healthy fingernails, and healthy hair:** Once you start to cut down unhealthy and processed foods from your diet, the appearance and condition of your skin, fingernails, and hair will improve drastically.

- **Increased energy:** It has been suggested that the Whole30 can triple a person's energy. This is because you are fueling your body with 100% pure natural energy. However, this increase in energy is not going to happen instantly. You will feel tired and lack energy during the first week of the Whole30, but after your body adjusts itself to the Whole30 diet, you soon will feel a boost in energy.

- **The Whole30 will help you lose weight:** Since you are getting rid of sugar, dairy,

wheat, and junk food from your diet, it will certainly help burn some fat.

- **Improve the quality of sleep.** The Whole30 has been proven to help to improve and to regulate the hormones in your body. It helps with how your body sleeps and improve your sleeping patterns.

- **Mental clarity and better focus:** When you are consuming whole foods, fresh meats, and organic vegetables, it will help you stay healthy, focused, and energized throughout the day.

- **The Whole30 can help fight certain diseases:** Multiple diseases such as diabetes, cerebral palsy, or certain psychological disorders can be eliminated while being on a Whole30 diet. Patients with such diseases and disorders have shown an improvement from these chronic diseases while on the Whole30 diet.

Food Standards Of The Whole Foods

The ingredients should not contain any artificial flavors

There should be no artificial preservatives, sweeteners, and colors.

There should be no use of hydrogenated fats

There should be no antibiotic use on animals providing meat. Also, avoid synthetic nitrates

Consider wild-caught seafood

All cleaning elements and products need to have ingredients that are safe for the environment.

Why Should You Choose Whole Foods?

- It's not as challenging as people perceive think it. Changing your diet is easy. Do you know what's difficult? Fighting off cancer. Giving birth. Losing a loved one. Choosing to drink black coffee pales in comparison to those. It's only thirty days, and these thirty days will allow you to get used to eating healthier and improve your lifestyle for the rest of your life.

- There are no accidents in diets. There are no "oops" moments when it comes to eating, unless someone shoved food in your mouth and forced you to swallow. Do not consider slipping up, as making excuses for yourself may cause you to have failed even before truly beginning.

- Similarly, you always have a choice when you eat. Even if there's a celebration, or a special occasion, whatever you eat is your choice. You could choose to eat healthy, or you could choose to give in to peer pressure like a high school kid. You choose.

- Becoming healthier requires effort. Putting more thoughts in your meals, planning groceries, finding out what's in your restaurant's food, all this needs time and effort. We have laid out the rules and what you need to do, but it's up to you to put it into action.

- It may sound intimidating, but you can do this. Tell your loved ones that you are undergoing this challenge, and they can serve as your support group when it comes to eating healthy.

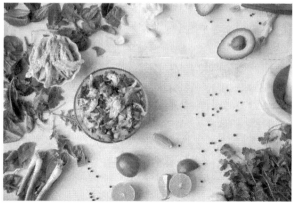

FAQs

What is the Whole30?

The Whole30 is a diet where you eliminate certain food groups from your diet for 30 days to reset your body and reevaluate your relationship with food.

What can I eat during the Whole30?

You can eat real whole food such as meat, seafood, eggs, vegetables, fruit, fats, oils, nuts, and seeds. Natural, unprocessed, and organic food is heavily encouraged on the Whole30.

What can I not eat during the Whole30?
For 30-days, you cannot eat any forms of sugar or sweetener, alcohol, grains, dairy, legumes, and any food that contains carrageenan, MSG, or sulfites.

Will I lose weight on the Whole30?

Most people on the Whole30 will lose weight, but the sole purpose of the Whole30 is not to lose weight but to remove foods and food groups that negatively affect your health.

Can the Whole30 cure diseases and illnesses?

Many people on the Whole30 claims that the Whole30 challenge helped prevent, improved, or cured illnesses such as:
High blood pressure / Type 1 Diabetes/ Type 2 diabetes / High cholesterol /Asthma / Allergies / Skin conditions / Infertility / Bipolar disorders / Depression / Leaky gut syndrome / Joint pain and other illnesses

Can I have a cheat day during the Whole30 challenge?

No, for a successful Whole30 diet, you must be strict not to eat any "cheat" or "junk" foods. Zero exceptions.

Can I adjust the Whole30 diet?

No one is forcing you not to eat the restricted foods. However, you may not experience all the benefits after the 30-days are up.

If I mess up, do I have to reset back to day one?

Most of the time, yes. If you ate birthday cake, drink alcohol, or something sugary, you should think about restarting the Whole30 challenge.

What if I am vegan?

Meat is highly encouraged on the Whole30, but you can still have a successful Whole30 by incorporating Whole30 compliant vegan sources such as nuts and seeds.

Chapter 2: Program Rules for 30 Days

Since Whole Food is not just a diet for losing weight, but a way to switch to a healthy lifestyle, it has several essential rules which are strictly obligatory. If you cannot follow them all; then, do not start the program. If you break even just one of them during the clearance, you should start your whole food challenge from the beginning.

- No any kind of alcohol – even as an additive to food
- No smoking – during the whole month
- No measuring. You are prohibited from weighing or doing any other measurements of your body during the diet. Weigh and measure the waist size on the first day of the program and then at the last one. But not in the middle of the diet
- No calories counting
- Three meals a day is an ideal option, although dried fruits and nuts as snacks are not prohibited. But in reasonable quantities!

Also, a critical thing to remember when doing the Wholefood diet is to check the label on each product you purchase as a lot of prepacked goods have additives or added sugar that you might not be aware of.

Let's say, bacon, sausages, mayonnaise, etc. You might be shocked at the ingredients included in the foods that you once ate. The levels of sodium, sugar, and additives that have names you cannot even pronounce could be preventing you from maintaining a healthy weight. Becoming conscious about every bite you put in your mouth can help you achieve the healthy weight you desire and stay that way!

Guidelines and Planning

Here are some tips to make your Whole Food journey as pleasant as possible.

- Make up your mind, be aware of all possible difficulties and start when you are fully committed
- Plan, plan, and plan one more time. Carefully prepare your first-week meal plan. Then go for the next ones
- Clear out your fridge off all foods that do not match with the Whole Food challenge
- Plan your meals and go shopping according to it. If you are busy, keep one day aside to create your meal plan for the rest of the week. Take your lunch to the office
- Do not cook something you should cook, but something that will make you happy and keep entertained throughout the month (check our recipes below, there are many decent ones to choose from)
- Have emergency snacks in your bag, car, office, parents' house. This could be some nuts or fruits
- Before starting your Whole Food journey, check out all the coming events. Birthdays, parties. The temptation is great. So keep your food-related socializing events at a minimum.
- Involve your friends, family, or housemates – it is always good to go on a diet with company, not alone.
- And most importantly, never give up!

Rules of Whole 30

The four general rules to follow on the Whole30 diet are:

1. No cheating
2. No recreating unhealthy options
3. No stepping on the scale or measuring your body
4. Avoid certain food groups

No cheating on the Whole30

To get the most out of the Whole30 program, it is highly recommended that you don't cheat. The Whole30 is all-or-nothing, so plan ahead – especially if it's around holidays, birthdays, traveling or socializing where you have no control over any available foods and drinks.

If you are a busy person, it's a good idea to have prepared meals in advance. Meals such as soups, stews, and salads can be stored in your refrigerator until ready to eat.

Don't recreate unhealthy foods or drinks.

Many people think that recreating a Whole30 cheesecake is fine as long as the ingredients are Whole30 compliant.

However, you must avoid recreating unhealthy food and drinks even if you are using Whole30 compliant ingredients. This can contribute to unintentional weight gain, physical illness, mental illness, and psychological disorders. Trying to recreate unhealthy food into healthy ones will defeat the purpose of the Whole30, and will only waste your time, energy, and money.

My advice for you is to keep an open mind about new recipes and ingredients. If you restrict yourself to a few meals, you will quickly tire out your taste buds and your patience. Luckily for you, in this book, you will find a diverse set of recipes that you can enjoy each day.

Don't weigh yourself

Daily weighing in and measuring your body is not allowed on the Whole30. The Whole30 diet encourages gradual and safe weight loss. You're not going to find any dramatic change in your weight if you check the scale each day. Instead, weigh and measure yourself before and after the Whole30 diet.

Avoid certain food items

The main rule of the Whole30 diet is to not consume any items from the following food groups:

- Any form of alcohol
- Any form of sugar or sweetener
- Any form of baked goods such as cakes, cupcakes, cheesecakes, cookies
- Dairy
- Processed foods
- Junk food
- Candies and sweets
- Pasta
- Grains
- Starchy foods
- Instant gravy mixes and sauces
- Processed Meats
- Legumes
- Processed snacks

You will find a fully comprehensive list in the "Whole30 Foods to Avoid" section.

Food to Eat:

1. Fruits: Fruits are important in the Whole 30 diets; it helps to fulfill your sugar carving. It contains vitamins, minerals, fiber, and antioxidants. Fruits help to stay hydrated during the summer months.
2. Best choices: Apples, Bananas, Figs, Grapefruit, Lemons, Cherries, Berries, Grapes, Pineapple etc.
3. Vegetables: Vegetables are low in calories and rich in fiber, which is very beneficial for maintaining your cholesterol level. Frozen vegetables also the best option in the Whole 30 diets. Frozen fruits are low cost and also find sometimes more nutrients compared to fresh ones.
4. Best choices: Brussels Sprouts, Carrot, Broccoli, Cauliflower, Kale, Eggplant, Mushrooms, Onion, Potatoes, Spinach, Tomatoes, Zucchini, etc.
5. Unprocessed Meats: During Whole 30 diet, your body needs a massive amount of proteins. Unprocessed meat is the best source of protein.
6. Best choices: Grass-fed beef, organic chicken and pork, etc.
7. Seafood's: Whole 30 diet recommends seafood, which contains omega-3 fatty acids. This helps to improve your brain and heart health.
8. Best choices: Wild-caught fish, Sardines, Salmon, Herring, etc.
9. Eggs: Eggs are the best choice for your breakfast; it is the best when it comes to the source of healthy protein.
10. Fats: You can use good and healthy fat during the Whole 30 diet
11. Best choices: Coconut oil, Avocado oils, Olive oils, Raw nuts, Organic Ghee, etc.
12. Coffee: You can add coffee into your Whole 30 diet. Don't add milk into coffee and add a dash of cinnamon into tour coffee to sweeten lightly.

More on Food to Avoid:

The more crucial aspect of the diet, however, is what the participant should avoid eating during the challenge. Getting rid of the following foods and drinks for the duration of the challenge will help reset yourself, allowing you to resist cravings, improve your metabolism, and get used to a healthier diet. Being able to do this successfully will undoubtedly be a step towards living a better, healthier life.

1. Dairy: Avoid dairy products during the Whole 30 diets except Ghee. You should avoid cheese, sour cream, butter, yogurt, milk, kefir, etc.

2. Added sugar: During Whole 30 diet, all types of sugar are prohibited for 30 days, whether it is artificial or real. You can avoid Maple syrup, Agave, Honey, Stevia, Splenda, Xylitol, etc. Check labels of any packaged product to ensure that they contain no added sugar.

3. Grains: Grains are a source of carbohydrates, and as such, you should try to eliminate them from your diet. Avoid all grains during Whole 30 diet even it is gluten-free. You should avoid Wheat, oats, corn, millet, sorghum, quinoa, sprouted grains, bulgur, rice, amaranth, buckwheat, rye, etc. Make sure to read the labels of any packaged product to ensure that you are not unwittingly consuming grain.

4. Legumes: During 30 days, you should not allow consuming any type of beans and soy. You should strictly avoid peas, lentils, peanut butter, lentils, chickpeas and soy like tofu, soy sauce, miso, tempeh, etc. Remember to check the label for bean products, as soy lecithin is a common component in many commercial foods.

5. Alcohol: Any types of alcohol are strictly avoided during 30 day's diet plans. Even you cannot use alcohol for cooking purposes. In addition to this, do not make use of tobacco products as well.

6. Junk Foods: Eliminate baked goods, treats, and junk food, even when they have "approved" ingredients. Trying to mimic processed junk foods by contorting them in ways that conform to the whole food diet is not what living a healthy whole food lifestyle is all about. There is such a thing as following the letter of the law while violating the spirit of the law, and this is one of those examples. Stay away from the types of foods that led you down the path of unhealthy eating and suboptimal living. Embrace the whole food lifestyle and don't try to "hack" it or "game" it. The point of the challenge is to cleanse your diet, and though certain treats may be from ingredients on the approved list, this defeats the purpose of the diet.

7. Eliminate Monosodium Glutamate and other additives. These additives include sulfites and carrageenan in addition to the aforementioned MSG.

Remember that the reason that you are removing these foods from your diet for the next thirty days is that you are trying to reset your palate and get yourself used to eating healthy. If you continue to indulge, then you will continue to crave these things and will have a harder time when it comes to eating properly. If you are not sure whether or not you should eat something, better leave it out to be safe. After all, you are only removing it 100% from your diet for only thirty days.

Exceptions

Though rules were mentioning what should be avoided 100%, there are certain exceptions.

- Ghee or clarified butter. This is the only type of dairy you may consume.
- Fruit juice. Some products use fruit juice as a sweetener, which is permissible.
- Some legumes. Green beans and snow peas are allowed.
- Vinegar. Most types of vinegar are permitted, such as white, red wine, balsamic, apple cider, and rice vinegar.
- Coconut aminos. These are allowed even if they may have coconut nectar as a listed ingredient.
- Salt. You may wonder why this is in the exception list, but iodized salt contains sugar

as well, and as salt is crucial and thus unavoidable, it is an exception to the no added sugar rule.

Shopping List

I remind you that all foods should be natural (organic is not a must, but the best option). Avoid factory-made products as they usually contain harmful substances such as MSG, sulfites, or added sugar.

Protein: Minced beef/lamb/pork Beef/lamb/pork joint Sausages/bacon/hamChicken /Turkey Salmon /Seafood /Eggs

Vegetables: Acorn squash / Asparagus Beetroots / Broccoli /Brussels sprouts /Butternut squash

Cabbage /Carrots /Cauliflower /Celery /Cucumber Eggplant /Garlic /Green beans /Lettuce /Mushrooms /Onion /Pumpkin /Peppers Radish /Spinach /Sweet potato /Tomato /Turnip /Zucchini

Fruits: Apples /Apricots /Bananas /Blackberries /Blueberries /Cherries /Dates /Grapefruits Grapes /Kiwi /Melon /Oranges /Pears /Plums /Raspberries /Strawberries /Watermelon

Oil: Coconut Oil /Ghee /Extra virgin olive oil /Clarified butter

Store Cupboard: Almonds /Cashew /Hazelnuts /Pistachio /Chili sauce /Coffee /Curry paste Coconut/Almond milk, Coconut/Almond flour Coconut water /Mustard/Walnuts Olives /Tahini /Vinegar /Herbs & Spices /Mayonnaise

Chapter 3: 30-Day Meal Plan

The 30-Day Meal Plan

Day 1
Breakfast: Keto Green Smoothie
Lunch: Creamy and Cheesy Chicken Salad
Dinner: Tilapia and Asparagus
Dessert/Snack: Chili Almond Coated Turkey Bites

Day 2
Breakfast: Bacon Omelets
Lunch: Baba Ghanoush
Dinner: Chinese-Style Turkey Meatballs
Dessert/Snack: Almond Bowls

Day 3
Breakfast: Cinnamon Crispy Waffle
Lunch: Chicken Nuggets
Dinner: Oven-Roasted Pork Cutlets with Veggies
Dessert/Snack: Watermelon Wraps

Day 4
Breakfast: Keto Breakfast Protein Smoothie
Lunch: Soft Cabbage with Garlic and Lemon
Dinner: Bacon Wrapped Chicken with Grilled Asparagus
Dessert/Snack: Spinach and Strawberry Salad

Day 5
Breakfast: Avocado Salmon
Lunch: Delicious and Easy Chicken Drumettes
Dinner: Roasted Salmon
Dessert/Snack: Asian Coconut Chutney

Day 6
Breakfast: Savory Coconut Pancake
Lunch: Grilled Rib Eye Steak
Dinner: Air Fried Chicken
Dessert/Snack: Portobello Mushrooms

Day 7
Breakfast: Fresh Red Jam
Lunch: Tasty Chicken Fajitas
Dinner: Thai Beef Recipe
Dessert/Snack: Squash and Cranberries

Day 8
Breakfast: Eggs and Brussels sprouts Breakfast
Lunch: Shrimp & Mushrooms
Dinner: Juicy and Tender Chicken Breasts
Dessert/Snack: Tomato Chicken Bites

Day 9
Breakfast: Delicious Chicken Frittata
Lunch: Turkey Balls
Dinner: Roasted Summer Squash
Dessert/Snack: Basil Zucchini Spaghetti

Day 10
Breakfast: Tomatoes Casserole
Lunch: Beef and Eggplant Casserole
Dinner: Simple Shredded Chicken
Dessert/Snack: Broiled Brussels Sprouts

Day 11
Breakfast: Squash and Zucchini Pudding
Lunch: Onion Garlic Chicken
Dinner: Lavender Lamb Chops
Dessert/Snack: Paprika Mushrooms with Coconut Flour Naan

Day 12
Breakfast: Breakfast Burger
Lunch: Roasted Herbed Sunchokes
Dinner: Spicy Buffalo Chicken
Dessert/Snack: Stuffed Mushrooms

Day 13
Breakfast: Breakfast Sandwich
Lunch: Spicy Shredded Chicken
Dinner: Dill and Artichoke Salad
Dessert/Snack: Kale Chips

Day 14
Breakfast: Chorizo Breakfast Skillet
Lunch: Pork Chops with Brussels sprouts
Dinner: Flavorful Chicken Curry
Dessert/Snack: Low Carb Cauliflower Hummus

Day 15
Breakfast: Steak and Veggie Breakfast
Lunch: Garlic Lemon Dump Chicken
Dinner: Healthy Beef Roast
Dessert/Snack: Baked Almond Crusted Zucchini Slices

Day 16
Breakfast: Breakfast Sliders
Lunch: Zucchini Hummus
Dinner: Mediterranean Turkey Cutlets
Dessert/Snack: Sweet Strawberry Cream

Day 17
Breakfast: Veggie Omelet Cupcakes
Lunch: Chicken Potato Curry
Dinner: Roasted Eggplant
Dessert/Snack: Stewed Pears

Day 18
Breakfast: Kale & banana smoothie
Lunch: Meatballs Stuffed with Brie
Dinner: Yummy Chicken Tacos
Dessert/Snack: Avocado Cake

Day 19
Breakfast: Super seed & nut butter smoothie
Lunch: Delicious Lemon Thyme Chicken
Dinner: Creamy Mushroom Pork Chops
Dessert/Snack: Avocado pops

Day 20
Breakfast: Endurance smoothie
Lunch: Coconut Ginger Pork
Dinner: Spicy and Juicy Pepperoncini Chicken
Dessert/Snack: Passion Fruit Dessert Cream

Day 21
Breakfast: Sunrise scramble
Lunch: Ginger Sweet Potatoes
Dinner: Spicy Beef with Tomato Sauce
Dessert/Snack: Simple Lemon Pudding

Day 22
Breakfast: Hard-Boiled Eggs
Lunch: Braised Pork with Paprika
Dinner: Sushi Shrimp Rolls
Dessert/Snack: Stuffed Apples

Day 23
Breakfast: Fajita Breakfast Casserole
Lunch: Sour Cream Salmon with Parmesan
Dinner: Classic Garlic Herb Pot Roast
Dessert/Snack: Pomegranate Fudge

Day 24
Breakfast: Blueberry Breakfast
Lunch: Jalapeno Beef
Dinner: Puréed Broccoli and Cauliflower
Dessert/Snack: Strawberry bliss bites

Day 25
Breakfast: Avocado breakfast boats
Lunch: Blackened Fish Tacos with Slaw
Dinner: Pork and Veggie Skewers
Dessert/Snack: Chocolate Cake

Day 26
Breakfast: Breakfast burrito jars
Lunch: Apple Cider Shredded Pork
Dinner: Grilled Shrimp
Dessert/Snack: Ricotta and Dates Cake

Day 27
Breakfast: Breakfast stuffed peppers
Lunch: Zoodles with Mushroom Sauce
Dinner: Yummy Ground Beef Casserole
Dessert/Snack: Simple Kimchi

Day 28
Breakfast: Crispy Potatoes
Lunch: Gluten-Free Beef Rice
Dinner: Lemon Herbed Salmon
Dessert/Snack: Awesome Coleslaw

Day 29
Breakfast: Meat Quiche
Lunch: Cod Coconut Curry
Dinner: Keto Beef Roast
Dessert/Snack: Fried Peppers

Day 30
Breakfast: Savory sweet potato toast
Lunch: Baked Juicy Pork Chunks with
Mushrooms
Dinner: Radish Hash Browns
Dessert/Snack: Apricot Bites

What To Do After 30 Days

After the monthly detox program, the second chapter of your Whole Food 30-day challenge begins – you have to reinstate those products that were eliminated from the diet slowly. Each group of products must be entered separately from the other. You can start with any, but the best is to choose dairy and milk products. So, on the first day after your one-month diet has finished, you start eating dairy products. You eat them throughout the day, and then for four days, you again go back to the whole food diet. It is a time to observe your condition.

You have to note any unpleasant symptoms that have not been seen all month, and now they have appeared again after the first day of reintroduction. It can be anything: bloating and diarrhea, itchy skin and queasiness, headache, and increased blood pressure. Anything that makes you feel bad.

If you did not notice any unpleasant symptoms within four days after the first "milk day," go on to reinstate into the diet, the second group of excluded foods, for example, legumes.

Theoretically, you can return all the excluded products. However, if you seriously approach to tracking your health after introducing a product group into the diet, you will find that not all of them are consumed by your body normally.

In addition, there are groups of products that you should never consume, like harmful vegetable oils, trans fats, sugar.

Chapter 4 Breakfast and Brunch

Keto Green Smoothie

Prep time: 5 minutes, Cook time: 5 minutes, Servings: 1

Ingredients:

1 oz. spinach
1½ cups almond milk
1.6 oz. celery
1.6 oz. cucumber
1/7 oz. avocado
10 drops liquid stevia
1 tbsp. coconut oil
½ tsp. chia seeds (for garnishing)

Instructions:

1. In your blender, add milk and spinach to blend until smooth.
2. Add in the rest of the ingredients and blend again to obtain a smooth and creamy consistency.
3. Set in a glass. Spread with chia seeds for garnishing and enjoy.

Nutritional Info: Calories: 375, Fat: 10.3g, Carbs: 4g, Protein: 30g

Bacon Omelets

Prep time: 10 minutes, Cook time: 10 minutes, Servings: 1

Ingredients:

½ cup chopped bacon
¼ tsp. salt
1 tbsp. olive oil
2 fresh eggs
½ tsp. pepper

Instructions:

1. Crack the eggs and set them in a bowl.
2. Add seasonings and whisk until incorporated.
3. To the egg mixture, add chopped bacon and stir gently.
4. Set up the sauce pan and preheat olive oil over medium heat.
5. Transfer the egg mixture into the sauce pan and cook well.
6. Set the bacon omelets into a serving dish and serve alongside tomato paste.
7. Enjoy.

Nutritional Info: Calories: 249, Carbs: 1.3g, Protein: 9.5g, Fat: 25g

Cinnamon Crispy Waffle

Prep time: 10 minutes, Cook time: 0 minutes, Servings: 2

Ingredients:

4 tbsps. Water
1½ tsps. Baking powder
¼ tsp. salt
3 fresh eggs
2 tsps. Cinnamon
¾ cup flaxseeds
2 tbsps. Avocado oil

Ingredients:

1. Combine flaxseeds, baking powder, and salt in bowl.
2. Pour water into the dry mixture then adds eggs and avocado oil. Stir in cinnamon then mix until smooth.
3. Preheat a waffle maker to moderate heat then pour a scoop of the mixture into it.
4. Once it is done, remove from the waffle maker then place on a serving dish.
5. Repeat with the remaining ingredients.
6. Serve right away.

Nutritional Info: Calories: 90, Fat: 4g, Carbs: 12g, Protein: 1.5g

Keto Breakfast Protein Smoothie

Prep time: 5 minutes, Cook time: 0 minutes, Servings: 1

Ingredients:

1 tbsp. MCT oil
½ tsp. cinnamon
½ cup coconut milk
½ cup water
1 tbsp. ground chia seeds
¼ cup plain whey protein powder

Instructions:

1. Put chia seeds, coconut milk, MCT oil, cinnamon and protein powder into the blender and blend until smooth and frothy.
2. Transfer to a serving glass and enjoy the delicious smoothie.

Nutritional Info: Calories: 467, Fat: 40.2g, Carbs: 4.6g, Proteins: 23.5g

Avocado Salmon

Prep time: 10 minutes, Cook time: 0 minutes, Servings: 1

Ingredients:

¼ cup wild-caught salmon chunks
2 tbsps. Lemon juice
1 ripe avocado
2 tbsps. Olive oil

Instructions:

1. Add lemon juice over salmon chunks and reserve for 10 minutes.
2. Preheat a saucepan and add olive oil in it.
3. Once olive oil is hot, add salmon chunks into the pan and sauté till cooked.
4. Cut avocado into halves and discard its seed.
5. Put the halved avocado on a serving dish and top with cooked salmon chunks.
6. Serve and enjoy.

Nutritional Info: Calories: 262.4, Fat: 16.9g, Carbs: 20.7g, Protein: 10.5g

Savory Coconut Pancake

Prep time: 10 minutes, Cook time: 4 minutes, Servings: 2

Ingredients:

1 tbsp. olive oil
¼ tsp. salt
1 cup coconut milk
½ tsp. baking powder
½ cup coconut flour
¼ tsp. cinnamon
1 fresh egg
1 tsp. vanilla

Instructions:

1. Put baking powder, coconut flour, cinnamon and vanilla in a bowl and stir until combined.
2. Pour egg and coconut milk into the mixture and combine until incorporated.
3. Preheat a nonstick saucepan then rub with olive oil.
4. Pour two tablespoons of the mixture and cook for 2 minutes.
5. Flip to cook for another 2 minutes until both sides are brown.
6. Transfer to a serving dish to serve while warm.

Nutritional Info: Calories: 31.5. Fat: 1.4g, Carbs: 2.2g, Protein: 2.1g

Fresh Red Jam

Prep time: 15 minutes, Cook time: 0 minutes, Servings: 4

Ingredients:

½ tsp. vanilla extract
3 tsps. Chia seeds
3 tsps. Water
1 cup fresh strawberries

Instructions:

1. In a food processor, add all the ingredients and blend well for about 1 minute.
2. Blend the mixture again to the desired consistency.
3. Pour the mixture into a jar and close tightly.
4. Refrigerate for 2 hours until set.
5. Serve and enjoy.

Nutritional Info: Calories: 55.6, Fat: 0g, Carbs: 13.8g, Protein: 0.1g

Eggs and Brussels sprouts Breakfast

Prep time: 10 minutes, Cook time: 4 hours, Servings: 4

Ingredients:

2 minced garlic cloves
Salt
1 tbsp. avocado oil
2 oz. chopped bacon
4 whisked eggs
12 oz. sliced Brussels sprouts
Black pepper
2 minced shallots

Instructions:

1. At the bottom of the Crock pot, drizzle oil and spread out garlic, Brussels sprouts, shallots and bacon.
2. Add pepper, salt, whisked eggs and cook on Low for 4 hours.
3. Divide into plates and serve immediately.
4. Enjoy.

Nutritional Info: Calories: 240, Fat 7g, Carbs: 7g, Protein: 13g

Delicious Chicken Frittata

Prep time: 10 minutes, Cook time: 5 hours, Servings: 5

Ingredients:

2 grated zucchinis
1 tsp. fennel seeds
3 tbsps. Almond flour
¼ tsp. salt
¼ tsp. black pepper
1 tsp. dried oregano
1 lb. ground chicken meat
7 eggs
1 tbsp. olive oil
½ cup coconut cream

Instructions:

1. Combine flour, seasonings, eggs, coconut cream, oregano, fennel, zucchini, meat and whisk well.
2. Pour the mixture into the Crockpot greased with oil and cook on Low for 5 hours.
3. Slice frittata and set into plates to serve.
4. Enjoy.

Nutritional Info: Calories: 300, Fat: 23g, Carbs: 4g, Protein: 18g

Different Chicken Omelet

Prep time: 10 minutes, Cook time: 3 hours, Servings: 2

Ingredients:

1 pitted, peeled and chopped small avocado
1 tsp. mustard
Salt
1 tbsp. homemade mayonnaise
4 eggs
Black pepper
1 chopped tomato
1 oz. shredded rotisserie chicken
2 cooked and crumbled bacon slices

Instructions:

1. Whisk together salt, pepper and eggs in a mixing bowl.
2. To the bowl, add chicken, tomato, avocado, mustard and mayo and toss.
3. Transfer everything into the Crockpot and cover to cook on Low for 3 hours.
4. Put into serving platters and serve.
5. Enjoy!

Nutritional Info: Calories: 270, Fat: 32g, Carbs: 4g, Protein: 25g

Tomatoes Casserole

Prep time: 10 minutes, Cook time: 4 hours, Servings: 4

Ingredients:

5 cubed tomatoes
1 chopped yellow onion
1 tsp. garlic powder
Salt

2 tbsps. Chopped parsley
3 minced garlic cloves
1 tbsp. olive oil
Black pepper

½ tsp. red pepper flakes
2 tsps. Onion powder
¾ cup soaked and drained cashews
½ tsp. dried sage

Instructions:
1. Mix garlic powder, sage, onion powder, cashews, pepper and salt in a blender.
2. Add oil to the crockpot and arrange parsley, garlic, salt and pepper, onion and tomatoes.
3. Add cashews sauce, toss and cover.
4. Cook for 4 hours on High until ready.
5. Serve for breakfast and enjoy.

Nutritional Info: Calories: 218, Fat: 6g, Carbs: 6g, Protein: 5g

---

Squash and Zucchini Pudding

Prep time: 10 minutes, Cook time: 8 hours, Servings: 4

Ingredients:
½ tsp. cinnamon powder
¼ cup chopped walnuts
1 ½ cups almond milk
1 grated zucchini
¼ tsp. ground cloves
1 tsp. vanilla extract
¼ tsp. ground nutmeg
5 oz. grated butternut squash
2 tbsps. Sugar-free maple syrup

Instructions:
1. Combine milk, nutmeg, cloves, zucchini, squash, walnuts, sugar-free maple syrup, cinnamon, and vanilla extract in your Crockpot and stir.
2. Cover to cook on Low for 8 hours.
3. Divide into bowls before serving for breakfast.
4. Enjoy.

Nutritional Info: Calories: 215, Fat: 4g, Carbs: 7g, Protein: 7g

---

Breakfast Burger

Prep time: 30 minutes, Cook time: 15 minutes, Servings: 4

Ingredients:
1 tsp. finely minced garlic
2 tbsps. Almond meal
½ cup ground sausages
8 slices bacon
Black pepper
3 chopped sun-dried tomatoes
5 eggs
2 tsps. Chopped basil leaves
1 lb. ground beef meat
Avocado oil

Instructions:
1. Mix beef meat with 1 egg, tomatoes, almond meal, basil, pepper and garlic in a bowl then stir well to form 4 burgers.
2. Set the pan over medium high heat and add burgers to cook for 4 minutes per side.
3. Heat the same pan over medium high heat and stir in sausages to cook for 5 minutes before transferring into plates.
4. Heat the pan once more and add bacon to cook for minutes, drain the excess grease and set aside.
5. In a pan drizzled with oil, fry the 4 eggs over medium high heat and top up with burgers.
6. Add bacon and sausage before serving.

Nutritional Info: Calories: 264, Fat: 12g, Carbs: 5g, Protein: 32g

---

Breakfast Sandwich

Prep time: 20 minutes, Cook time: 10 minutes, Servings: 2

Ingredients:
1 torn lettuce leaf
3.5 oz. peeled pumpkin flesh
1 pitted and peeled small avocado
4 slices paleo coconut bread
1 finely grated carrot

Instructions:
1. Place the pumpkin flesh in a tray and introduce in the oven to bake for minutes at 350°F.

2. Remove pumpkin from the oven and set aside for 3 minutes.
3. Transfer into a bowl and slightly mash it.
4. Put avocado in a separate bowl to mash with a fork.

5. Spread the avocado on 2 bread slices then add mashed pumpkin, grated carrot and 2 lettuce pieces on each slice.
6. Top them with the remaining bread slices.
7. Serve and enjoy.

Nutritional Info: Calories: 340, Fat: 7g, Protein: 4g, Carbs: 13g

Burger

Prep time: 30 minutes, Cook time: 10 minutes, Servings: 4
Ingredients:
2 tbsps. almond meal
2 tbsps. coconut oil
1 tsp. minced garlic
8 chopped and cooked bacon slices
5 eggs
1 lb. ground beef
2 tsps. basil
3 chopped sun-dried tomatoes
½ cup ground sausage
Instructions:
1. Mix beef with tomatoes, basil, garlic, almond meal and 1 egg in a bowl, stir well and mould into 4 burgers.

2. Heat up a grill over medium high heat and add the burgers to cook for 5 minutes on each side then reserve in plates.
3. Heat a pan over medium high heat and add sausage to cook until done then divide into burgers.
4. Top cooked bacon on sausages and reserve.
5. Heat a pan with coconut oil over medium high heat.
6. Crack one egg at a time to fry them well.
7. Divide the fried eggs on burgers and serve.
8. Enjoy.

Nutritional Info: Calories: 340, Fat: 20g, Carbs: 7g, Protein: 20g

Chorizo Breakfast Skillet

Prep time: 40 minutes, Cook time: 25 minutes, Servings: 2
Ingredients:
3 minced garlic cloves
½ cup chopped cilantro
1 peeled, pitted and chopped small avocado
1 cup chopped kale
8 chopped mushrooms
½ chopped yellow onion
4 chopped bacon slices
½ cup beef stock
2 chopped poblano peppers
4 eggs
1 lb. chopped chorizo
Instructions:
1. Heat up a pan over medium heat, add bacon and chorizo, stir to cook until brown.

2. Stir in peppers, garlic and onions to cook for 6 minutes.
3. Stir in mushroom, kale and stock to cook for 4 more minutes.
4. Make holes in the mix and crack an egg in each hole.
5. Put in an oven to bake for 12 minutes at 350°F.
6. Divide the mix into plates sprinkled with cilantro and avocado topping.
7. Serve and enjoy.

Nutritional Info: Calories: 200, Fat: 6g, Carbs: 6g, Protein: 10g

Steak and Veggie Breakfast

Prep time: 5 minutes, Cook time: 30 minutes, Servings: 4

Ingredients:

2 chopped sweet potatoes
¼ tsp. sea salt
¾ lb. sliced sirloin steak
2 tbsps. Bacon fat
1 chopped red bell pepper
Black pepper
1 chopped yellow onion
1 sliced tomato
4 eggs
1 chopped green bell pepper

Instructions:

1. Heat up a pan with half of the fat over medium high heat, add steak, cook for some minutes until brown and remove from heat.

2. Heat up the pan again with the remaining fat over medium high heat

3. Stir in green and red peppers and onions to cook for 5 minutes.

4. Stir in sweet potatoes to cook for 10 more minutes.

5. Add pieces of steak then make holes to crack an egg in each.

6. Arrange tomato slices and sprinkle with black pepper and salt.

7. Put in an oven to bake for 12 minutes at 350⁰F.

8. Serve warm and enjoy.

Nutritional Info: Calories: 180, Fat: 4g, Carbs: 6g, Protein: 8g

Breakfast Sliders

Prep time: 25 minutes, Cook time: 9 minutes, Servings: 3

Ingredients:

4 bacon slices
3 eggs
3 Portobello mushroom caps
4 oz. smoked salmon

Instructions:

1. Heat up a pan over medium high heat, add bacon, cook until it is crispy, transfer to paper towels and drain grease.

2. Heat up the pan with the bacon grease over medium heat and place egg rings in it.

3. Crack and egg in each, cook them for 6 minutes and transfer them to a plate.

4. Heat up the pan again over medium high heat, add mushroom caps, cook for 5 minutes and transfer them to a platter.

5. Top each mushroom cap with bacon, salmon and eggs. Serve hot.

Nutritional Info: Calories: 180, Fat: 3g, Carbs: 7g, Protein: 8g

Kale & banana smoothie

Prep time: 5 minutes, Cook time: 0 minutes, Servings: 4

Ingredients:

4 ripe bananas
1 peeled and pitted avocado
Ice
4 pitted dates
2 cups kale
¼ tsp. salt
4 cups almond milk

Instructions:

1. In a blender, pulse the dates until broken up.

2. Add the milk, kale, bananas, avocado, salt, and blend until smooth.

3. Add ice or water to increase the volume if desired, blend again, pour into glasses, and serve.

Nutritional Info: Calories: 278, Fat: 6g, Carbs: 54g, Protein: 9g

Veggie Omelet Cupcakes

Prep time: 30 minutes, Cook time: 20 minutes, Servings: 4

Ingredients:

1 chopped yellow bell pepper
4 chopped bacon slices
Black pepper
Chopped spinach
1 chopped green bell pepper
1 chopped tomato
1 chopped red bell pepper
8 eggs
¼ tsp. sea salt
1 chopped white onion

Instructions:

1. Heat up a pan over medium high heat, add bacon, stir; cook until it's crispy, transfer to paper towels, drain grease and leave aside for now.

2. Heat up the same pan with the bacon fat over medium high heat, add onion, stir and cook for 3 minutes.

3. Add tomato, all bell peppers, a pinch of salt and black pepper, stir; cook for a couple more minutes and take off heat.

4. In a bowl; whisk eggs with a pinch of salt and black pepper and mix with veggies and bacon.

5. Stir, divide this into a lined muffin tray, place in the oven at 350 °F and bake for 17 minutes. Leave you special muffins to cool down, divide between plates and serve.

Nutritional Info: Calories: 200, Fat: 4g, Carbs: 5g, Protein: 7g

Super seed & nut butter smoothie

Prep time: 5 minutes, Cook time: 0 minutes, Servings: 4

Ingredients:

1 tsp. vanilla extract
6 cups almond milk
Ice
2 cups cubed cooked sweet potato
2 cups frozen cauliflower florets
¼ cup super-seed and nut butter

Instructions:

1. In a blender, combine the milk, cauliflower, sweet potato, Super Seed & Nut Butter, and vanilla.

2. Blend until smooth.

3. Add ice or water to increase the volume if desired, blend again, pour into glasses, and serve.

Nutritional Info: Calories: 427, Fat: 13g, Carbs: 51g, Protein: 30g

Endurance smoothie

Prep time: 5 minutes, Cook time: 0 minutes, Servings: 4

Ingredients:

2 tbsps. coconut oil
1 tbsp. hemp seeds
1 tbsp. bee pollen
2 bananas
2 cups coconut milk
2 peeled and pitted avocados
2 cups coconut water
Ice
2 cups fresh orange juice

Instructions:

1. In a blender, combine the avocados, bananas, orange juice, coconut milk, coconut water, coconut oil, bee pollen, and hemp seeds, and blend until smooth.

2. Add ice to the blender if desired, blend again, pour into glasses, and serve.

Nutritional Info: Calories: 285, Fat: 3g, Carbs: 61g, Protein: 11g

Sunrise Scramble

Prep time: 10 minutes, Cook time: 15 minutes, Servings: 4

Ingredients:

2 cups spinach
½ tsp. freshly ground black pepper
1 shredded sweet potato
2 minced garlic cloves
2 tsps. ground turmeric
1 tbsp. coconut oil
2 tsps. Balti seasoning
16 oz. drained and dried extra-firm block tofu
1 tsp. salt
¼ cup nutritional yeast
1 cup finely chopped red onion
Chopped avocado or tomatoes

Instructions:

1. In a large skillet over medium heat, heat the coconut oil.

2. Add the onion and sweet potato and cook for 3 to 4 minutes, until the onion softens slightly.
3. Crumble the tofu into the skillet, using your fingers.
4. Add the garlic, turmeric, Balti seasoning, salt, and pepper and cook, stirring occasionally, for about 10 minutes.
5. Stir in the spinach, cooking until wilted.
6. Remove from the heat, sprinkle with the nutritional yeast, and serve.
7. Add avocado or chopped tomatoes, if using.

Nutritional Info: Calories: 335, Fat: 8.1g, Carbs: 36g, Protein: 24.25g

Hard-Boiled Eggs

Prep time: 5 minutes, Cook time: 10 minutes, Servings: 6

Ingredients:

1 tbsp. chopped parsley
6 eggs
1 cup water

Instructions:

1. Place a steamer rack in the Instant Pot.
2. Add the water into the pot.
3. Place the eggs on the rack.
4. Seal the pot.

5. Choose the manual mode.
6. Cook at high pressure for 4 minutes.
7. Release the pressure naturally.
8. Let sit for 5 minutes before peeling.
9. Sprinkle with the parsley.

Nutritional Info: Calories: 63, Fat: 4.4g, Carbs: 0.3g, Protein: 5.5g

Eggs Benedict with Cauliflower

Prep time: 15 minutes, Cook time: 10 minutes, Servings: 2

Ingredients:

2 tsps. Lemon juice
2 eggs
Cooking spray
1 cup water
1 egg yolk
Salt
1 cup sliced cauliflower
Pepper

Instructions:

1. Spray egg cup molds with oil.
2. Add the cauliflower in the Instant Pot.
3. Pour in the water. Place a steamer rack inside the pot.

4. Put the egg molds on top of the rack. Crack the eggs into a bowl.
5. Transfer each without breaking the yolk into the egg molds. Cover the pot
6. Set it to manual. Cook at high pressure for 2 minutes.
7. Release the pressure quickly.
8. Drain the cauliflower and take out the egg cups.
9. In a blender, put the lemon juice, egg yolk, salt and pepper.
10. Blend for 30 seconds.
11. Serve the eggs with the cauliflower and sauce.

Nutritional Info: Calories: 160, Fat: 13.1g, Carbs: 3.4g, Protein: 8g

Fajita Breakfast Casserole

Prep time: 15 minutes, Cook time: 10 minutes, Servings:4

Ingredients:

½ cup sliced green bell pepper
½ cup sliced orange bell pepper
Pepper
1 tbsp. olive oil
Salt
1 tbsp. minced garlic
4 eggs
½ cup sliced onion
½ cup sliced red bell pepper
1 cup water

Instructions:

1. Set the Instant Pot to sauté setting. Pour in the olive oil.
2. Add the onion, garlic and bell peppers. Cook for 5 minutes.
3. Transfer the contents of the Instant Pot to a small baking pan.
4. Crack the eggs on top of the vegetables.
5. Season with the salt and pepper.
6. Cover the pan with foil. Add a steamer rack inside the pot.
7. Pour the water into the bottom of the pot. Place the baking pan on top.
8. Lock the lid in place. Set it to manual. Cook at high pressure for 2 minutes. Release the pressure quickly.

Nutritional Info: Calories: 116, Fat: 8g, Carbs: 5.8g, Protein: 6.3g

Scotch Eggs

Prep time: 20 minutes, Cook time: 10 minutes, Servings: 4

Ingredients:

1 lb. ground sausage
2 cups divided water
1 tbsp. olive oil
4 eggs

Instructions:

1. Place a steamer rack inside the Instant Pot.
2. Add 1 cup water.
3. Put the eggs on top of the rack.
4. Cover the pot. Choose manual setting. Cook at high pressure for 6 minutes. Release the pressure naturally.
5. Place the eggs in a bowl with cold water.
6. Let sit for 5 minutes and peel. Divide the sausage into 4 portions.
7. Flatten each. Wrap the sausage around the egg.
8. Press the sauté setting in the Instant Pot. Add the oil.
9. Cook the eggs with sausage until brown on all sides.
10. Place the steamer rack back to the pot.
11. Add another cup of water into the bottom of the pot.
12. Add the eggs on top of the rack.
13. Seal the pot. Set it to manual. Cook at high pressure for 5 minutes.
14. Do a quick pressure release.

Nutritional Info: Calories: 318, Fat: 26.7g, Carbs: 0.2g, Protein 18.4g

Turkey Sausage & Egg Casserole

Prep time: 15 minutes, Cook time: 3 hours, Servings: 8

Ingredients:

1 cup crumbled turkey breakfast sausage
Salt
Cooking spray
32 oz. cubed frozen hash browns
1 cup almond milk
1 diced onion
Pepper
10 eggs

Instructions:

1. Spray the Instant Pot with oil.
2. Arrange 1/3 of the cubed hash browns on the bottom of the pot.
3. Top with 1/3 of onion and 1/3 of turkey sausage.
4. Repeat the layers.

5. In a bowl, beat the eggs and milk.
6. Season with the salt and pepper.
7. Pour this mixture over the layers.
8. Cover the pot.

9. Press slow cooker function.
10. Cook for 3 hours.
Nutritional Info: Calories: 454, Fat: 26.8g, Carbs: 43.2g, Protein: 11.2g

Meat Quiche

Prep time: 20 minutes, Cook time: 30 minutes, Servings: 4
Ingredients:
1 cup cooked ground beef
Salt
2 chopped green onions
1 cup water
½ cup almond milk
Pepper
6 beaten eggs
1 slice diced ham
Instructions:
1. Place a steamer rack inside the Instant Pot.
2. Add the water.
3. In a bowl, beat the eggs and milk.

4. Season with the salt and pepper.
5. Place the ground beef, ham and green onion in a small baking dish.
6. Pour the egg mixture on top.
7. Cover with foil.
8. Place the baking dish on top of the rack.
9. Cover the pot and set to manual.
10. Cook at high pressure for 30 minutes.
11. Release the pressure quickly.
Nutritional Info: Calories: 377, Fat: 14.3g, Carbs: 3g, Protein: 10.3g

Blueberry Breakfast

Prep time: 10 minutes, Cook time: 3 minutes, Servings:1
Ingredients:
¼ cup sliced blueberries
1 tbsp. chia seeds
1 ½ cup water
¼ tsp. cinnamon powder
¼ cup vegan yogurt
½ cup almond milk
Drops vanilla extract
Instructions:
1. Pour the water into the Instant Pot.

2. Place all the ingredients in a mason jar.
3. Cover with the foil.
4. Seal the pot.
5. Choose manual.
6. Cook at high pressure for 3 minutes.
7. Release the pressure naturally.
Nutritional Info: Calories: 339, Fat: 31g, Carbs: 16.7g, Protein: 4g

Veggie Scrambled Eggs

Prep time: 5 minutes, Cook time: 10 minutes, Servings: 2
Ingredients:
¼ cup chopped tomato
1 tbsp. olive oil
4 beaten eggs
Pepper.
1 tbsp. almond milk
1 diced onion
Salt
Instructions:
1. Beat the eggs, milk, salt and pepper in a bowl.

2. Set the Instant Pot to sauté.
3. Pour in the oil.
4. Add the onion and tomato.
5. Cook until soft.
6. Pour in the egg mixture.
7. Cook, stirring frequently.
Nutritional Info: Calories: 229, Fat: 17.7g, Carbs: 7.2g, Protein: 12.1g

Avocado breakfast boats

Prep time: 10 minutes, Cook time: 0 minutes, Servings: 4

Ingredients:

2 halved and pitted avocados
½ tbsp. flaxseed
2 chopped bananas
¼ cup nut butter
¼ cup super-seed
½ tbsp. hemp seeds

Instructions:

1. In a medium bowl, mix the banana chunks together with the Super Seed & Nut Butter.
2. Place a scoop of the banana mixture into each avocado half.
3. Top each with a sprinkle of hemp and flaxseed and serve.

Nutritional Info: Calories: 220, Fat: 18g, Carbs: 9g, Protein: 12g

Savory sweet potato toast

Prep time: 10 minutes, Cook time: 25 minutes, Servings: 4

Ingredients:

Pinch chipotle pepper flakes
2 sliced sweet potatoes
¼ tsp. salt
4 hard-boiled eggs
1 cup corn and bean salsa
1 avocado

Instructions:

1. Preheat the oven to 350°F.
2. Set a wire baking rack over a baking sheet. Lay each sweet potato slice on the wire rack.
3. Bake for 20 to 25 minutes, until the potato slices start to soften.
4. Remove from the oven. (Steps 1 through 4 can be completed ahead of time. Store the baked slices in the refrigerator to make morning sweet potato toast super quick.).
5. Toast each slice in a toaster.
6. In a medium bowl, mash the avocado together with the eggs (if using).
7. Top each sweet potato slice with a scoop of the salsa and avocado.
8. Sprinkle with salt and chipotle pepper flakes to taste (if using) and serve.

Nutritional Info: Calories: 160, Fat: 7.9g, Carbs: 20.3g, Protein: 3.9g

Super food smoothie bowls

Prep time: 10 minutes, Cook time: 0 minutes, Servings: 4

Ingredients:

½ cup unsweetened shredded coconut
8 pitted dates
½ tsp. salt
2 bananas
Sunflower-oat granola
1 peeled and pitted avocado
2 cups coconut water
2 zucchinis
2 cups almond milk
2 tbsps. cacao powder
1 tbsp. spirulina
2 peeled kiwis
1 tsp. vanilla extract

Instructions:

1. Roughly chop the zucchini, kiwis, bananas, avocado, and dates. (You can place all solid ingredients in a freezer-safe bag and freeze until ready to blend.)
2. In a blender, combine the chopped zucchini, kiwis, bananas, avocado, and dates with the coconut water, milk, shredded coconut, cacao powder, spirulina, vanilla, and salt, and blend until smooth.
3. Pour into bowls, top each bowl with a handful of granolas, and serve.

Nutritional Info: Calories: 510, Fat: 23g, Carbs: 49g, Protein: 32g

Breakfast burrito jars

Prep time: 10 minutes, Cook time: 35 minutes, Servings: 4

Ingredients:

1 cup corn kernels
1 diced red bell pepper
½ diced sweet yellow onion
15 oz. drained and rinsed pinto beans
1 cup quinoa
2 minced garlic cloves
1 tsp. ground cumin
1 tsp. chili powder
Water
Juice of 1 lime
Salt
1 chopped avocado
1 handful fresh cilantro leaves

Instructions:

1. In a slow cooker or large pot with a lid, combine the corn, pepper, onion, beans, quinoa, garlic, cumin, and chili powder.
2. Fill with enough water or broth to cover the ingredients by about 1 inch.
3. If using a slow cooker, cook on low for about 5 hours. If cooking on the stovetop, simmer over low heat for about 30 minutes.
4. Add the lime juice and salt to taste.
5. Portion into jars.
6. Top each with the avocado and cilantro, cover, and refrigerate.

Nutritional Info: Calories: 865, Fat: 68g, Carbs: 35g, Protein: 33g

Breakfast stuffed peppers

Prep time: 10 minutes, Cook time: 30 minutes, Servings: 4

Ingredients:

½ tsp. dried oregano
4 large eggs
2 tbsps. extra-virgin olive oil
1 diced zucchini
½ diced sweet yellow onion
2 diced Yukon Gold potatoes
1 cup spinach
½ tsp. red pepper flakes
Salt
4 bell peppers
Freshly ground black pepper

Instructions:

1. Preheat the oven to 350°F, and line a baking sheet with aluminum foil.
2. Brush the peppers with olive oil and set them on the baking sheet, then cover with foil and bake for about 10 minutes.
3. Meanwhile, in a large skillet over medium-high heat, sauté the potatoes, zucchini, and onion in 2 tablespoons of oil.
4. Once golden, after about 7 minutes, add the spinach, oregano, and red pepper flakes, and sauté until the spinach is wilted. Season to taste with salt and pepper.
5. Remove the peppers from the oven.
6. Divide the filling among each pepper, and crack 1 egg into each half.
7. Cover with foil
8. Bake for 15 minutes, or until the eggs are cooked to your desired consistency. Serve or cool and refrigerate.

Nutritional Info: Calories: 201.0, Fat: 12.1g. Carbs: 9.1g, Protein: 14.8g

Crispy Potatoes

Prep time: 10 minutes, Cook time: 5 minutes, Servings: 4

Ingredients:

1 cup water
1 lb. sliced potatoes
2 tbsps. ghee
Sea salt
Black pepper
¼ cup chopped chives

Instructions:

1. Pour the water into the Instant Pot.
2. Add the potatoes. Cover the pot. Choose manual mode.
3. Cook at high pressure for 5 minutes. Release the pressure naturally.
4. Press the sauté setting. Add the ghee.
5. Add the boiled potatoes.
6. Season with the salt and pepper. Cook until brown and crispy.
7. Toss with the chives.

Nutritional Info: Calories: 135, Fat: 6.5g, Carbs: 18g, Protein: 2g

Potato Egg Frittata

Prep time: 20 minutes, Cook time: 20 minutes, Servings: 4

Ingredients:

4 oz. potatoes, sliced into thin strips
6 eggs
Salt
Black pepper
¼ cup almond milk
1 tsp. tomato paste
¼ cup chopped onion
1 minced clove garlic
Cooking spray
1 tbsp. ghee
1½ cups water

Instructions:

1. Soak the potato strips in water for 20 minutes.
2. While waiting, beat the eggs and season with the salt and pepper.
3. In another bowl, blend the milk and tomato paste.
4. Add this to the egg mixture.
5. Add the onions and garlic to the egg mixture.
6. Spray a small baking dish with oil.
7. Pat the potato sticks with paper towel to dry.
8. Add the potatoes to the egg mixture. Stir in the ghee.
9. Pour this mixture into a baking dish.
10. Add the water to the Instant Pot.
11. Place a steamer rack inside.
12. Put the baking dish on top of the rack.
13. Seal the pot. Choose manual. Cook at high pressure for 20 minutes.
14. Release the pressure naturally.

Nutritional Info: Calories: 183, Fat: 13.5g, Carbs: 7g, Protein: 9.3g

Chapter 5 Soups and Stews

Butternut Squash Soup

Prep time: 15 minutes, Cook time: 3 hours, Servings: 6

Ingredients:

4 cups vegetable broth
1 chopped large butternut squash
3 peeled and chopped large carrots
3 minced garlic cloves
Fresh ground black pepper
1 chopped onion

Instructions:

1. Add all the ingredients to the slow cooker.

2. Cover the slow cooker to cook on low for 3 hours until the squash becomes tender.
3. Blend the mixture to a desired consistency using an immersion blender.
4. Serve in bowls garnished with pepper.

Nutritional Info: Calories: 100, Fat: 2.5g, Carbs: 20g, Protein: 2g

Turkey Cauliflower Soup

Prep time: 25 minutes, Cook time: 45 minutes, Servings: 4

Ingredients:

1 ½ cups minced cauliflower
4 cups coarsely chopped kale
Pepper
1 lb. ground turkey
5 cups chicken stock
3 sliced carrots
15 oz. can diced tomatoes
1 sliced bell pepper
4 chopped shallots
2 tbsps. coconut oil
Salt

Instructions:

1. Heat up your saucepan with coconut oil. Add the shallots, carrots, cauliflower, and bell pepper.

2. Cook for about 8-10 min. until the vegetables are slightly soft, stirring frequently. Add the turkey and cook for about 6-8 min. until the meat is cooked through.
3. Pour the chicken stock in the saucepan. Add tomatoes. Sprinkle everything with pepper and salt.
4. Bring the soup to a boil. Stir in the kale, reduce the heat to low, and let it simmer, covered, for 12-15 min.

Nutritional Info: Calories: 245, Fat: 20 g, Carbs: 28 g, Protein: 37 g

Easy Red Curry Soup

Prep time: 10 minutes, Cook time: 5 minutes, Servings: 1

Ingredients:

½ tbsp. powdered ginger
Cooked spaghetti squash
2 tbsps. red curry paste
Leftover cooked veggies
½ can fire-roasted diced tomatoes
Leftover cooked meat
½ cup coconut milk

Instructions:

1. Add coconut milk, tomatoes, curry paste and ginger to a small saucepan. Stir with a whisk to combine.
2. Cook for about 5 minutes until the mixture bubbles.
3. Add cooked veggies and meat until heated through. Pour over spaghetti squash to serve.

Nutritional Info: Calories: 165, Fat: 10g, Carbs: 11g, Protein: 6g

Stuffed Pepper Soup

Prep time: 15 minutes, Cook time: 45 minutes, Servings: 6

Ingredients:

2 cups chicken broth
1 lb. ground beef
15 oz. unsweetened tomato sauce
4 cups cauliflower florets
1 diced green bell pepper
1 tsp. garlic powder
Salt
14.5 oz. diced tomatoes
Pepper
1 diced onion
2 tsps. coconut oil

Instructions:

1. Heat coconut oil in a large pot. Add onion, bell pepper, and ground beef. Cook breaking up the beef until no pink remains.

2. Add in tomatoes, the broth, garlic powder, and tomato sauce. Season with salt and pepper. Bring to a boil; cover and simmer for 20 minutes.

3. Meanwhile, grate your cauliflower (or process in a food processor) to make cauliflower rice.

4. Heat the coconut oil. Add the grated cauliflower and season with salt and pepper. Cook, frequently stirring, for 3-5 minutes or until the cauliflower rice has softened.

Nutritional Info: Calories: 170, Fat: 3g, Carbs: 10g, Protein: 12g

Aromatic Beef Stew

Prep time: 20 minutes, Cook time: 45 minutes, Servings: 6

Ingredients:

½ cup cremini mushrooms
2 quarts beef broth
2 lbs. beef stew
3 chopped celery stalks
4 cubed potatoes
Herbs
Extra virgin olive oil
1 roughly chopped big yellow onion
2 garlic cloves
3 chopped carrots
32 oz. peeled tomatoes

Instructions:

1. Heat up a sauté' pan with olive oil, put garlic in, stir and fry for 1-2 minutes.

2. Add beef, brown from both sides. When it is ready, drain the liquid off and set aside.

3. Wipe pan clean quickly, add some more olive oil to the pan, and turn the heat on. Add onion, carrot, celery stalks, and sauté'. Add beef, stir it well and keep sautéing.

4. Take out a 16-quart stockpot. Add 2 quarts of broth. After, add the potatoes, mushrooms, and peeled tomatoes.

5. Simmer on the stove for 45-55 minutes.

6. Top with herbs and serve.

Nutritional Info: Calories: 320, Fat: 12.2 g, Carbs: 27 g, Protein: 26g

Sunday Beef Stew

Prep time: 8 hours, Cook time: Servings: 6

Ingredients:

½ lb. chopped broccoli
1 bay leaf
1 tsp. pepper
6 sliced carrots
4 minced garlic cloves
1 tbsp. balsamic vinegar
1 diced yellow onion
1½ lbs. cubed beef chuck

½ tsp. dried rosemary
1¾ lbs. peeled and cubed red potatoes
1½ cup beef stock
4 tbsps. tomato paste
1 tsp. salt

Instructions:

1. First, slice up the beef chuck, and place the pieces in the bottom of the slow cooker. Season with salt and pepper.
2. Next, add the tomato paste, the vinegar, and the stock to the slow cooker, and stir well with a wooden spoon.
3. Add the bay leaf, rosemary, and garlic next, along with the potatoes, and the onions. Add the carrots last. Don't stir.
4. Next, place the lid on the slow cooker, and cook on HIGH for five hours or LOW for 8 hours.
5. During the last 40 minutes of cooking, add the broccoli. Serve the stew warm, and enjoy.

Nutritional Info: Calories: 306, Carbs: 34 g, Protein: 27 g, Fat: 7 g

Asian Turkey Soup

Prep time: 40 minutes, Cook time: 5 hours, Servings: 4

Ingredients:

1 tbsp. grated ginger
1 cup chopped broccoli
26 oz. coconut milk
1 sliced lime
2 cups chopped cooked turkey breast
2 cups low-sodium chicken broth
2 cups peeled and cubed butternut squash
1 diced onion
2 tbsps. red curry paste
1 diced onion

Instructions:

1. First, add all of the ingredients, except for the lime, to the slow cooker.
2. Cover the slow cooker and cook on HIGH for five hours or on LOW for seven hours. The vegetables should be tender.
3. At this time, serve the soup warm, with a few bits of lime on the top. Enjoy.

Nutritional Info: Calories: 331, Carbs: 19 g, Protein: 26 g, Fat: 15 g

Butternut Squash Soup

Prep time: 40 minutes, Cook time: 8 hours, Servings: 6

Ingredients:

3 peeled and chopped carrots
1 tsp. dried thyme
2 minced garlic cloves
½ tsp. sea salt
1 cup almond milk
½ tsp. pepper
6 cups chopped butternut squash
2 cups vegetable stock
2 cored, peeled, and chopped apples

Instructions:

1. First, add the carrots, squash, apples, garlic, stock, onion, and the spices to the bottom of the slow cooker. Stir well, and then add the stock. Place the lid on the slow cooker and cook on LOW for eight hours.
2. Next, add the almond milk. Stir well. Add the soup to a blender and blend until smooth, or use an immersion blender if you have one. If you want to have a thinner consistency, feel free to add additional vegetable stock.
3. Season to taste, and enjoy.

Nutritional Info: calories: 211, Carbs: 32 g, Protein: 3 g, Fat: 10 g

Cacao Chili

Prep time: 40 minutes, Cook time: 3 hours, Servings: 12

Ingredients:

6 diced and deseeded jalapeno peppers
1 tbsp. olive oil
½ tbsp. cacao powder
2 diced onions
4 ½ lbs. ground beef

2 tbsps. arrowroot powder
2 tbsps. cumin, ground
2 tbsps. garlic powder
28 oz. diced tomatoes
3 tbsps. ground ancho chili powder

1/3 cup beef stock
2 diced poblano peppers
2 tbsps. chopped oregano leaves
2 tbsps. water

Instructions:

1. First, add the ground beef to a skillet and brown it in batches before adding it to the slow cooker. Chop all the vegetables as you cook the beef and set them to the side.
2. Next, after the beef is browned, add the olive oil to the skillet, and add the vegetables, sautéing until the onions begin to turn clear.
3. Next, add the seasonings to the skillet, and cook until fragrant. When finished, there shouldn't be any liquid at the bottom of the pan.
4. At this time, drain the tomatoes and add them to the skillet, stirring well. At this time, pour this skillet mixture over the ground beef, without stirring.
5. Add the beef stock to the slow cooker, place the lid on, and then cook on HIGH for three hours.
6. Afterwards, stir together the arrowroot powder and the water in a small bowl to create a slurry. Add the slurry, along with the cacao powder, to the slow cooker, and stir well.
7. Season to taste, adding salt if you desire, and then cook on HIGH for an additional hour. Serve warm, and enjoy.

Nutritional Info: Calories: 362, Carbs: 8 g, Fat: 12 g, Protein: 53 g

Roasted Red Pepper Soup with Garden Tomatoes

Prep time: 30 minutes, Cook time: 8 hours, Servings: 8

Ingredients:

3 chopped celery stalks
½ cup coconut milk
1 tsp. pepper
15 oz. roasted red peppers
80 oz. tomatoes
1/3 cup chopped basil, fresh
1 diced onion
4 cups vegetable broth
1 bay leaf
2 chopped and peeled carrots
1 tsp. salt

Instructions:

1. Add the entire list of ingredients to the slow cooker and give the mixture a good stir, incorporating everything.
2. Place the lid on the slow cooker. Cook on LOW for eight hours. Afterwards, blend the soup in batches in the blender, or else use an immersion blender within the actual pot. Season the soup with salt and pepper to taste.
3. If you want a creamier tomato soup, feel free to use a half-cup of coconut milk after it's cooked. Blend well.

Nutritional Info: Calories: 75, Carbs: 16 g, Protein: 3 g, Fat: 1 g

Lemon and Kale Chicken Soup

Prep time: 20 minutes, Cook time: 6 hours, Servings: 6

Ingredients:

3 tbsps. lemon juice
1 tsp. sea salt
1 bunch kale
Zest from 3 lemons
1 cup diced onion
6 cups chicken broth
½ cup olive oil
4 cups shredded chicken

Instructions:

1. First, wash the kale and slice it.
2. Next, add two cups of the stock, olive oil, and onion to a blender and blend for two minutes, or until it's smooth. Add this mixture to the slow cooker, along with the rest of the broth, kale, chicken, lemon juice, and lemon zest. Add the salt and give the mixture a stir.
3. Allow the soup to cook on LOW for six hours. Stir occasionally.
4. Serve warm, and enjoy.

Nutritional Info: Calories: 349, Carbs: 6 g, Protein: 33 g, Fat: 21 g

Show the Love to Sweet Potato Chili

Prep time: 30 minutes, Cook time: 4 hours, Servings: 10

Ingredients:

3 minced garlic cloves
2 diced sweet potatoes
1 diced onion
4 tbsps. chili powder
2 lbs. ground beef
28 oz. tomato sauce
3 cups beef stock
½ tsp. oregano
2 tsp. salt
½ tsp. black pepper
14 oz. minced tomatoes

Instructions:

1. First, place the ground beef in a skillet over medium heat. Brown until cooked all the way through, and then drain the fat. Add the beef to the slow cooker, along with the rest of the ingredients. Stir the mixture to combine well.
2. Next, cook on LOW for eight hours or on HIGH for four hours. Afterwards, stir to incorporate the meat, and then serve warm.

Nutritional Info: Calories: 286, Carbs: 25 g, Protein: 31 g, Fat: 6 g

Southern Texas Chicken Soup

Prep time: 30 minutes, Cook time: 4 hours, Servings: 8

Ingredients:

½ pint halved cherry tomatoes
4 cups spinach
Lime juice
1 diced onion
2 lbs. boneless and skinless chicken breasts
1 tsp. cumin
32 oz. chicken stock
4 cups water
½ tsp. chili powder
3 chopped zucchinis
15 oz. tomato sauce
3 tsps. salt
½ cup cilantro

Instructions:

1. First, add the chicken, onion, tomato sauce, spices, stock, and the water to the slow cooker. Cover the slow cooker and cook on HIGH for four hours or on LOW for seven hours. The chicken should be completely cooked through.
2. When it's finished, remove the chicken and shred it using two forks. Then, add the chicken back to the slow cooker. Add the greens and the zucchini, and cover once more. Cook for an extra 30 minutes. The zucchini and spinach should be tender.
3. Next, add the lime juice, and serve the soup topped with the tomatoes, and the cilantro. Enjoy.

Nutritional Info: Calories: 259, Carbs: 8 g, Protein: 35 g, Fat: 9 g

Asian Turkey Soup

Prep time: 20 minutes, Cook time: 7 hours, Servings: 4

Ingredients:

1 cup chopped broccoli
1 sliced lime
26 oz. coconut milk
2 tbsps. red curry paste
2 cups cubed and peeled butternut squash
2 cups cooked and chopped turkey breast
1 diced onion
1 tbsp. grated ginger
2 cups low-sodium chicken broth

Instructions:

1. First, add all of the ingredients, except for the lime, to the slow cooker.
2. Cover the slow cooker and cook on HIGH for five hours or on LOW for seven hours. The vegetables should be tender.
3. At this time, serve the soup warm, with a few bits of lime on the top. Enjoy.

Nutritional Info: Calories: 331, Protein: 26g, Fat: 15g, Carbs: 19g

Artichoke Chicken Soup

Prep time: 40 minutes, Cook time: 8 hours, Servings: 6

Ingredients:
2 lbs. skinless and boneless chicken breasts
1/3 cup chopped parsley
3 diced celery stalks
1 diced onion
1 tsp. pepper
1/3 cup lemon juice
14 oz. artichoke hearts
1 bay leaf
3 cups peeled and cubed turnips
7 cups chicken broth
4 minced garlic cloves
2 diced carrots
1 tsp. salt

Instructions:
1. Add everything listed above to the slow cooker—except for the parsley and the lemon juice. Cover the slow cooker and cook on LOW for eight hours.
2. Afterwards, remove the chicken. Shred the chicken and add it back to the slow cooker and give the soup a good stir.
3. To serve, salt and pepper the soup well, and then add the lemon juice and the parsley. Stir, and enjoy.

Nutritional Info: calories: 280, Carbs: 14 g, Protein: 37 g, Fat: 5 g

Sunday Beef Stew

Prep time: 20 minutes, Cook time: 5 hours, Servings: 6

Ingredients:
1½ c. beef stock
½ tsp. dried rosemary
Salt
1¾ lbs. cubed and peeled red potatoes
½ lb. chopped broccoli
1 tbsp. balsamic vinegar
1 diced yellow onion
1½ lbs. cubed beef chuck
Pepper
4 tbsps. tomato paste
1 bay leaf
4 minced garlic cloves
6 sliced carrots
Instructions:

1. First, slice up the beef chuck, and place the pieces in the bottom of the slow cooker. Season with salt and pepper.
2. Next, add the tomato paste, the vinegar, and the stock to the slow cooker, and stir well with a wooden spoon.
3. Add the bay leaf, rosemary, and garlic next, along with the potatoes, and the onions. Add the carrots last. Don't stir.
4. Next, place the lid on the slow cooker, and cook on HIGH for five hours or LOW for eight hours.
5. During the last 40 minutes of cooking, add the broccoli. Serve the stew warm, and enjoy.

Nutritional Info: Calories: 306, Protein: 27g, Fat: 7g, Carbs: 34g

Whole Food Cacao Chili

Prep time: 20 minutes, Cook time: Servings: 12

Ingredients:
2 tbsps. chopped oregano leaves
28 oz. diced tomatoes
Beef stock
1 tbsp. olive oil
2 diced onions
4½ lbs. ground beef
6 seedless and diced jalapeno peppers
2 tbsps. garlic powder
2 tbsps. ground cumin

2 tbsps. arrowroot powder
2 tbsps. water
2 diced seedless poblano peppers
3 tbsps. ground ancho chili powder
½ tbsp. cacao powder

Instructions:
1. First, add the ground beef to a skillet and brown it in batches before adding it to the

slow cooker. Chop all the vegetables as you cook the beef and set them to the side.

2. Next, after the beef is browned, add the olive oil to the skillet, and add the vegetables, sautéing until the onions begin to turn clear.

3. Next, add the seasonings to the skillet, and cook until fragrant. When finished, there shouldn't be any liquid at the bottom of the pan. Add this mixture to the slow cooker.

4. At this time, drain the tomatoes and add them to the skillet, stirring well for a few minutes. Next, pour this tomato mixture over the ground beef, without stirring.

5. Add the beef stock to the slow cooker, place the lid on, and then cook on HIGH for three hours.

6. Afterwards, stir together the arrowroot powder and the water in a small bowl to create a slurry. Add the slurry, along with the cacao powder, to the slow cooker, and stir well.

7. Season to taste, adding salt if you desire, and then cook on HIGH for an additional hour. Serve warm, and enjoy.

Nutritional Info: Calories: 362, Protein: 53g, Fat: 12g, Carbs: 8g

Southern Texas Chicken Soup

Prep time: 20 minutes, Cook time: 4 hours, Servings: 8

Ingredients:

½ cup cilantro
Juice from 2 limes
4 cups water
½ tsp. chili powder
15 oz. tomato sauce
½ pint halved cherry tomatoes
1 diced onion
3 tsps. salt
1 tsp. cumin
4 cups spinach
2 lbs. skinless and boneless chicken breasts
3 chopped zucchinis
32 oz. chicken stock

Instructions:

1. First, add the chicken, onion, tomato sauce, spices, stock, and the water to the slow cooker.

Cover the slow cooker and cook on HIGH for four hours or on LOW for seven hours. The chicken should be completely cooked through.

2. When it's finished, remove the chicken and shred it using two forks. Then, add the chicken back to the slow cooker. Add the greens and the zucchini, and cover once more. Cook for an extra 30 minutes. The zucchini and spinach should be tender.

3. Next, add the lime juice, and serve the soup topped with the cherry tomatoes, and the cilantro.

Nutritional Info: Calories: 259, Protein: 35g, Fat: 9g, Carbs: 8g

Butternut and Apple Soup with Crispy Leeks

Prep time: 20 minutes, Cook time: 4 hours, Servings: 6

Ingredients:

2 ½ cups chicken broth
2 lbs. peeled, cubed and seeded butternut squash
½ cup coconut milk
1 diced medium carrot
1 peeled, cored and diced medium Granny Smith apple
1 chopped leek

Instructions:

1. To the slow cooker add: broth, squash, apples, and leeks. Place the lid on the slow cooker

and cook on HIGH for four hours or LOW for eight hours.

2. Stir in the coconut milk after the cooking time is completed. Using an immersion blender, blend the soup inside the slow cooker until smooth. Alternatively, you could use a regular blender and blend the soup in batches.

3. Serve warm garnished with extra leeks, drizzled with olive oil and coconut milk.

Nutritional Info: Calories: 150, Protein: 4g, Fat 7g, Carbs: 20g

Full Body Cleansing Vegetable Soup

Prep time: 13 minutes, Cook time: 8 minutes, Servings: 4

Ingredients:

2 finely chopped small-sized yellow onions
1 chopped medium-sized red pepper
4 minced garlic cloves
2 finely chopped medium-sized celery stalks
6 cups low sodium vegetable stock
2 tbsps. olive oil
1 tsp. freshly ground black pepper
2 peeled and chopped large carrots
14.5 oz. undrained crushed tomatoes
1 finely chopped small fresh broccoli head
1 chopped medium-sized fresh zucchini
1 chopped medium-sized yellow pepper
2 tsps. Italian seasoning
1 tsp. sea salt

Instructions:

1. Add all the ingredients to your Instant Pot besides the zucchini, bell pepper, and broccoli.
2. Lock the lid and ensure the valve is closed.
3. Press the "Manual" button and cook for 2 minutes on High Pressure.
4. When the cooking is done, quick release the pressure and remove the lid.
5. Stir the broccoli, zucchini, and bell pepper to your Instant Pot.
6. Place the lid on your Instant Pot and allow to sit in your Instant Pot for 5 minutes or until the vegetables have softened. Serve and enjoy!

Nutritional Info: Calories: 223, Fat: 0.8g, Carbs: 16.3g, Protein: 13g

Heroic Cauliflower and Fennel Soup

Prep time: 10 minutes, Cook time: 20 minutes, Servings: 4

Ingredients:

3 cups homemade low-sodium vegetable broth
1 finely chopped medium-sized onion
1 tsp. freshly ground black pepper
2 medium-sized fennel bulbs
1 tbsp. coconut oil
3 minced garlic cloves
1 lb. chopped raw cauliflower florets
1 tsp. sea salt

Instructions:

1. Press the "Sauté" function on your Instant Pot and add the coconut oil.
2. Once the display reads hot, add the onion and sauté for 5 minutes or until translucent, stirring occasionally.
3. Add the cauliflower, fennel, and garlic to your Instant Pot and sauté for 5 to 10 minutes or until golden brown, stirring occasionally.
4. Add the vegetable broth to your Instant Pot.
5. Lock the lid and ensure the valve is closed. Press the "Manual" button and cook for 5 minutes on High Pressure.
6. When the cooking is done, quick release the pressure and remove the lid.
7. Use an immersion blender to blend the soup until smooth. Alternatively, you can transfer the contents to a blender and blend until reach your desired consistency.
8. Season the soup with salt and black pepper. Serve and enjoy!

Nutritional Info: Calories: 276, Fat: 19.1g, Carbs: 21.9g, Protein: 9.2g

Celebrated Sweet Potato Soup

Prep time: 16 minutes, Cook time: 15 minutes, Servings: 6

Ingredients:

½ tsp. organic ground cinnamon powder
1 tsp. freshly ground black pepper
4 cups low-sodium vegetable
2 cups plain water
1 finely chopped medium-sized yellow onion
2 lbs. peeled and sliced sweet potatoes
4 minced garlic cloves
1 tbsp. olive oil

1 tsp. organic smoked paprika
1 tsp. sea salt
Instructions:
1. Press the "Sauté" function on your Instant Pot and add 1 tablespoon of olive oil.
2. Once the display reads hot, add the onions and sauté for 4 minutes or until translucent, stirring occasionally.
3. Add the minced garlic and sauté for 1 minute, stirring occasionally.
4. Add the 2 pounds of sweet potatoes, vegetable or chicken stock, smoked paprika, and

cinnamon powder to your Instant Pot. Give a good stir.
5. Place and seal the lid on your Instant Pot. Press the "Manual" button and cook for 10 minutes on High Pressure.
6. When the cooking is done, quick release the pressure and carefully remove the lid.
7. Use an immersion blender to blend the contents in your Instant Pot until smooth.
8. Stir in salt, and black pepper.
9. Serve and enjoy!
Nutritional Info: Calories: 261, Fat: 7.8g, Carbs: 46.1g, Protein: 3.6g

Pleasurable and Healthy Green Chicken Soup

Prep time: 15 minutes, Cook time: 8 minutes, Servings: 8
Ingredients:
1 tbsp. dried oregano
1 lb. fresh boneless and skinless chicken breasts
1 tsp. garlic powder
1 cup sliced shiitake mushrooms
1 tsp. onion powder
4 peeled and sliced carrots
1 tsp. sea salt
1 stemmed and chopped large bunch kale
8 cups homemade low-sodium chicken stock
1 tsp. freshly ground black pepper
Instructions:
1. In a blender or food processor, add 6 cups of homemade low-sodium chicken stock and a large bunch of chopped kale. Pulse until smooth and relatively creamy.

2. Add the kale mixture and the remaining ingredients to your Instant Pot.
3. Place and seal the lid on your Instant Pot. Press the "Manual" button and cook for 8 minutes on High Pressure.
4. When the cooking is done, naturally release the pressure and remove the lid.
5. Transfer the chicken to a serving platter and shred using two forks.
6. Return the shredded chicken to your Instant Pot and stir until well combined with the kale-stock mixture.
7. Serve and enjoy
Nutritional Info: Calories: 126, Fat: 2.3g, Carbs: 7.5g, Protein: 18.6g

Brazilian Shrimp Stew

Prep time: 25 minutes, Cook time: 13 minutes, Servings: 6
Ingredients:
¼ cup roasted and diced red pepper
1 minced garlic clove
¼ cup chopped fresh cilantro
¼ cup olive oil
1½ lbs. peeled and deveined raw shrimp
14 oz. diced tomatoes with chilies
2 tbsps. Sriracha hot sauce
1 cup coconut milk
Salt
2 tbsps. lemon juice
¼ cup diced onions
Black pepper

Instructions:
1. Heat olive oil in a medium saucepan and add garlic and onions.
2. Sauté for about 3 minutes and add peppers, tomatoes, shrimp and cilantro.
3. Simmer for about 5 minutes and add coconut milk and Sriracha sauce.
4. Cook for about 5 minutes and stir in lime juice, salt and black pepper.
5. Garnish with fresh cilantro and serve hot.
Nutritional Info: Calories: 316, Carbs: 7.4g, Fat: 19.9g, Proteins: 26.

Lovely Polish-Inspired Cabbage Soup

Prep time: 21 minutes, Cook time: 15 minutes, Servings: 6

Ingredients:

1 tsp. onion powder
1 lb. sliced pork
1 tsp. sea salt
4 cups low-sodium chicken stock
1 tsp. freshly ground black pepper
2 tbsps. olive oil
14 oz. undrained diced tomatoes
2 lbs. rinsed sauerkraut
14 oz. tomato sauce
1 cored and thinly sliced large head fresh green cabbage
1 tsp. garlic powder

Instructions:

1. Press the "Sauté" function on your Instant Pot and add the olive oil.
2. Once the display reads hot, working in batches if necessary, add the pork strips and sauté until brown. Turn off "Sauté" function and add all the pork strips back to the inner pot.
3. Add the sauerkraut, green cabbage, diced tomatoes, tomato sauce, chicken stock, onion powder, and garlic powder to your Instant Pot.
4. Lock the lid and ensure the valve is closed on your Instant Pot. Press the "Manual" button and cook for 15 minutes on High Pressure.
5. When the cooking is done, naturally release the pressure and carefully remove the lid.
6. Give the cabbage soup a good stir and season the soup with salt and pepper.
7. Serve and enjoy!

Nutritional Info: Calories: 245, Fat: 8.3g, Carbs: 20.9g, Protein: 24.7g

Bacon Cabbage Chuck Beef Stew

Prep time: 10 minutes, Cook time: 7 hours, Servings: 6

Ingredients:

1 small Napa cabbage
1 cup homemade beef bone broth
½ lb. bacon strips
1 minced garlic clove
Salt
2 lbs. sliced grass-fed chuck roast
2 peeled and sliced small red onions
Black pepper
1 sprig fresh thyme

Instructions:

1. Put bacon slices, onion slices and garlic at the bottom of the slow cooker.
2. Layer with the chuck roast, followed by the cabbage slices, thyme and broth.
3. Season with salt and black pepper, and cook on LOW for 7 hours.
4. Dish out and serve hot.

Nutritional Info: Calories: 170, Carbs: 3.7g, Fat: 9g, Protein: 19.6g

Thai Pumpkin Seafood Stew

Prep time: 5 minutes, Cook time: 45 minutes, Servings: 12

Ingredients:

32 fresh and alive medium-sized mussels
32 fresh and alive medium-sized clams
1½ tbsps. roughly chopped fresh galangal
1 tsp. lime zest
1 small kabocha squash
1 lb. shrimp
1½ lbs. fresh salmon
16 leaves Thai basil
1 tbsp. minced lemongrass
2 tbsps. coconut oil
Salt
4 roughly chopped garlic cloves
13.5 oz. coconut milk
Black pepper.

Instructions:

1. Add coconut milk, lemongrass, galangal, garlic and lime leaves in a small saucepan, and bring to a boil. Allow to simmer for about 25 minutes, stirring occasionally.

2. Strain this mixture through a fine sieve into a large soup pot and bring to a simmer.
3. Meanwhile, heat oil in a pan and add kabocha squash.
4. Season with a bit of salt and pepper and sauté for about 5 minutes. Add this mixture to the coconut milk mixture. Heat oil again in a pan and add fish and shrimp.
5. Season with salt and pepper and sauté for about 4 minutes.
6. Throw this mixture into the coconut milk mixture along with clams and mussels.
7. Simmer for about 8 minutes and garnish with Thai basil to serve.

Nutritional Info: Calories: 389, Carbs: 9.7g, Fat: 16.8g, Protein: 48.8g

Italian Beef Stew with Zucchini, Mushrooms, and Basil

Prep time: 40 minutes, Cook time: 1 hour, Servings: 8

Ingredients:
29 oz. diced tomatoes with juice
4 tbsps. chopped fresh basil
14 oz. beef broth
Black pepper
5 tsps. Olive oil
1 tsp. ground fennel seed
1 tbsp. Italian Herb Blend
1 diced large onion
2 lbs. cubed chuck roast
Salt
½ lb. sliced mushrooms
2 sliced small zucchini

Instructions:
1. Heat olive oil in a large non-stick pan over medium-high heat and add onions, green peppers and beef cubes.
2. Brown beef on all sides for about 10 minutes and season with salt and black pepper.
3. Add the browned meat mixture to the stew pot along with beef broth, Italian Herb Blend, diced tomatoes with juice and ground fennel.
4. Heat oil again in a non-stick pan and add zucchini and mushroom slices.
5. Cook for about 5 minutes and add to the stew pot.
6. Simmer for about 1 hour and add the chopped basil. Simmer for about 15 more minutes and dish out to serve.

Nutritional Info: Calories: 318, Carbs: 5g, Fat: 13.5g, Protein: 42.3g

Mexico Green Chile Pork Stew

Prep time: 5 minutes, Cook time: 1 hour 40 minutes, Servings: 8

Ingredients:
2 garlic cloves
27 oz. whole Hatch green chilies and liquid
2 tsps. ground cumin
2 lbs. cubed pork loin
½ cup chopped onions
2 cups water
2 tsps. garlic powder
1 tsp. chili powder
3 tbsps. olive oil

Instructions:
1. Put onions, garlic and green chilies in a blender and blend to make a paste.
2. Heat oil in a pan and add cubed pork loin and onion paste.
3. Sauté for about 8 minutes and add cumin, chili powder and garlic powder.
4. Sauté for about 1 minute and add water.
5. Reduce heat to low and simmer for about 1 hour 30 minutes.
6. Dish out in a bowl and serve hot.

Nutritional Info: Calories: 329, Carbs: 1.9g, Fats: 21.3g, Proteins: 31.3g

Mediterranean Beef Stew with Rosemary and Balsamic Vinegar

Prep time: 15 minutes, Cook time: 8 hours 5 minutes, Servings: 8

Ingredients:

¼ cup balsamic vinegar
1 tbsp. capers
2 tbsps. finely chopped fresh parsley
Salt
2 lbs. sliced chuck steak
2 tbsps. olive oil
1 diced onion
1 cup beef stock
½ cup tomato sauce
14.5 oz. diced tomatoes with juice
1 can halved black olives
8 oz. sliced mushrooms
2 tbsps. finely chopped fresh rosemary
½ cup thinly sliced garlic cloves
Black pepper

Instructions:

1. Heat olive oil in a frying pan over medium-high heat and add onions and mushrooms.
2. Cook for about 5 minutes and transfer into a slow cooker. Add a little more oil and add beef.
3. Cook for about 10 minutes until brown and transfer into a slow cooker along with diced tomatoes and juice, beef stock, tomato sauce, olives, garlic, balsamic vinegar, rosemary, capers, parsley, salt and black pepper. Stir well and cook, covered for about 8 hours on LOW.

Nutritional Info: Calories: 357, Carbs: 7g, Fats: 19.4g, Protein: 37.5g

Belizean Stewed Chicken

Prep time: 15 minutes, Cook time: 25 minutes, Servings: 6

Ingredients:

4 whole chicken legs
1 cup sliced yellow onions
2 tbsps. white vinegar
3 garlic cloves
1 tbsp. coconut oil
3 tbsps. Worcestershire sauce
2 tbsps. recadorojo seasoning
1 tsp. dried oregano
1 tbsp. erythritol
½ cup cilantro
2 cups chicken stock
1 tsp. ground cumin
½ tsp. black pepper

Instructions:

1. Mix together the vinegar, recadorojo paste, Worcestershire sauce, oregano, cumin, erythritol and pepper in a large bowl.
2. Add chicken pieces and rub the marinade into it.
3. Marinate overnight and transfer into an Instant Pot.
4. Select "Sauté" and add coconut oil and chicken.
5. Sauté for about 2 minutes per side and dish out.
6. Add garlic and onions and sauté for about 3 minutes.
7. Return chicken pieces to the Instant Pot and stir in broth.
8. Lock the lid and set to "Manual" at high pressure for about 20 minutes.
9. Release the pressure naturally and garnish with cilantro to serve.

Nutritional Info: Calories: 184, Carbs: 7g, Fat: 11.9g, Protein: 14.7g

Southwestern Beef Stew with Tomatoes, Olives and Chiles

Prep time: 15 minutes, Cook time: 7 hours 16 minutes, Servings: 6

Ingredients:

1 crushed tomato
4 oz. diced green chiles
Fresh lime slices
1 chopped large onion
2 tsps. olive oil
2 tsps. ground cumin
1 tbsp. crushed garlic
2 lbs. sliced lean beef cubes
1 cup salsa
1 cup beef broth

1 tsp. Mexican oregano
1 can drained and halved olives
Instructions:
1. Heat the olive oil in a large heavy frying pan and add beef.
2. Sauté for about 10 minutes and add beef broth.
3. Cook for about 5 minutes and transfer to the slow cooker along with onions, cumin, salsa, garlic and Mexican oregano.

4. Cook on LOW for about 7 hours and add olives, crushed tomatoes and green chiles.
5. Cook for about 1 more hour and top with fresh lime slices.
6. Dish out to serve hot.

Nutritional Info: Calories: 320, Carbs: 8.2g, Fat: 10.3g, Proteins: 46.6g

Tomato Soup

Prep time: 15 minutes, Cook time: 7 minutes, Servings: 4

Ingredients:
¾ cup unsweetened coconut milk
2 tbsps. chopped fresh basil leaves
2 cups peeled, seeded and chopped tomatoes
¼ tsp. baking soda
¼ cup coconut cream
Salt.
½ cup vegetable broth
Ground black pepper
Instructions:
1. In the pot with the Instant Pot, pour the tomatoes and broth.
2. Secure the lid and turn to "Seal" position. Select "Manual" and cook under medium pressure for about 3 minutes.

3. Press the "Cancel" and permit a "Quick" release.
4. Carefully, get rid of the lid and immediately, stir in baking soda until well combined.
5. Stir inside milk and cream.
6. With an immersion blender, puree the soup well.
7. Select "Sauté" and cook for around 3-4 minutes or until heated completely.
8. Select the "Cancel" and serve hot with the garnishing of basil.

Nutritional Info: Calories: 112, Fat: 191g, Protein 2.7g, Carbs: 17g

Beef Neck Stew

Prep time: 15 minutes, Cook time: 7 minutes, Servings: 4

Ingredients:
½ tsp. chili powder
3 cups beef broth
2 bay leaves
4 tbsps. essential olive oil
1 cup fire-roasted tomatoes
2 lbs. chopped beef neck
1 cup chopped cauliflower
4 tbsps. Parmesan cheese
1 tbsp. cayenne pepper
½ tsp. salt
Instructions:
1. Rinse the meat and pat dry with a kitchen paper. Place on a large cutting board and cut into bite-sized pieces and put in a large bowl. Season with salt, cayenne, and chili pepper. Set aside.
2. Plug in the instant pot and press the "Sauté" button. Grease the bottom in the inner pot

with extra virgin olive oil and add the meat. Cook for 5 - 7 minutes, stirring constantly.
3. Now add remaining ingredients and seal the lid. Adjust the steam release handle on the "Sealing" position and press the "Meat" button. Cook for 35 minutes on high pressure.
4. When done, press the "Cancel" button to show off the heat and release pressure naturally. Make sure the pot stays covered for an additional 10 minutes before detaching the lid.
5. Carefully, get rid of the lid and chill for a while. Divide the stew between serving bowls and sprinkle each with parmesan cheese to take pleasure from. Serve it immediately.

Nutritional Info: Calories: 414, Fat 20.6g, Protein: 50.8g, Carbs: 5.4g

Hamburger Stew

Prep time: 10 minutes, Cook time: 7 minutes, Servings: 6

Ingredients:

½ cup tomato sauce

2 tbsps. tomato paste

1 tbsp. powdered chicken broth base

2 tsps. freshly ground black pepper

Lemon juice

1 cup sliced onions

1 lb. lean ground beef

3 tbsps. using apple cider vinegar

1 tsp. salt

Instructions:

1. Preheat the Instant Pot by selecting "Sauté" and adapting to high heat.
2. When the inner cooking pot is hot, add the soil beef. Break up any clumps and cook for 2 to 3 minutes.
3. You don't need to brown the beef, because Maillard reaction in the pressure cooker will take care of computer in your case.
4. Add the tomato sauce, tomato paste, chicken broth base, green beans, onions, vinegar, salt, and pepper.
5. Latch the lid. Select "Pressure Cook" or "Manual" and hang up pressure to high and cook for 5 minutes. After some time finishes, allow 10 minutes to naturally release pressure to succeed.
6. For any remaining pressure, just quick-release it. Open the lid.
7. Stir inside lemon juice and serve.

Nutritional Info: Calories: 276, Fat: 20.0g, Protein: 16.7g, Carbs: 8.0g

Zucchini Soup

Prep time: 15 minutes, Cook time: 15 minutes, Servings: 6

Ingredients:

1/3 cup chopped and divided fresh basil

4 cups vegetable broth

3 tbsps. essential olive oil

1 chopped large leek

2 chopped medium zucchinis

1 tbsp. fresh freshly squeezed lemon juice

Sea salt.

Instructions:

1. Add oil within the Instant Pot and select "Sauté." Now, add the zucchini and cook approximately 4-5 minutes. Add leek and ¼ cup of basil and cook approximately 2 minutes.
2. Select the "Cancel" and stir in the remaining
3. Secure the lid and use "Seal" position. Cook on "Manual" with underhand approximately 8 minutes.
4. Press the "Cancel" and invite a "Natural" release. Carefully take away the lid sufficient reason for an immersion blender, puree the soup.
5. Serve immediately with the garnishing of remaining basil.

Nutritional Info: Calories: 106, Fat: 8.1g, Protein: 4.3g, Carbs: 5.0g

Beef and Cabbage Stew

Prep time: 5 minutes, Cook time: 20 minutes, Servings: 4

Ingredients:

2 tbsps. butter

1 chopped onion

2 minced garlic cloves

1½ lbs. cubed beef stew meat

2½ cups beef stock

½ lb. sugar-free tomato sauce

2 cups shredded red cabbage

1 tbsp. coconut aminos

2 bay leaves

1 tsp. dried parsley flakes

½ tsp. crushed red pepper flakes

Sea salt

Black pepper

Instructions:

1. Press the "Sauté" button to heat the Instant Pot. Then, melt the butter. Cook the onion and garlic until softened.
2. Add beef stew meat and cook yet another 3 minutes or until browned. Stir the residual ingredients into the Instant Pot.
3. Secure the lid. Choose "Manual" mode and ruthless; cook for fifteen minutes. Once cooking is complete, use a quick pressure release; carefully eliminate the lid.
4. Discard bay leaves and ladle into individual bowls. Enjoy!

Nutritional Info: Calories: 320, Fat: 7.0g, Protein: 3.7g, Carbs: 39.1g

Chicken and Kale Soup

Prep time: 5 minutes, Cook time: 5 minutes, Servings: 4

Ingredients:

2 cups chopped cooked chicken breast

¾ lb. frozen kale

1 chopped onion

2 cups water

1 tbsp. powdered chicken broth base

½ tsp. ground cinnamon

Pinch ground cloves

2 tsps. minced garlic

1 tsp. black pepper

1 teaspoon salt

2 cups full-fat coconut milk

Instructions:

1. Place the chicken, kale, onion, water, chicken broth base, cinnamon, cloves, garlic, pepper, and salt within the inner cooking pot.
2. Latch the lid. Select "Pressure Cook" or "Manual" and set pressure to high and cook for 5 minutes. After some time finishes, allow 10 minutes to naturally release the pressure. For any remaining pressure, just quick-release it. Open the lid.
3. Stir inside coconut milk. Taste and adjust any seasonings, when needed, before serving.

Nutritional Info: Calories: 387, Fat: 27.0g, Protein: 26.0g, Carbs: 10.0g

Zucchini and Yellow Squash Soup

Prep time: 10 minutes, Cook time: 20 minutes, Servings: 6

Ingredients

8 cups Green and yellow squash
8 cups Vegetable stock/chicken stock
1 tbsp. Butter
2 tbsps. Olive oil
1 chopped onion
1 minced garlic
1 tbsp. Italian herb blend
4 tbsps. Chopped rosemary
Salt
Black pepper

Instructions:

1. Melt the butter as well as the extra virgin olive oil within the Pressure cooker and set it to "Sauté"; add the onion and cook for 5 minutes.
2. Add Italian Herb Blend, garlic and rosemary, and cook for 5 more minutes.
3. Meanwhile, chop the zucchini and yellow squash (you'll need 8 cups), cook it for the short while with all the herbs and garlic; add the vegetable or chicken stock towards the onion mix and permit it to simmer for 10 mins.
4. Release the stress while using quick-release method once some time in order to smoke has ended.
5. Blend a combination; simmer it again (it will gain your preferred thickness); you'll need about twenty minutes in "Sauté" setting.
6. Add salt and pepper by preference and serve it while it's still hot

Nutritional Info: Calories: 250; Fats: 20g, Carbs: 15g, Fats: 4.9g

Carrot Soup

Prep time: 10 minutes, Cook time: 10 minutes, Servings: 3

Ingredients:

1 chopped Potato
6 cups vegetable broth
2 tbsps. Carrot Olive oil
2 cups chopped onion
1 lb. Carrots
2 garlic cloves
2 tbsps. Turmeric
2 tbsps. Curry powder
½ tsp. Cumin
½ tsp. Salt
½ cup Apple juice
1 tbsp. Lemon juice
¼ cup toasted Pumpkin seeds
Cilantro

Instructions:

1. Add as well as heat the oil inside pressure cooker; put within the carrots, garlic, and onion (they should all be chopped and stir well. Set to "Sauté" for 5 minutes.
2. Add and stir the cumin, turmeric, salt, and curry powder and cook it to get a minute then put inside vegetable broth, apple juice, and potatoes.
3. Close and secure the coverage; cook on ruthless for 5 minutes. Release the stress while using quick-release method.
4. Once it's cool blend the mixture until it can be smooth.
5. Add the freshly squeezed lemon juice and season with salt and pepper as needed.
6. Serve it while using pumpkin seeds and cilantro while it's still hot.

Nutritional Info: Calories: 169, Fats: 4.2g, Carbs: 28.5g, Proteins: 6.5g

Chapter 6 Vegan and Vegetable

Ginger Sweet Potatoes

Prep time: 10 minutes, Cook time: 2 hours, Servings: 8
Ingredients:
1 grated fresh ginger
Fresh parsley
Salt
2½ lbs. diced sweet potatoes
½ tbsp. ghee
Pepper.
1 cup water
Instructions:
1. Put the potatoes in slow cooker
2. Add fresh ginger and water and stir well.
3. Cover the lid and cook on High for 2 hours until the potatoes are tender.
4. Drain the water once the potatoes are cooked.
5. Add the ghee and mash the potatoes.
6. Add pepper and salt.
7. Serve in a bowl and garnish with parsley.
8. Enjoy.

Nutritional Info: Calories: 100, Fat: 0.5g, Carbs: 23g, Protein: 2g

Stewed Tomatoes

Prep time: 10 minutes, Cook time: 3 hours, Servings: 6
Ingredients:
1 tsp. oregano
2 diced celery stalks
28 oz. whole tomatoes
1 minced small onion
Fresh cilantro
1 minced garlic clove
1 tsp. thyme
Instructions:
1. Add all the ingredients to slow cooker and stir well.
2. Cover the lid and let the mixture cook on Low for 3 hours.
3. Serve on a platter and garnish with cilantro.
4. Enjoy!

Nutritional Info: Calories: 100, Fat: 0.5g, Carbs: 23g, Protein: 2g

Oven–fried Green Beans

Prep time: 10 minutes, Cook time: 10 minutes, Servings: 4
Ingredients:
12 oz. green beans
Salt
½ tsp. garlic powder
⅔ cup grated parmesan cheese
Ground black pepper
¼ tsp. paprika
1 egg
Instructions:
1. In a bowl, mix Parmesan cheese with salt, pepper, garlic powder, and paprika. In another bowl, whisk egg with salt and pepper.
2. Coat the green beans in egg, and then in the Parmesan mixture.
3. Place green beans on a lined baking sheet, place in an oven at 400ºF for 10 minutes. Serve hot.

Nutritional Info: Calories: 66, Fat: 2.7g, Carbs: 6.7g, Protein: 5.3g

Dill Carrots

Prep time: 10 minutes, Cook time: 2 hours, Servings: 6

Ingredients:

1 tbsp. minced fresh dill

3 tbsps. water

1 lb. sliced carrots

½ tsp. ghee

Instructions:

1. Add all the ingredients to the slow cooker and stir well.

2. Cover the cooker with a lid and cook on Low for 2 hours.

3. Serve on a platter and add fresh parsley to garnish.

4. Enjoy.

Nutritional Info: Calories: 35, Fat: 0g, Carbs: 8g, Protein: 1g

Garlic Mashed Potatoes

Prep time: 5 minutes, Cook time: 2 hours, Servings: 10

Ingredients:

1 tbsp. ghee

Pepper.

1 cup chicken broth

4 minced garlic cloves

Salt

Fresh parsley

3 lbs. peeled and cubed red skin potatoes

Instructions:

1. To the slow cooker, add chicken broth, garlic and potatoes and stir well.

2. Cover the cooker with the lid and cook for 2 hours on Low to make the potatoes fork tender.

3. Drain off the liquid once everything is well cooked.

4. Mash the potatoes and add salt and pepper to season.

5. Serve in a bowl and garnish with fresh cilantro.

Nutritional Info: Calories: 130, Fat: 2g, Carbs: 23g, Protein: 4g

Stewed Squash

Prep time: 10 minutes, Cook time: 3 hours 30 minutes, Servings: 4

Ingredients:

3 tbsps. Lemon juice

Fresh dill

Pepper.

¼ inch. Yellow onion slices

Salt

3 cups peeled and sliced zucchini

1 tsp. ghee

Instructions:

1. Put the onion slices along the bottom of slow cooker.

2. Add dill, zucchini, lemon juice and seasonings.

3. Cover with the lid and cook on Low for 3 hours.

4. Add ghee to the slow cooker and stir.

5. Recover the slow cooker to cook on High for 30 minutes.

Nutritional Info: Calories: 70, Fat: 2g, Carbs: 14g, Protein: 2g

Stewed Okra

Prep time: 10 minutes, Cook time: 3 hours, Servings: 4

Ingredients:

1 tsp. hot sauce

1½ cups diced okra

2 minced garlic cloves

2 diced large tomatoes

1 diced small onion

Instructions:

1. Add all the ingredients to the slow cooker and stir well.

2. Cover with the lid and cook on Low for 3 hours.

3. Serve on a platter and enjoy.

Nutritional Info: Calories: 40, Fat: 0g, Carbs: 8g, Protein: 2g

Puréed Broccoli and Cauliflower

Prep time: 10 minutes, Cook time: 15 minutes, Servings: 5

Ingredients:

2 tbsps. butter
1 head broccoli florets
Salt
2 chopped bacon slices
Black pepper.
1 head cauliflower florets
2 peeled and minced garlic cloves

Instructions:

1. Heat the saucepan over medium high heat.
2. Add bacon and garlic then stir to cook for 3 minutes.
3. Add broccoli and cauliflower florets and stir to cook for 2 minutes.
4. Add water to the mixture until full and cover the pot to simmer for 10 minutes.
5. Stir in the pepper and salt and blend the soup using an immersion blender.
6. Let it simmer for some minutes over medium heat.
7. Ladle into bowls and serve to enjoy.

Nutritional Info: Calories: 128, Fat: 8.2g, Carbs: 9.4g, Protein: 6.6g

Broccoli Stew

Prep time: 10 minutes, Cook time: 40 minutes, Servings: 4

Ingredients:

1 peeled and chopped small ginger piece
28 oz. pureed tomatoes
Olive oil
Salt
¼ tsp. crushed red pepper
1 peeled and minced garlic clove
2 tsps. coriander seeds
1 head broccoli florets
1 peeled and chopped onion
Ground black pepper.

Instructions:

1. Set up water in a saucepan, add salt and boil over medium high heat.
2. Add broccoli florets and steam for 2 minutes.
3. Transfer them into a bowl full of ice water and drain them to set aside.
4. Set a pan on fire over medium high heat then add coriander seeds and toast them for 4 minutes.
5. Transfer the seeds to a grinder and grind to reserve.
6. Set a pot with oil over medium heat and stir in red pepper, onions and seasonings to cook for 7 minutes.
7. Stir in coriander seeds, ginger and garlic to cook for 3 minutes.
8. Add tomatoes and bring to a boil then simmer for 10 minutes.
9. Stir in broccoli and cook stew for 12 minutes.
10. Divide into bowls and serve.

Nutritional Info: Calories: 152, Fat: 0.9g, Carbs: 4.1g, Protein: 7.9g

Turnips and Sauce

Prep time: 11 minutes, Cook time: 14 minutes, Servings: 4

Ingredients:

1 tbsp. chopped rosemary
Orange zest
3 tbsps. coconut oil
¼ tsp. sea salt
1 tbsp. lemon juice
16 oz. thinly sliced turnips
Black pepper

Instructions:

1. Heat up a pan with the oil over medium high heat, add turnips, stir and cook for 4 minutes.
2. Add lemon juice, a pinch of salt, black pepper and rosemary, stir and cook for 10 minutes more. Take off heat, add orange zest, stir; divide between plates and serve.

Nutritional Info: Calories: 90, Fat: 1g, Carbs: 3g, Protein: 4g

Mushroom Boats

Prep time: 10 minutes, Cook time: 30 minutes, Servings: 4

Ingredients:

1 chopped yellow onion
1 lb. separated and chopped big white mushroom caps
3 tbsps. coconut oil
¼ tsp. black pepper
1 lb. chopped turkey meat

Instructions:

1. Heat up a pan with 2 tablespoons oil over medium heat, add mushrooms stems, stir and cook them for 3 minutes.
2. Add the rest of the oil, onion and a pinch of black pepper, stir and cook for 7 minutes.
3. Transfer this mix to a bowl, add turkey meat and stir well.
4. Stuff mushrooms with this mix, place them on a lined baking sheet and bake in the oven at 400 degrees F for 30 minutes.
5. Arrange mushrooms on a platter and serve them.
6. Enjoy!

Nutritional Info: Calories: 317, Fat: 15.9g, Carbs: 6.3g, Protein: 37.2g

Eggplant Fries

Prep time: 15 minutes, Cook time: 20 minutes, Servings: 2

Ingredients:

1/8 tsp. parsley flakes
½ peeled and sliced large eggplant
1 beaten egg
Black pepper
1/8 cup coconut flour
Salt
1/8 cup grated parmesan cheese
1/8 cup olive oil
1/8 tsp. garlic powder

Instructions:

1. In a small bowl, beat the egg and set aside.
2. Combine parmesan, parsley flakes, parmesan cheese, coconut flour, garlic powder, salt and black pepper in another medium bowl.
3. Pass the eggplant through the egg mixture for 1 minute and then dredge in coconut flour mixture.
4. Heat olive oil in a pan and drop some eggplant fries.
5. Cook on both sides until brown and dish out in a serving platter.
6. Serve and enjoy.

Nutritional Info: Calories: 204, Carbs: 12.1g, Fats: 16.1g, Protein: 5.5g

Bok Choy Stir–fry

Prep time: 10 minutes, Cook time: 7 minutes, Servings: 2

Ingredients:

2 chopped bacon slices
Salt
2 peeled and minced garlic cloves
Avocado oil
2 cups chopped bok choy
Ground black pepper.

Instructions:

1. Set a pan over medium heat.
2. Add bacon then stir and brown until crispy before transferring to paper towels.
3. Drain the grease from the bacon.
4. Return the pan to medium heat and stir in bok choy and garlic to cook for 4 minutes.
5. Season with pepper and salt and return the bacon to pan.
6. Stir in to cook for 1 minute before serving.
7. Enjoy.

Nutritional Info: Calories: 116, Fat: 8.1g, Carbs: 2.8g, Protein: 8.3g

Mushroom and Broccoli Skewers

Prep time: 20 minutes, Cook time: 10 minutes, Servings: 4

Ingredients:

10 mushroom caps
½ tsp. turmeric powder
Garlic paste
¼ tsp. sea salt
½ tsp. chili powder
Olive oil
Black pepper
1 tsp. garam masala
1 tsp. ginger
1 cup broccoli florets

Instructions:

1. In a bowl, mix chili powder, garam masala, ginger paste, turmeric, salt, pepper and oil and stir.

2. Add mushroom caps and broccoli florets, toss to coat well and keep in the fridge for 20 minutes.

3. Arrange these on skewers, place them on preheated grill over medium-high heat, cook for 5 minutes on each side and transfer to a platter.

4. Serve them as an appetizer.

5. Enjoy!

Nutritional Info: Calories: 20, Fat: 1.5g, Carbs: 1.3g, Protein: 0.9g

Zoodles with Mushroom Sauce

Prep time: 10 minutes, Cook time: 5 minutes, Servings: 4

Ingredients:

1 cup chicken stock
1 lb. chopped mushrooms
¼ tsp. chili powder
2 zucchinis
2 chopped ripe tomatoes
½ tsp. dried oregano
1 tbsp. minced shallots
1 tsp. minced garlic
2 tbsps. avocado oil
1 tsp. dried basil

Instructions:

1. Firstly, cut off the ends of each zucchini. Make zucchini noodles by using your spiralizer, a julienne peeler or mandoline.

2. Now, bring a pot of lightly salted water to a boil; cook your zucchini noodles for one minute. Reserve.

3. In the meantime, heat avocado oil in a large-sized pan over a moderate flame. Cook the shallot and garlic for 2 minutes. Add the mushrooms and cook an additional 3 minutes.

4. Now, stir in the remaining ingredients; cover the pot and bring the mixture to a simmer over a medium-low heat. Cook until everything is warmed through.

5. Top your zoodles with the prepared mushroom sauce and serve immediately. Enjoy!

Nutritional Info: Calories: 85, Fat: 3.5g, Carbs: 6.4g, Protein: 5.8g

Celery Stew

Prep time: 10 minutes, Cook time: 30 minutes, Servings: 6

Ingredients:

2 tsps. chicken bouillon
2 chopped fresh mint bunches
4 peeled and minced garlic cloves
1 chopped celery bunch
3 dried Persian lemons
Ground black pepper.
1 bunch chopped parsley

Salt
4 tbsps. olive oil
1 peeled and chopped onion
1 bunch peeled and chopped green onion
2 cups water

Instructions:

1. Set a saucepan with oil over medium high heat.
2. Stir in green onions, garlic and onions to cook for 6 minutes.
3. Add chicken bouillon, Persian lemons, water, pepper and salt then cover before simmering on medium heat for 20 minutes.
4. Stir in mint and parsley to cook for 10 minutes.
5. Divide into bowls before serving.
6. Enjoy.

Nutritional Info: Calories: 100, Fat: 9.5g, Carbs: 4.4g, Protein: 0.9g

Mediterranean Pasta with Avocado

Prep time: 13 minutes, Cook time: 10 minutes, Servings: 2

Ingredients:
1 tbsp. roughly chopped fresh parsley
2 spiralized zucchinis
½ cup chopped Kalamata olives
1 tbsp. chopped oregano
2 tbsps. chopped capers
¼ cup chopped sun-dried tomatoes
1 tsp. minced garlic
2 tbsps. butter
1 tsp. chopped fresh rosemary
¼ cup grated parmesan cheese
1 cup baby spinach
1 pitted and sliced avocado

Instructions:

1. Press the Sauté function to melt the butter.
2. When sizzling, add the garlic and cook for 45 seconds, until fragrant.
3. Stir in the spinach and zucchini, and cook for about 5 minutes.
4. Add the remaining ingredients except parmesan cheese and avocado and stir well to combine before cooking for 2 more minutes.
5. Sprinkle with parmesan cheese and avocado slices
6. Serve and enjoy!

Nutritional Info: Calories 315, Protein: 15g, Carbs: 6.5g, Fat: 28g

Mini Pesto Cake

Prep time: 6 minutes, Cook time: 10 minutes, Servings: 1

Ingredients:
3 tbsps. almond flour
¼ tsp. red pepper flakes
1 ½ tbsps. Pesto Sauce
2 tbsps. butter
½ tsp. baking powder
¼ tsp. salt
1 egg
1 cup water

Instructions:
1. Pour in the water and lower the trivet.

2. In a small jar, whisk together the remaining ingredients.
3. Seal the jar and set it on top of the trivet.
4. Set it to cook on High pressure for 3 minutes.
5. Release the pressure quickly when it goes off.
6. Cook the cake for 5 minutes before serving.
7. Enjoy.

Nutritional Info: Calories 431, Protein: 12g, Carbs: 5g, Fat: 38g

Stuffed Mushrooms with Walnuts

Prep time: 30 minutes, Cook time: 20 minutes, Servings: 2

Ingredients:
1 beaten egg
2 tsps. chopped fresh dill
1½ cups water
4 portobello mushrooms
Pepper.
1 minced garlic clove

1 chopped onion
Salt.
1 tbsp. olive oil
¼ cup roughly chopped walnuts

Instructions:
1. Pour in the water and lower the trivet.

2. Rub the baking dish with cooking spray and set aside.
3. Set up a medium mixing bowl to combine dill, walnuts, garlic and onion.
4. Stuff the mushrooms with the walnut mixture and drizzle with oil before seasoning.
5. Arrange the stuffed portobellos in the baking dish.
6. Put the dish on top of the trivet and seal the lid to cook on High pressure for 20 minutes.
7. Once ready, do a quick release and open the lid carefully.
8. Serve and enjoy.

Nutritional Info: Calories 326, Protein: 15g, Carbs: 5g, Fat: 29g

---

Tofu and Swiss chard Bowl

Prep time: 60 minutes, Cook time: 1 hour, Servings: 4

Ingredients:
1 diced green onion
1 tbsp. chopped parsley
9 oz. chopped Swiss chard
3 tbsps. olive oil
1 tsp. sweetener
Juice of ½ lime
2 tbsps. tamari
For the tofu:
1½ cups water
15 oz. cubed tofu
2 tsps. minced garlic
1 tbsp. sesame oil
1 tbsp. vinegar
1 tbsp. tamari

Instructions:
1. Pour the water in the trivet and lower it.
2. Put all the ingredients in the Ziploc bag, shake well and set aside for 30 minutes to marinate.
3. Rub the baking dish with cooking spray after 30 minutes and arrange the tofu on it.
4. Set the dish on top of the trivet and seal the lid to cook on High pressure for 30 minutes.
5. Do a quick pressure release after the beep.
6. Remove the dish and set aside to cool for 2 minutes.
7. Stir in the tofu.

Nutritional Info: Calories 415, Protein 24g, Carbs 6.6g, Fat 31g

---

Smoked Paprika Cauliflower Cakes

Prep time: 10 minutes, Cook time: 15 minutes, Servings: 4

Ingredients:
¼ tsp. onion powder
1 lb. cauliflower rice
½ tsp. baking powder
½ tsp. salt
2 tbsps. butter
½ cup almond flour
1 tsp. smoked paprika
¼ tsp. garlic powder
3 eggs
1 tsp. pepper
Instructions:

1. In a large mixing bowl, combine all the ingredients except butter.
2. Mold the mixture into 4 cakes.
3. Melt the butter on Sauté and add 2 cauliflower cakes inside the pot.
4. Let them cook on all sides until crispy.
5. Melt the rest of butter and repeat the same process with the remaining two cakes.
6. Serve and enjoy!

Nutritional Info: Calories 215, Protein 9g, Carbs 4.5g, Fat 15g

---

Beet and Pecan Bowl

Prep time: 15 minutes, Cook time: 25 minutes, Servings: 4

Ingredients:
1 cup veggie broth
½ cup grated parmesan cheese
½ minced shallot

½ cup chopped walnuts
2 minced garlic cloves
1 tbsp. olive oil

4 chopped large beets

Instructions:

1. Put the beets in a food processor and pulse to a rice-like consistency.
2. Heat olive oil on Sauté and add shallots to cook for 2 minutes.
3. Add garlic and stir to cook for 1 more minute.
4. Pour the broth over and stir in the beet rice to cook on High pressure for 20 minutes under a sealed lid.
5. Do a quick release once it goes off.
6. Stir in parmesan cheese and divide among 4 bowls.
7. Top up with walnuts and serve.

Nutritional Info: Calories 273, Protein: 9g, Carbs: 8.5g, Fat: 22g

Broccoli with Tomatoes

Prep time: 10 minutes, Cook time: 15 minutes, Servings: 4

Ingredients:

1 tbsp. olive oil
Pepper.
1 tsp. garlic powder
½ tsp. celery seeds
1 head broccoli florets
14 oz. diced tomatoes
Salt
½ diced onion

Instructions:

1. Heat the oil on Sauté.
2. Once the oil is sizzling hot, add onions to cook for 3 minutes.
3. Add spices and tomatoes then stir well to cook for 2 more minutes.
4. Stir in broccoli and seal the lid.
5. Tap the Manual function and cook for 8 minutes on High pressure.
6. Do a quick pressure release once it is off.
7. Let the broccoli with tomatoes chill before serving.
8. Enjoy.

Nutritional Info: Calories: 153, Protein: 9g, Carbs: 5g, Fat: 12g

Asparagus Zoodles with Pesto & Soft Boiled Eggs

Prep time: 5 minutes, Cook time: 10 minutes, Servings: 2

Ingredients:

1 tbsp. fresh chopped dill
1 minced garlic clove
4 eggs
Pepper.
2 tsps. olive oil
¼ cup pesto sauce
1 cup water
2 spiralized zucchinis
4 sliced asparagus spears
Salt

Instructions:

1. Add water to the pot and lower the trivet.
2. Carefully arrange the eggs in a steamer basket and seal the lid to cook on low pressure for 3 minutes.
3. Do a quick release once ready.
4. Let the eggs cool and peel the eggs into halves.
5. Heat olive oil on Sauté and add garlic to cook for 1 minute until fragrant.
6. Add zoodles and asparagus to cook for 3 minutes before seasoning with salt and pepper.
7. Add pesto sauce to cook until it becomes heated through.
8. Serve on plates topped with halved eggs and fresh dill.
9. Enjoy!

Nutritional Info: Calories: 312, Protein: 8g, Carbs: 4g, Fat: 25g

Squash Spaghetti with Mint and Almond Pesto

Prep time: 5 minutes, Cook time: 4 minutes, Servings: 2

Ingredients:

3 spiralized yellow summer squashes
1 tbsp. toasted and chopped almonds
¼ tsp. grated lemon zest
¼ cup olive oil
Salt
1 diced celery stalk
1 tbsp. olive oil
Juice of ½ lemon
2 tbsps. finely chopped mint
Pepper.
1 ½ cups water

Instructions:

1. In the food processor, add celery, lemon juice, mint and half of the almonds to blend until combined.
2. Add seasonings and set aside.
3. Pour water in the pot and lower the trivet.
4. Grease the baking dish with cooking spray and set the spiralized squash inside.
5. Put the dish on top of the trivet and seal the lid to cook for 4 minutes on High pressure.
6. Do a quick release when everything is ready.
7. Transfer the squash noodles in a large bowl to top up with lemon zest, pesto and the remaining almonds.
8. Serve and enjoy.

Nutritional Info: Calories: 174, Protein: 5g, Carbs: 5g, Fat: 8g

Radish Hash Browns

Prep time: 15 minutes, Cook time: 20 minutes, Servings: 4

Ingredients:

¼ tsp. garlic powder
1 ½ cups water
Pepper.
4 eggs
Salt
1lb. shredded radishes

Instructions:

1. Add water to the pot and lower the trivet.
2. Grease the baking dish with cooking spray and set aside.
3. Beat eggs in a large bowl along salt, pepper and garlic powder.
4. Add radishes and stir well.
5. Transfer the mixture into the greased baking dish and put the dish on top of the trivet to cook on High pressure for 20 minutes under a sealed lid.
6. Do a quick pressure release once it beeps.
7. Carefully open the lid and cut the hash browns into 4 squares.
8. Serve with aioli and enjoy.

Nutritional Info: Calories: 80, Protein: 7g, Carbs: 5g, Fat: 5g

Jalapeno Lunch 'Waffles'

Prep time: 5 minutes, Cook time: 6 minutes, Servings: 2

Ingredients:

1 tsp. psyllium husk powder
¼ tsp. salt
1 tbsp. butter
1 tbsp. coconut flour
1 seeded and diced jalapeno
3 eggs
1 tsp. baking powder

Instructions:

1. Put all the ingredients in the food processor and process until smooth and well incorporated.
2. Melt the butter on Sauté then add half of the initially processed batter to cook until golden on all sides.
3. Set aside and repeat the same for the other "waffle".
4. Serve with chicken breast and enjoy.

Nutritional Info: Calories: 331, Protein: 16g, Carbs: 4.3g, Fat: 25g

Mint Zucchini

Prep time: 10 minutes, Cook time: 7 minutes, Servings: 4

Ingredients:

¼ tsp. cayenne pepper
2 tbsps. mint
1 tbsp. coconut oil
2 halved and sliced zucchinis
½ tbsp. chopped dill

Instructions:

1. Heat up a pan with the oil over medium high heat, add zucchinis, stir and cook for 6 minutes.
2. Add cayenne, dill and mint, stir; cook for 1 minute more, divide between plates and serve.

Nutritional Info: Calories: 80, Fat: 0g, Carbs: 1g, Protein: 5g

Kale and Cauliflower Stew

Prep time: 10 minutes, Cook time: 8 minutes, Servings: 4

Ingredients:

2 tbsps. olive oil
Salt
2 minced garlic cloves
14 oz. canned diced tomatoes
2 diced celery stalks
3 cups cauliflower rice
Pepper.
2 sliced carrots
4 cups veggie broth
2 cups chopped kale
1 diced onion
2 tsps. cumin

Instructions:

1. Heat the olive oil on Sauté and add onions, celery, and carrots to cook for a few minutes, until softened.
2. Add garlic and stir to cook for 45 more seconds.
3. Stir the remaining ingredients to combine in the pot.
4. Seal the lid to cook on High pressure for 8 minutes.
5. Do a natural pressure release when the timer goes off.
6. Carefully open the lid and ladle into bowls.
7. Enjoy.

Nutritional Info: Calories: 320, Protein: 12g, Carbs: 4g, Fat: 14g

Flax and Swiss chard Patties

Prep time: 10 minutes, Cook time: 12 minutes, Servings: 4

Ingredients:

1 tsp. chopped thyme
1 cup chopped Swiss chard
2 chopped green onions
Pepper.
½ cauliflower head
1 tbsp. flaxseed meal
2 eggs
2 tbsps. butter
1 tbsp. olive oil
Salt

Instructions:

1. In a food processor, blend the cauliflower until rice-like consistency forms.
2. Add green onions, Swiss chard and thyme and stir well.
3. Process the mixture until smooth and transfer it into a bowl.
4. Stir in the rest of the ingredients.
5. Melt half of the butter on Sauté and put ¼ of batter in the pot to cook on both sides until golden and crispy.
6. Repeat the process once more and melt the rest of batter to do the same with the remaining batch.
7. Serve with garlic-yoghurt sauce and enjoy.

Nutritional Info: Calories: 281, Protein: 16g, Carbs: 3.5g, Fat: 20g

Portobello Burgers

Prep time: 5 minutes, Cook time: 10 minutes, Servings: 2

Ingredients:

2 whisked eggs

2 keto buns

2 tbsps. butter

Pepper.

2 portobello mushrooms

2 lettuce leaves

Salt

2 tbsps. mayonnaise

Instructions:

1. Melt half of the butter on Sauté.
2. Add eggs and season with salt and pepper to cook for a few minutes.
3. Put the eggs on a plate.
4. Melt the rest of butter and add in the portobellos to cook for 3 minutes on each side then season with salt and pepper,
5. Cut the buns open and stuff lettuce leaves inside.
6. Add a portobello mushroom and spread the mayo over.
7. Add eggs topping then close the sandwich.
8. Top with the eggs and close the sandwich.
9. Serve immediately and enjoy.

Nutritional Info: Calories: 531, Protein: 23g, Carbs: 7.4g, Fat: 50g

---

Dill and Artichoke Salad

Prep time: 10 minutes, Cook time: 10 minutes, Servings: 4

Ingredients:

¼ tsp. sweetener

1 tbsp. chopped capers

6 baby artichokes

¼ cup olive oil

1 ½ tbsps. chopped dill

Pepper.

½ tsp. lemon zest

½ tsp. capers brine

1 ½ cups water

Salt

1 tbsp. lemon juice

Instructions:

1. Add water to the Instant pot then add artichokes.
2. Seal the lid and tap the Manual function to cook for 10 minutes on High pressure.
3. Put the artichokes on a chopping board to chop finely before transferring into a bowl.
4. Add the remaining ingredients into the bowl and toss with hands until everything is combined.'
5. Serve with chicken breasts and enjoy.

Nutritional Info: Calories: 173, Protein: 1g, Carbs: 5g, Fat: 13g

---

Cauliflower and Leeks

Prep time: 10 minutes, Cook time: 20 minutes, Servings: 4

Ingredients:

2 tbsps. bacon grease

1½ cups cauliflower florets

1½ cups artichoke hearts

Black pepper

1½ cups chopped leeks

2 minced garlic cloves

Instructions:

1. Heat up a pan with the bacon grease over medium high heat, add garlic, leeks, cauliflower florets and artichoke hearts, stir and cook for 20 minutes.
2. Add black pepper, stir; divide between plates and serve.

Nutritional Info: Calories: 110, Fat: 2g, Carbs: 6g, Protein: 3g

Eggplant Burgers

Prep time: 10 minutes, Cook time: 10 minutes, Servings: 4

Ingredients:

Tomato sauce

2 tbsps. mustard

1 ½ cups water

1 large eggplant

½ cup grated parmesan cheese

2 tbsps. olive oil

For the slaw:

½ cup shredded red cabbage

½ cup shredded white cabbage

Instructions:

1. Add water to the instant pot.
2. Wash the eggplants and slice them into 4 rounds.
3. Put the eggplants into the pot, seal the lid to cook on High pressure for 2 minutes.
4. Do a quick pressure release once the timer goes off.
5. Drain the egg plants and discard the cooking liquid.
6. Rub the eggplants with mustard.
7. Heat the oil on Sauté then add the egg plants after the oil starts sizzling.
8. Let it cook for few minutes on both sides.
9. Serve with tomato sauce.

Nutritional Info: Calories: 183, Protein: 5g, Carbs: 3.5g, Fat: 5g

---

Soft Cabbage with Garlic and Lemon

Prep time: 17 minutes, Cook time: 6 minutes, Servings: 4

Ingredients:

2 tsps. minced garlic

¼ tsp. onion powder

1 tbsp. olive oil

1 cup veggie broth

2 cups chopped cabbage

Pepper.

¼ cup lemon juice

Salt.

Instructions:

1. In the Instant pot, combine cabbage and broth.
2. Seal the lid and cook for 5 minutes on High pressure.
3. Do a quick pressure release once the timer goes off.
4. Carefully open the lid, transfer the cabbage to a plate and discard the broth wiping the pot clean.
5. Warm the olive oil on Sauté and add garlic to cook for 1 minute.
6. Add cabbage and all seasonings and stir.
7. Drizzle with the lemon juice and serve.
8. Enjoy.

Nutritional Info: Calories: 83, Protein: 3g, Carbs: 2g, Fat: 7g

---

Lemon Basil Ratatouille

Prep time: 10 minutes, Cook time: 10 minutes, Servings: 8

Ingredients:

2 cubed summer squash

1 chopped white onion

3 minced garlic cloves

1 sliced eggplant

2 cubed zucchinis

2 tbsps. white wine vinegar

1 tbsp. lemon juice

¼ cup olive oil

1 cup basil

1 cup cherry tomatoes

2 tbsps. tomato paste

Salt

Instructions:

1. Add all the vegetables in the Instant Pot.
2. Put the rest of the ingredients in a food processor. Blend until smooth.
3. Pour the sauce over the vegetables.
4. Seal the pot.
5. Choose manual function.
6. Cook at high pressure for 10 minutes.
7. Release the pressure naturally.

Nutritional Info: Calories: 117, Fat: 7g, Carbs: 13.4g, Protein: 3.1g

Vegetable Stew

Prep time: 15 minutes, Cook time: 35 minutes, Servings:4

Ingredients:

1 cup sliced carrots
2 cups bone broth
2 tbsps. avocado oil
Pepper
1 sliced onion
4 cups cubed potatoes
2 cups diced zucchini
1 cup sliced mushrooms
Salt

Instructions:

1. Set the Instant Pot to sauté.
2. Add the avocado oil.
3. Cook the vegetables until soft.
4. Season with the salt and pepper.
5. Pour in the broth.
6. Cover the pot.
7. Choose manual mode.
8. Cook at high pressure for 35 minutes.
9. Release the pressure naturally.

Nutritional Info: Calories: 148, Fat: 1.2g, Carbs: 31.7g, Protein 4.4g

Spicy Spinach & Mushroom

Prep time: 20 minutes, Cook time: 20 minutes, Servings: 4

Ingredients:

1 cup chopped tomatoes
3 cups chopped spinach
1 tbsp. olive oil
Pepper
4 minced cloves garlic
2 cups diced mushrooms
1 tsp. red pepper flakes
Garlic salt
1 diced onion
1 tsp. dried basil

Instructions:

1. Blend the tomatoes in a food processor.
2. Season with the garlic salt and pepper.
3. Choose the sauté mode in the Instant Pot.
4. Pour in the olive oil. Add the onion and garlic.
5. Cook for 2 minutes.
6. Add the spinach, mushrooms and red pepper flakes.
7. Cook for another 2 minutes or until spinach has wilted.
8. Add the tomato puree.
9. Simmer for 15 minutes.

Nutritional Info: Calories: 135, Fat: 7.8g, Carbs: 15.1g, Protein: 5.4g

Spaghetti Squash

Prep time: 15 minutes, Cook time: 6 minutes, Servings: 2

Ingredients:

1 cup cold water
1 whole spaghetti squash

Instructions:

1. Slice the spaghetti squash in half.
2. Remove the seeds.
3. Pour the water into the Instant Pot.
4. Add the steamer rack.
5. Put the spaghetti squash on top of the rack.
6. Cover the pot.
7. Choose manual setting.
8. Cook at high pressure for 6 minutes.
9. Release the pressure quickly.
10. Shred the squash to create spaghetti strands.

Nutritional Info: Calories: 90, Fat: 1g, Carbs: 18.9g, Protein: 6.8g

Eggplant Stir Fry

Prep time: 10 minutes, Cook time: 25 minutes, Servings: 4

Ingredients:

1 chopped onion
4 cups sliced eggplant
½ tsp. red pepper flakes
½ tsp. ground ginger
1 tbsp. olive oil
1 sliced bell pepper
5 tbsps. tamari sauce
3 minced garlic cloves

Instructions:

1. Heat oil in a pan over medium-high heat.
2. Add onion and garlic and sauté for 6-8 minutes.
3. Turn heat to medium and add eggplant and bell pepper.
4. Stir well and cook for few minutes.
5. Add red pepper flakes, ginger, and tamari and stir well.
6. Cook for 12 minutes. Stir occasionally.
7. Serve and enjoy.

Nutritional Info: Calories: 85, Fat: 3 g, Carbs: 10 g, Protein: 4 g

Easy Grilled Veggies

Prep time: 10 minutes, Cook time: 15 minutes, Servings: 4

Ingredients:

2 cups sliced mushrooms
1 tsp. Cajun seasoning
4 diced bell peppers
2 tbsps. olive oil
¼ tsp. pepper
2 diced eggplants
1 tsp. salt

Instructions:

1. Add all vegetables in a baking dish and drizzle with olive oil and season with seasoning, pepper and salt.
2. Cook at 392^0 F for 15-20 minutes
3. Serve and enjoy.

Nutritional Info: Calories 55, Fat 3 g, Carbs: 5 g, Protein: 2 g

Avocado Green Beans

Prep time: 10 minutes, Cook time: 5 minutes, Servings: 6

Ingredients:

3 peel and mashed avocado
4 tbsps. olive oil
1 lb. trimmed fresh green beans
¼ tsp. pepper
¼ cup chopped green onion
¼ tsp. salt

Instructions:

1. Heat olive oil in pan over medium high heat.
2. Add green beans in pan and sauté for 4 minutes.
3. Season beans with pepper and salt and set aside.
4. In a mixing bowl, add green beans, avocado, and green onion and mix well.
5. Serve and enjoy.

Nutritional Info: Calories: 315, Fat: 30 g, Carbs: 14 g, Protein: 3.6 g

Spicy Eggplant

Prep time: 10 minutes, Cook time: 2 hours 30 minutes, Servings: 8

Ingredients:

1 tsp. turmeric powder
1 chopped onion
2 sliced medium eggplants
1 tbsp. garam masala
2 seeded and minced jalapeno pepper
5 chopped garlic cloves
1 tbsp. chili powder
1 tsp. ginger paste
1 tbsp. ground cumin
1 tbsp. chopped fresh parsley

¼ cup olive oil
½ tbsp. salt
Instructions:
1. Add all ingredients except salt and parsley into the crock pot and stir well.
2. Cover and cook on high for 2 hours. Stir after 1 hour.
3. Stir well and cook on low for 30 minutes more.
4. Add parsley and salt and stir well.
5. Serve and enjoy.

Nutritional Info: Calories: 100, Fat: 7 g, Carbs: 10 g, Protein: 2 g

Tofu Skewers

Prep time: 10 minutes, Cook time: 15 minutes, Servings: 6

Ingredients:
2 tbsps. tomato paste
1 cup unsweetened coconut milk
2 tbsps. lemon juice
1 sliced red bell pepper
¼ tsp. pepper
¼ tsp. cayenne pepper
2 tsps. ground cumin
2 tsps. paprika
14 oz. pressed and sliced tofu
1 sliced small zucchini
½ tsp. turmeric
2 minced garlic cloves
¾ tsp. salt

Instructions:
1. Preheat the grill over medium-high heat.
2. Add all ingredients into the mixing bowl and mix well.
3. Cover bowl and place in fridge for 1 hour.
4. Arrange marinated tofu, bell pepper, and zucchini pieces on soaked wooden skewers.
5. Place tofu skewers on hot grill and cook for 10 minutes or until lightly golden brown.
6. Serve and enjoy.

Nutritional Info: Calories: 160, Fat: 12 g, Carbs: 8 g, Protein: 8 g

Healthy Vegetables Roast

Prep time: 10 minutes, Cook time: 25 minutes, Servings: 4

Ingredients:
2 minced garlic cloves
1 cup diced eggplant
½ tsp. pepper
4 sliced mushrooms
2 tbsps. chopped parsley
1 tsp. salt
8 small asparagus spears
¼ cup olive oil
2 sliced bell pepper
1 cup sliced zucchini

Instructions:
1. Preheat the oven to 375 F.
2. In a large bowl, whisk together oil, garlic, parsley, pepper, salt.
3. Add vegetables in a bowl and toss well.
4. Place vegetables in an aluminum foil container and pour remaining marinade over vegetables. Seal container.
5. Bake in oven for 25 minutes. Season with pepper and salt.
6. Serve and enjoy.

Nutritional Info: Calories: 150, Fat: 13 g, Carbs: 8 g, Protein: 2 g

Spaghetti Squash

Prep time: 10 minutes, Cook time: 15 minutes, Servings: 4

Ingredients:
4 cups cooked spaghetti squash
2 tbsps. chopped fresh parsley
½ tsp. dried thyme
½ tsp. dried rosemary
½ tsp. garlic powder
2 tbsps. olive oil
½ tsp. pepper
1 tsp. salt

Instructions:
1. Preheat the oven to 350 F.
2. Add all ingredients into the large bowl and mix well to combine.
3. Transfer bowl mixture to the baking dish and cook in oven for 15 minutes.
4. Stir well and serve.

Nutritional Info: Calories: 95, Fat: 7 g, Carbs: 8 g, Protein: 0.9 g

Creamy Asparagus Mash

Prep time: 10 minutes, Cook time: 10 minutes, Servings: 2

Ingredients:
2 tbsps. chopped fresh parsley
10 trimmed and chopped asparagus spears
Salt
1 diced small onion
1 tbsp. olive oil
1 tsp. lemon juice
Pepper

Instructions:
1. Sauté onion in pan over medium heat until onion is softened.
2. Blanch chopped asparagus in boiling water for 2 minutes and drain well.
3. Add sautéed onion, lemon juice, parsley, asparagus, pepper, and salt into the blender and blend until smooth.
4. Serve and enjoy.

Nutritional Info: Calories: 124, Fat: 10 g, Carbs: 7 g, Protein: 3 g

Roasted Summer Squash

Prep time: 10 minutes, Cook time: 60 minutes, Servings: 3

Ingredients:
1 tbsp. lemon juice
Pepper
2 lbs. sliced summer squash
3 tbsps. olive oil
¼ tsp. paprika
¼ tsp. garlic powder
Salt

Instructions:
1. Preheat the oven to 400 F.
2. Place squash pieces onto a baking tray and drizzle with olive oil.
3. Season with garlic powder, paprika, pepper, and salt.
4. Drizzle with lemon juice and bake in oven for 50-60 minutes.
5. Serve and enjoy.

Nutritional Info: Calories: 180, Fat: 15 g, Carbs: 12 g, Protein: 3 g

Simple Spinach Omelet

Prep time: 10 minutes, Cook time: 5 minutes, Servings: 1

Ingredients:
1 tsp. olive oil
Salt
2 eggs
½ cup baby spinach
Pepper

Instructions:
1. Add eggs, spinach, pepper, and salt in the blender and blend until well combined.
2. Heat olive oil in a pan over medium heat.
3. Pour egg mixture into a hot pan and cook for 2-3 minutes then flip to other side and cook for 2 minutes more.
4. Serve and enjoy.

Nutritional Info: Calories: 375, Fat: 30 g, Carbs: 8 g, Protein: 12 g

Zucchini Hummus

Prep time: 10 minutes, Cook time: 10 minutes, Servings: 4

Ingredients:

1 tbsp. olive oil
Salt
2½ tbsps. tahini
4 halved zucchinis
1 tbsp. lemon juice
2 garlic cloves
¼ cup chopped parsley
1 tsp. cumin
Pepper

Instructions:

1. Place zucchini on hot grill and season with pepper and salt.
2. Grilled zucchini for 10 minutes.
3. Add grilled zucchini, parsley, cumin, tahini, lemon juice, olive oil, garlic, pepper and salt in a blender and blend until smooth.
4. Pour zucchini mixture in a bowl and sprinkle with paprika.
5. Serve and enjoy.

Nutritional Info: Calories: 135, Fat: 10 g, Carbs: 10 g, Protein: 5 g

Veggie Medley

Prep time: 10 minutes, Cook time: 6 hours, Servings: 8

Ingredients:

14.5 oz. diced tomatoes
1/8 tsp. pepper
2 cups sliced mushrooms
1 chopped bell pepper
½ tsp. oregano
¼ tsp. dried thyme
1 chopped onion
1 chopped zucchini
¼ tsp. garlic powder

Instructions:

1. Add all ingredients into the crock pot and stir well.
2. Cover and cook on low for 6 hours.
3. Stir well and serve.

Nutritional Info: Calories 30, Fat 0.2 g, Carbs 6 g, Protein: 2 g

Asian Vegetable Medley

Prep time: 10 minutes, Cook time: 3 hours, Servings: 8

Ingredients:

½ cup sliced leeks
¼ cup fresh basil leaves
12 oz. halved and sliced zucchini
1/3 cup unsweetened coconut milk
2 tbsps. curry paste
2 tbsps. vegetable stock
½ tbsp. grated fresh ginger
8 oz. halved and sliced squash
2 cups quartered mushrooms
3 minced garlic cloves
1 seeded and sliced sweet pepper

Instructions:

1. Add all ingredients except ginger, coconut milk, and basil into the crock pot and stir well.
2. Cover and cook on low for 3 hours.
3. Add ginger and coconut milk and stir well.
4. Garnish with basil and serve.

Nutritional Info: Calories: 65, Fat: 4 g, Carbs: 7 g, Protein: 2 g

Collard Greens Dish

Prep time: 25 minutes, Cook time: 2 hours, Servings: 10

Ingredients:

1 turkey leg
Black pepper
1 tbsp. crushed red pepper flakes.
2 tbsps. minced garlic
¼ cup olive oil
5 bunches chopped collard greens.
5 cups chicken stock
Salt

Instructions:

1. Heat up a pot with the oil over medium heat; add garlic; stir and cook for 1 minute
2. Add stock, salt, pepper and turkey leg; stir, cover and simmer for 30 minutes
3. Add collard greens, cover pot again and cook for 45 minutes more
4. Reduce heat to medium, add more salt and pepper; stir and cook for 1 hour.
5. Drain greens, mix them with red pepper flakes; stir, divide between plates and serve as a side dish.

Nutritional Info: Calories: 143, Fat: 3g, Carbs: 3g, Protein: 6g

Baba Ghanoush

Prep time: 10 minutes, Cook time: 60 minutes, Servings: 6

Ingredients:

¼ cup chopped fresh parsley
Salt
1 peeled and diced medium eggplant
2 minced garlic cloves
2 tbsps. lemon juice
1 tbsp. tahini
½ tsp. olive oil
¼ tsp. liquid smoke
Pepper

Instructions:

1. Add all ingredients into the crock pot and stir well.
2. Cover and cook on high for 1 hour.
3. Mash eggplant mixture using masher until smooth.
4. Serve and enjoy.

Nutritional Info: Calories: 40, Fat: 2 g, Carbs: 5 g, Protein: 1 g

Quick Guacamole

Prep time: 5 minutes, Cook time: 5 minutes, Servings: 8

Ingredients:

1 minced small onion
Salt
3 pitted and halved avocados
2 minced garlic cloves
2 tbsps. fresh lime juice
Pepper
2 tbsps. chopped fresh parsley

Instructions:

1. Remove avocado pulp using a spoon and place in bowl.
2. Mash avocado pulp using a fork.
3. Add remaining ingredients and stir well.
4. Serve and enjoy.

Nutritional Info: Calories: 92, Fat: 8 g, Carbs: 6 g, Protein: 1 g

Flavorful Baked Okra

Prep time: 10 minutes, Cook time: 15 minutes, Servings: 4

Ingredients:

2 tbsps. olive oil
1 lb. sliced okra
½ tsp. paprika
Salt
1/8 tsp. cayenne pepper

Instructions:

1. Preheat the oven to 450 F.
2. Spread okra on baking tray and drizzle with olive oil.
3. Season with cayenne pepper, paprika, and salt. Stir well.
4. Bake in preheated oven for 15 minutes.
5. Serve and enjoy.

Nutritional Info: Calories: 105, Fat: 7 g, Carbs: 8 g, Protein: 2.2 g

Curried Cauliflower Rice

Prep time: 10 minutes, Cook time: 10 minutes, Servings: 4

Ingredients:

1 tbsp. olive oil
½ tbsp. curry powder
4 cups cauliflower rice
1 tsp. turmeric powder
½ cup vegetable stock
Salt

Instructions:

1. Heat oil in a saucepan over medium heat.
2. Add turmeric and curry powder and sauté for 30 seconds.
3. Add remaining ingredients and stir well and cook until stock is completely absorbed.
4. Stir well and serve.

Nutritional Info: Calories: 92, Fat: 8 g, Carbs: 6 g, Protein: 1 g

Grilled Eggplant

Prep time: 10 minutes, Cook time: 10 minutes, Servings: 6

Ingredients:

4 tbsps. olive oil
1 tsp. Italian seasoning
2 minced garlic cloves
Pepper
2 sliced medium eggplant
Salt

Instructions:

1. Preheat the grill to medium-high heat.
2. In a small bowl, mix together Italian seasoning, garlic, and olive oil.
3. Brush eggplant slices with olive oil mixture and place on hot grill.
4. Grill for 3-5 minutes on each side.
5. Serve and enjoy.

Nutritional Info: Calories: 120, Fat: 9 g, Carbs: 8 g, Protein: 2 g

Roasted Eggplant

Prep time: 10 minutes, Cook time: 25 minutes, Servings: 4

Ingredients:

1 tsp. kosher salt
2 tbsps. olive oil
½ tsp. pepper
1 lb. peeled and cubed eggplant

Instructions:

1. Preheat the oven to 425 F.
2. Place eggplant cubes on baking tray and drizzle with olive oil. Season with pepper and salt.
3. Roast in preheated oven for 25 minutes.
4. Serve and enjoy.

Nutritional Info: Calories: 90, Fat: 7 g, Carbs: 7 g, Protein: 1 g

Sautéed Bell Peppers

Prep time: 10 minutes, Cook time: 10 minutes, Servings: 3

Ingredients:

1 sliced onion
3 sliced bell peppers
Pepper
1 tbsp. olive oil
½ tsp. chipotle powder
Salt

Instructions:

1. Heat oil in a pan over medium-high heat.
2. Add onion and bell peppers to the pan and sauté for 10 minutes.
3. Season with chipotle powder, pepper, and salt.
4. Stir well and serve.

Nutritional Info: Calories: 90, Fat: 5 g, Carbs: 12 g, Protein: 1.6 g

Chapter 7 Fish and Seafood

Shrimp Curry

Prep time: 5 minutes, Cook time: 1 hour 20 minutes, Servings: 4

Ingredients:

½ cup Thai red curry sauce
¼ cup fresh cilantro
2½ tsps. lemon garlic seasoning
1½ cups water
1 lb. deveined shrimp
3 cups light coconut milk

Instructions:

1. Add red curry sauce, water, lemon garlic seasoning, water and coconut milk to the slow cooker and stir well.
2. Cover the lid to cook for 1 hour on Low.
3. Add shrimp to cook for 20 minutes.
4. Serve on platter garnished with fresh cilantro.

Nutritional Info: Calories: 576, Fat: 22g, Carbs: 63g, Protein: 32g

Salmon Fillet

Prep time: 5 minutes, Cook time: 1 hour, Servings: 4

Ingredients:

1 cup frozen vegetables
1 tbsp. fresh lemon juice
2 tbsps. ghee
Fresh dill
¼ tsp. pepper
1 cup water
Lemon wedges
4 salmon fillets
1 sprig fresh dill
¼ tsp. salt
1 thinly sliced small onion

Instructions:

1. Grease the slow cooker with ghee
2. Add dill and onion slices to the cooker then add chicken broth, water and lemon juice.
3. Cover the cooker with the lid to cook for 30 minutes on High.
4. Open the cooker and add frozen vegetables and fillets.
5. Cover with lid to cook for 30 minutes on High.
6. Serve on platter garnished with fresh dill and lemon wedges.
7. Enjoy.

Nutritional Info: Calories: 381, Fat: 25g, Carbs: 4g, Protein: 35g

Tilapia and Asparagus

Prep time: 20 minutes, Cook time: 2 hours, Servings: 4

Ingredients:

Lemon juice
Pepper
12 asparagus
12 tbsps. lemon juice
6 tilapia Fillets
3 tbsps. clarified butter

Instructions:

1. Make single pieces of foil for the fillets.
2. Put each piece of fillet on each foil and season with pepper then squeeze of the lemon juice.
3. Drizzle clarified butter over the fillet and top with asparagus.
4. Fold the foil over the fish and seal the ends.
5. Transfer foil packets to the slow cooker.
6. Cover the lid to cook for 2 hours on High.
7. Serve while hot and enjoy.

Nutritional Info: Calories: 229, Fat: 10g, Carbs: 1g, Protein: 28g

Shrimp Scampi

Prep time: 20 minutes, Cook time: 2 hours, Servings: 3

Ingredients:

2 tsps. minced parsley

¼ cup chicken broth

1 lb. large raw shrimp

2 tbsps. olive oil

2 tsps. chopped garlic

½ cup white wine vinegar

Instructions:

1. Put all the ingredients in the slow cooker.
2. Cover the lid to cook on Low for 2 hours.
3. Serve the rice garnished with lemon wedges and fresh parsley.

Nutritional Info: Calories: 293, Fat: 24g, Carbohydrates: 4g, Protein: 16g

Fish Broth

Prep time: 10 minutes, Cook time: 8 hours, Servings: 3

Ingredients:

2 tbsps. peppercorns

3 quarts water

Parsley bunch

Head of bones from 3 different fish

1 tsp. salt

2 quartered onions

1 tsp. pepper

2 roughly chopped celery stalks

Instructions:

1. Put all the ingredients in the slow cooker.
2. Cover the cooker to cook on Low for 8 hours.
3. Drain the liquid and leave to chill overnight.
4. Skim any foam to use as needed.

Nutritional Info: Calories: 401, Fat: 20g, Carbs: 9g, Protein: 40g

Easy Pan Sea Bass

Prep time: 10 minutes, Cook time: 15 minutes, Servings: 2

Ingredients:

3 tbsps. olive oil

1 peeled and sliced orange

¼ tsp. salt

2 boneless and skinless sea bass fillets

4 tbsps. capers

Juice of 1 lemon

1 head broccoli florets

¼ tsp. black pepper

Instructions:

1. Set a pan on fire with 2 tablespoons oil to heat over medium high heat.
2. Add seasonings and fish fillets to cook for 4 minutes with the skin side down then flip to cook for 2 more minutes and divide into plates.
3. Heat another pan on fire with the remaining oil over medium high heat.
4. Add broccoli, salt and pepper, orange segments, lemon juice and capers then toss to cook for 6 more minutes.
5. Divide next to the fish and serve.
6. Enjoy.

Nutritional Info: Calories: 322, Fat: 6g, Carbs: 9g, Protein: 18g

Roasted Char

Prep time: 10 minutes, Cook time: 10 minutes, Servings: 4

Ingredients:

2 tbsps. chopped red onion

¼ tsp. black pepper

¼ cup orange juice

5 tsps. Olive oil

¼ tsp. salt

¼ cup chopped mint

1 tbsp. balsamic vinegar

4 skinless and boneless char fillets

1 tsp. grated orange zest

Instructions:

1. Combine orange juice with orange zest, oil, mint, vinegar, salt, pepper and onion in a bowl and whisk well.
2. Arrange the fish on a baking tray and spray orange mix all over.
3. Put in the oven to cook for 10 minutes at 400⁰F.
4. Divide the fish between plates and serve.
5. Enjoy.

Nutritional Info: Calories: 345, Fat: 10g, Carbs: 13g, Protein: 27g

Easy Baked Salmon

Prep time: 10 minutes, Cook time: 15 minutes, Servings: 4

Ingredients:

1 cup chopped parsley
½ cup toasted and chopped almonds
4 boneless medium salmon fillets
¼ tsp. black pepper
1 tbsp. red vinegar
Olive oil
¼ tsp. salt
1 chopped shallot

Instructions:

1. Add salt and pepper to the salmon and arrange on a lined baking tray.
2. Set into the oven to cook for 15 minutes at 450⁰F.
3. Combine shallot with vinegar, almonds, a drizzle of oil and almonds and stir well.
4. Divide the salmon between plates and drizzle the parsley mix over and serve.
5. Enjoy.

Nutritional Info: Calories: 361, Fat: 4g, Carbs: 16g, Protein: 28g

Lemony Swordfish

Prep time: 10 minutes, Cook time: 20 minutes, Servings: 6

Ingredients:

Hot sauce
¼ tsp. sweet paprika
½ cup olive oil
¼ tsp. salt
¼ cup lemon juice
6 swordfish steaks
¼ tsp. black pepper

Instructions:

1. Combine oil with seasonings, paprika and hot sauce and whisk well.
2. Rub the fish steaks with the mix and arrange them in a baking tray then drizzle with lemon juice all over.
3. Introduce into the oven to bake for 20 minutes at 350⁰F.
4. Divide between plates and serve.
5. Enjoy.

Nutritional Info: Calories: 299, Fat: 4g, Carbs: 16g, Protein: 7g

Baked Haddock

Prep time: 10 minutes, Cook time: 30 minutes, Servings: 4

Ingredients:

1 tsp. dill weed
Vegetable oil cooking spray
3 tsps. water
Salt
2 tbsps. mayonnaise
Old Bay Seasoning
1 lb. haddock
2 tbsps. lemon juice
Ground black pepper.

Instructions:

1. Rub the baking dish with cooking oil.
2. Add fish, water and lemon juice and toss to coat.
3. Add dill, salt, pepper and Old bay seasoning then add mayonnaise and spread well.
4. Put in an oven to bake for 30 minutes at 350⁰F.
5. Divide into plates and serve.

Nutritional Info: Calories: 121, Fat: 3.5g, Carbs: 1.9g, Protein: 20.1g

Tilapia

Prep time: 10 minutes, Cook time: 10 minutes, Servings: 4

Ingredients:

¼ cup butter

4 tbsps. mayonnaise

¼ tsp. onion powder

4 boneless tilapia fillets

Ground black pepper

½ cup grated parmesan cheese

¼ tsp. garlic powder

Salt

2 tbsps. lemon juice

¼ tsp. dried basil

Vegetable oil cooking spray

Instructions:

1. Spray a baking sheet with cooking spray, and arrange the tilapia on the tray.
2. Season with salt, pepper, place under a preheated broiler, and cook for 3 minutes.
3. Turn the fish and broil for 3 minutes.
4. In a bowl, mix Parmesan cheese with mayonnaise, basil, garlic, lemon juice, onion powder, butter, and stir well.
5. Add fish to mixture, toss to coat well, place on baking sheet again, and broil for 3 minutes. Transfer to plates and serve.

Nutritional Info: Calories: 300, Fat: 20.5g, Carbs: 4.3g, Protein: 25.9g

Trout with Special Sauce

Prep time: 10 minutes, Cook time: 10 minutes, Servings: 1

Ingredients:

1 tbsp. butter

Ground black pepper

1 tbsp. olive oil

Zest, and juice from 1 lemon

½ cup chopped pecans

1 trout fillet

½ cup chopped fresh parsley

Salt

Instructions:

1. Heat a pan with the oil over medium–high heat, add fish fillet, season with salt, pepper, cook for 4 minutes on each side, transfer to a plate and keep warm.
2. Heat the same pan with butter over medium heat, add pecans, stir, and toast for 1 minutes.
3. Add lemon juice, lemon zest, some salt, pepper, and chopped parsley, stir, cook for 1 minute, and pour over the fish fillets, and serve.

Nutritional Info: Calories: 838, Fat: 81g, Carbs: 11.9g, Protein: 25g

Trout with Butter Sauce

Prep time: 10 minutes, Cook time: 10 minutes, Servings: 4

Ingredients:

6 tbsps. butter

4 trout fillets

Salt

2 tbsps. olive oil

2 tsps. lemon juice

3 tsps. grated lemon zest

Ground black pepper

3 tbsps. chopped fresh chives

Instructions:

1. Season trout with salt, pepper, drizzle olive oil, and massage into fish.
2. Heat a kitchen grill over medium–high heat, add fish fillets, cook for 4 minutes, flip, and cook for 4 minutes.
3. Heat a pan with the butter over medium heat, add salt, pepper, chives, lemon juice, lemon zest, and stir well.
4. Divide fish fillets on plates, drizzle the butter sauce over them, and serve.

Nutritional Info: Calories: 333, Fat: 29.6g, Carbs: 0.5g, Protein: 16.8g

Roasted Salmon

Prep time: 10 minutes, Cook time: 12 minutes, Servings: 4

Ingredients:

2 oz. diced kimchi
Salt
Ground black pepper
2 tbsps. softened butter
1¼ lbs. salmon fillet

Instructions:

1. In a food processor, mix butter with kimchi and blend well.
2. Rub salmon with salt, pepper, and kimchi mixture, and place into a baking dish.
3. Place in an oven at 425°F and bake for 15 minutes. Divide on plates and serve.

Nutritional Info: Calories: 467, Fat: 25g, Carbs: 0.5g, Protein: 60.6g

Breakfast Avocado and Tuna Balls

Prep time: 5 minutes, Cook time: 0 minutes, Servings: 4

Ingredients:

1 pitted and peeled avocado
½ tsp. dried dill
½ cup chopped onion
½ tsp. freshly ground black pepper
3 oz. sunflower seeds
1 can tuna
Salt.
½ tsp. smoked paprika

Instructions:

1. Thoroughly mix all ingredients in a mixing dish. Shape the mixture into 8 balls.
2. Serve well chilled and enjoy!

Nutritional Info: Calories: 316, Fat: 24.4g, Carbs: 5.9g, Protein: 17.4g

Hot and Spicy Fish Stew

Prep time: 15 minutes, Cook time: 17 minutes, Servings: 4

Ingredients:

1 cup pureed fresh tomato
2 chopped rosemary sprigs
1/8 tsp. Tabasco sauce
½ cup Sauvignon blanc
1 tbsp. chicken bouillon granules
1 tbsp. sesame oil
1 tsp. smashed garlic
1 cup chopped onions
Sea salt
4 cups water
1/3 lb. sliced halibut
½ lb. sliced sea bass

Instructions:

1. Heat the oil in a large stockpot that is preheated over medium heat. Now, sauté the onions and garlic until they're softened and aromatic.
2. Add the salt, water, tomato and chicken bouillon granules; cook an additional 13 minutes.
3. Stir in the remaining ingredients and bring to a rolling boil.
4. After that, turn the heat to medium-low and let it simmer until the fish easily flakes apart, about 4 minutes.
5. Taste and adjust the seasonings. Ladle the soup into individual bowls and serve hot.

Nutritional Info: Calories: 296, Fat: 8.6g, Carbs: 5.5g, Protein: 41.4g

Easy Oven-Baked Cod Fillets

Prep time: 8 minutes, Cook time: 22 minutes, Servings: 4

Ingredients:

Ground black pepper
2 tbsps. olive oil
½ tbsp. yellow mustard
1 tsp. garlic paste
½ tbsp. fresh lemon juice
½ tsp. shallot powder

Salt
4 cod fillets
¼ cup chopped fresh cilantro
½ tsp. crushed red pepper flakes
Instructions:
1. Start by preheating your oven to 420 degrees F. Lightly grease a baking dish with a nonstick cooking spray.
2. In a small mixing dish, thoroughly combine the oil, mustard, garlic paste, lemon juice,

shallot powder, salt, black pepper and red pepper.
3. Rub this mixture on all sides of your fish.
4. Bake 15 to 22 minutes in the middle of the preheated oven. Serve sprinkled with fresh cilantro.

Nutritional Info: Calories: 195, Fat: 8.2g, Carbs: 0.5g, Protein: 28.7g

Ricotta and Tuna Spread

Prep time: 10 minutes, Cook time: 0 minutes, Servings: 6
Ingredients:
2 oz. ground pecans
6 oz. drained tuna in oil
½ tsp. turmeric
1 tbsp. chopped fresh cilantro
½ cup Ricotta cheese
Instructions:

1. Blend tuna, Ricotta cheese, turmeric powder and pecans in your blender.
2. Transfer to a serving bowl and serve garnished with fresh cilantro.
3. Serve with veggie sticks. Bon appétit!

Nutritional Info: Calories: 384, Fat: 20.4g, Carbs: 2.5g, Protein: 0.4g

Colorful Scallop Dinner

Prep time: 10 minutes, Cook time: 3 minutes, Servings: 4
Ingredients:
Freshly ground pepper
½ cup pitted and sliced ripe olives
Sea salt
½ tsp. dried dill weed
4 roughly chopped spring garlic
1 sliced Iceberg lettuce head
½ tbsp. deli mustard
¼ cup extra-virgin olive oil
2 tbsps. fresh lemon juice
1 sliced cucumber
2 sliced plum tomatoes
1 lb. halved sea scallops
Instructions:

1. Add the scallops to a pot of a lightly salted water; cook for 1 to 3 minutes or until opaque; rinse under running water and transfer to a salad bowl.
2. Stir in spring garlic, tomatoes, cucumber, and lettuce; gently toss to combine.
3. In a mixing dish, thoroughly combine the mustard, olive oil, lemon, salt, pepper and dill. Drizzle this mixture over the vegetables in the salad bowl.
4. Serve topped with ripe olives and enjoy!

Nutritional Info: Calories: 260, Fat: 13.6g, Carbs: 5.9g, Protein: 28.1g

Trout and Fennel Parcels

Prep time: 5 minutes, Cook time: 15 minutes, Servings: 4
Ingredients:
½ lb. butterflied deboned trout
1 cup thinly sliced fennel
3 tsps. capers
Salt
3 tbsps. olive oil
4 sprigs rosemary

4 butter cubes
1 sliced medium red onion
Black pepper
4 sprigs thyme
8 lemon slices
Instructions:

1. Preheat the oven to 400°F and cut out parchment paper wide enough for each trout and in a bowl. Toss the fennel and onion with a little of olive oil and share into the middle parts of the papers.
2. Place the fish on each veggie mound, top with a drizzle of olive oil each, a season of salt and pepper, a sprig of rosemary and thyme each, and 1 cube of butter each. Also, lay the lemon slices on the fish. Wrap and close the fish packets securely, and place them on a baking sheet.
3. Bake in the oven for 15 minutes, remove once ready, and immediately plate them. Garnish the fish with capers and serve with a squash mash.

Nutritional Info: Calories: 234, Fat: 9.3g, Carbs: 2.8g, Protein: 17g

Shrimp & Mushrooms

Prep time: 5 minutes, Cook time: 7 minutes, Servings: 4

Ingredients:

1 lb. cubed potato
2 cups chicken broth
Salt
Pepper
1 tbsp. minced garlic
1 cup sliced mushrooms
½ tbsp. onion powder
½ tbsp. garlic powder
1 ½ lb. shrimp, peeled and deveined
1 cup water

Instructions:
1. Place the potatoes in the Instant Pot.
2. Pour in the chicken broth.
3. Add the salt and pepper.
4. Cover the pot.
5. Choose manual mode.
6. Cook at high pressure for 3 minutes.
7. Release the pressure naturally.
8. Add the garlic, mushrooms, onion powder, garlic powder, shrimp and water. Mix well.
9. Cover the pot and cook at high pressure for 4 minutes.

Nutritional Info: Calories: 322, Fat: 3.7g, Carbs: 25.6g, Protein: 44.4g

Red Cabbage Tilapia Taco Bowl

Prep time: 17 minutes, Cook time: Servings: 4

Ingredients:

Chili pepper
Water
¼ shredded red cabbage head
2 tsps. ghee
4 cubed tilapia fillets
2 cups cauli rice
¼ tsp. taco seasoning
Pink salt
1 pitted and chopped ripe avocado

Instructions:
1. Sprinkle cauli rice in a bowl with a little water and microwave for 3 minutes. Fluff after with a fork and set aside. Melt ghee in a skillet over medium heat, rub the tilapia with the taco seasoning, salt, and chili pepper, and fry until brown on all sides, for about 8 minutes in total.
2. Transfer to a plate and set aside. In 4 serving bowls, share the cauli rice, cabbage, fish, and avocado. Serve with chipotle lime sour cream dressing.

Nutritional Info: Calories: 269, Fat: 23.4g, Carbs: 4g, Protein: 16.5g

Sour Cream Salmon with Parmesan

Prep time: 25 minutes, Cook time: 17 minutes, Servings: 4

Ingredients:

½ cup grated parmesan cheese
1 cup sour cream
4 salmon steaks
½ zested and juiced lemon
Pink salt
½ tbsp. minced dill

Black pepper
Instructions:
1. Preheat oven to 400°F and line a baking sheet with parchment paper; set aside. In a bowl, mix the sour cream, dill, lemon zest, Juice, salt, and pepper, and set aside.
2. Season the fish with salt and black pepper, drizzle lemon juice on both sides of the fish and arrange them in the baking sheet. Spread the sour cream mixture on each fish and sprinkle with Parmesan.
3. Bake fish for 15 minutes and after broil the top for 2 minutes with a close watch for a nice a brown color. Plate the fish and serve with buttery green beans.

Nutritional Info: Calories: 288, Fat: 23.4g, Carbs: 1.2g, Protein: 16.2g

Spicy Sea Bass with Hazelnuts

Prep time: 15 minutes, Cook time: 15 minutes, Servings: 2
Ingredients:
⅓ cup roasted hazelnuts
2 sea bass fillets
¼ tsp. cayenne pepper
2 tbsps. butter
Instructions:
1. Preheat your oven to 425 °F. Line a baking dish with waxed paper. Melt the butter and brush it over the fish. In a food processor, combine the rest of the ingredients.
2. Coat the sea bass with the hazelnut mixture.
3. Place in the oven and bake for about 15 minutes.

Nutritional Info: Calories: 467, Fat: 31g, Carbs: 2.8g, Protein: 40g

Sushi Shrimp Rolls

Prep time: 10 minutes, Cook time: 0 minutes, Servings: 5
Ingredients:
¼ cup mayonnaise
2 cups cooked and chopped shrimp
¼ julienned cucumber
5 hand roll nori sheets
1 tbsp. sriracha sauce
Instructions:
1. Combine shrimp, mayonnaise, and sriracha in a bowl. Lay out a single nori sheet on a flat surface and spread about 1/5 of the shrimp mixture.
2. Roll the nori sheet as desired. Repeat with the other ingredients.

Nutritional Info: Calories: 216, Fat: 10g, Carbs: 1g, Protein: 18.7g

Sicilian-Style Zoodle Spaghetti

Prep time: 10 minutes, Cook time: 10 minutes, Servings: 2
Ingredients:
½ cup canned chopped tomatoes
1 tsp. minced garlic
1 tbsp. parsley
4 cups zoodles
4 oz. chopped canned sardines
2 oz. cubed bacon
1 tbsp. capers
Instructions:
1. Pour some of the sardine oil in a pan. Add garlic and cook for 1 minute.
2. Add the bacon and cook for 2 more minutes.
3. Stir in the tomatoes and let simmer for 5 minutes.
4. Add zoodles and sardines and cook for 3 minutes.

Nutritional Info: Calories: 355, Fat: 31g, Carbs: 6g, Protein: 20g

Blackened Fish Tacos with Slaw

Prep time: 14 minutes, Cook time: 6 minutes, Servings: 4

Ingredients:
2 tilapia fillets
4 low carb tortillas
1 tbsp. olive oil
1 tsp. paprika
1 tsp. chili powder
For the slaw:
1 tsp. apple cider vinegar
1 tbsp. olive oil
½ cup shredded red cabbage
1 tbsp. lemon juice
Instructions:

1. Season the tilapia with chili powder and paprika. Heat the olive oil in a skillet over medium heat.
2. Add tilapia and cook until blackened, about 3 minutes per side. Cut into strips.
3. Divide the tilapia between the tortillas.
4. Combine all slaw ingredients in a bowl. Split the slaw among the tortillas.

Nutritional Info: Calories: 268, Fat: 20g, Carbs: 3.5g, Protein: 13.8g

Oven Baked Fish-balls with Red Sauce

Prep time: 10 minutes, Cook time: 35 minutes, Servings: 6

Ingredients:
1 lemon
1 grated tomato
½ cup fresh chopped parsley
1 lb. white fish filet
1 egg
2 tbsps. almond flour
Sea salt
2 finely sliced garlic cloves
1 chopped scallion
2 tbsps. white wine
½ cup olive oil
Ground white pepper
Instructions:

1. Preheat your oven to 360 F/180C.
2. In a bowl combine minced fish filet, scallion finely chopped, almond flour, egg, garlic and season with the salt and white pepper.
3. Shape a fish mixture in small balls.
4. Place the fish-balls in a greased baking dish.
5. In a bowl, combine grated tomato, white wine, olive oil, fresh parsley and lemon juice.
6. Pour prepared sauce evenly over fish-balls.
7. Bake for 25 - 35 minutes and until golden brown. Serve hot.

Nutritional Info: Calories: 298, Carbs: 3.8g, Proteins: 18g, Fat: 24g

Delicious Tartar Salmon

Prep time: 10 minutes, Cook time: 0 minutes, Servings: 4

Ingredients:
Handful fresh dill
1 ½ tbsps. lemon juice
2 tbsps. olive oil
Salt
1 ½ lbs. skinless salmon fillet
Black pepper
Zest of 1 lemon
Instructions:
1. Remove the salmon bones.

2. Once cleaned, cut into small cubes with a sharp knife.
3. In a bowl, combine salmon with olive oil, dill, lemon juice, lemon zest, and salt and pepper to taste.;
4. Put the mixture in a round shape and refrigerate for 2 - 3 hours.
5. Serve cold.

Nutritional Info: Calories: 328, Carbs: 0.6g, Proteins: 37.3g, Fat: 19g

Roasted Herbed Sunchokes

Prep time: 10 minutes, Cook time: 45 minutes, Servings: 6

Ingredients:

2 tbsps. olive oil
1 tbsp. finely chopped fresh mint leaves
2 lbs. sunchokes
1 tbsp. fresh lime juice
2 tbsps. chopped fresh parsley
Salt
2 finely chopped garlic cloves
Freshly black pepper

Instructions:

1. Pre-heat oven to 375 F/190 C.
2. Just scrub the sunchokes, clean, rinse and chop into chunks.
3. Arrange on a baking sheet together with olive oil, garlic and lime juice.
4. Bake sunchokes for 35-45 minutes or until soft completely.
5. Season with the salt and pepper to taste.
6. Sprinkle with parsley and mint and serve warm.

Nutritional Info: Calories: 121, Carbs: 10.1g, Proteins: 6g, Fat: 13g

Roasted Barramundi

Prep time: 22 minutes, Cook time: 12 minutes, Servings: 4

Ingredients:

¼ cup chopped cherry tomatoes.
Black pepper
2 tsps. olive oil
2 tbsps. lemon zest
1 tbsp. lemon zest
2 tbsps. chopped parsley.
1 tbsp. olive oil
¼ cup chopped black olives.
2 barramundi fillets
2 tsps. Italian seasoning
Salt
¼ cup pitted and chopped green olives.

Instructions:

1. Rub fish with salt, pepper, Italian seasoning and 2 teaspoons olive oil, transfer to a baking dish and leave aside for now.
2. Meanwhile; in a bowl, mix tomatoes with all the olives, salt, pepper, lemon zest and lemon juice, parsley and 1 tablespoon olive oil and toss everything well.
3. Introduce fish in the oven at 400 degrees F and bake for 12 minutes
4. Divide fish on plates, top with tomato relish and serve

Nutritional Info: Calories: 150, Fat: 4g, Carbs: 1g; Protein: 10g

Spicy Shrimp

Prep time: 10 minutes, Cook time: 8 minutes, Servings: 2

Ingredients:

2 tsps. olive oil
½ lb. peeled and deveined big shrimp
Salt
1 tsp. Creole seasoning
Juice of 1 lemon
2 tsps. Worcestershire sauce
Black pepper

Instructions:

1. Arrange shrimp in one layer in a baking dish, season with salt and pepper and drizzle the oil.
2. Add Worcestershire sauce, lemon juice and sprinkle Creole seasoning.
3. Toss shrimp a bit, introduce in the oven, set it on the broiler and cook for 8 minutes
4. Divide between 2 plates and serve

Nutritional Info: Calories: 120, Fat: 3g, Carbs: 2g, Protein: 6g

Fish Curry

Prep time: 20 minutes, Cook time: 35 minutes, Servings: 4

Ingredients:

¼ cup cilantro
½ tsp. mustard seeds
1 chopped small red onion.
Black pepper.
1 tsp. curry powder
4 white fish fillets
4 tbsps. coconut oil
1-inch grated turmeric root
1½ cups coconut cream
2 chopped green chilies.
1 tsp. grated ginger
¼ tsp. ground cumin
Salt
3 minced garlic cloves

Instructions:

1. Heat up a pot with half of the coconut oil over medium heat; add mustard seeds and cook for 2 minutes
2. Add ginger, onion and garlic; stir and cook for 5 minutes
3. Add turmeric, curry powder, chilies and cumin; stir and cook for 5 minutes more
4. Add coconut milk, salt and pepper; stir, bring to a boil and cook for 15 minutes
5. Heat up another pan with the rest of the oil over medium heat; add fish; stir and cook for 3 minutes
6. Add this to the curry sauce; stir and cook for 5 minutes more
7. Add cilantro; stir, divide into bowls and serve

Nutritional Info: Calories: 500, Fat: 34g, Carbs: 6g, Protein: 44g

Mussels Soup Recipe

Prep time: 15 minutes, Cook time: 5 minutes, Servings: 8

Ingredients:

1 chopped yellow onion.
Black pepper
1 handful chopped parsley.
3 minced garlic cloves
28 oz. chopped canned tomatoes.
1 tsp. crushed red pepper flakes.
1 tbsp. olive oil
2 lbs. mussels
28 oz. crushed canned tomatoes.
2 cup chicken stock
Salt

Instructions:

1. Heat up a Dutch oven with the oil over medium high heat; add onion; stir and cook for 3 minutes
2. Add garlic and red pepper flakes; stir and cook for 1 minute
3. Add crushed and chopped tomatoes and stir.
4. Add chicken stock, salt and pepper; stir and bring to a boil.
5. Add rinsed mussels, salt and pepper, cook until they open, discard unopened ones and mix with parsley.
6. Stir, divide into bowls and serve

Nutritional Info: Calories: 250; Fat: 3g, Carbs: 2g, Protein: 8g

Grilled Shrimp

Prep time: 20 minutes, Cook time: 6 minutes, Servings: 4

Ingredients:

1 minced garlic clove
Black pepper.
2 tbsps. grated parmesan
1 lb. peeled and deveined shrimp
2 tbsps. olive oil
½ cup basil leaves

1 tbsp. lemon juice
1 tbsp. toasted pine nuts
Salt

Instructions:

1. In your food processor, mix parmesan with basil, garlic, pine nuts, oil, salt, pepper and lemon juice and blend well.
2. Transfer this to a bowl, add shrimp, toss to coat and leave aside for 20 minutes
3. Thread skewers with marinated shrimp, place them on preheated grill over medium high heat; cook for 3 minutes, flip and cook for 3 more minutes
4. Arrange on plates and serve

Nutritional Info: Calories: 185, Fat: 11g, Carbs: 2g; Protein: 13g

Sardines Salad

Prep time: 10 minutes, Cook time: 0 minutes, Servings: 1

Ingredients:
Black pepper.
1 tbsp. lemon juice
5 oz. canned sardines in oil
½ tbsp. mustard
Salt
1 chopped small cucumber.

Instructions:

1. Drain sardines, put them in a bowl and mash using a fork.
2. Add salt, pepper, cucumber, lemon juice and mustard; stir well and serve cold.

Nutritional Info: Calories: 200, Fat: 20g, Carbs: 0g, Protein: 20g

Fried Calamari and Tasty Sauce

Prep time: 30 minutes, Cook time: 0 minutes, Servings: 2

Ingredients:
Coconut oil
Salt
1 tsp. sriracha sauce
1 sliced squid
1 whisked egg
2 tbsps. coconut flour
1 tbsps. lemon juice
4 tbsps. mayo
Black pepper.

Instructions:
1. Season squid rings with salt pepper and cayenne and put them in a bowl.
2. In a bowl, whisk the egg with salt, pepper and coconut flour and whisk well.
3. Dredge calamari rings in this mix.
4. Heat up a pan with enough coconut oil over medium heat; add calamari rings, cook them until they become gold on both sides
5. Transfer to paper towels, drain grease and put in a bowl.
6. In another bowl, mix mayo with lemon juice and sriracha sauce; stir well and serve your calamari rings with this sauce on the side

Nutritional Info: Calories: 345, Fat: 32g, Carbs: 3g, Protein: 13g

Sea Bass with Capers

Prep time: 10 minutes, Cook time: 15 minutes, Servings: 4

Ingredients:
Black pepper.
2 tbsps. dill
1 lb. sea bass fillet
2 tbsps. capers
Salt
1 sliced lemon

Instructions:

1. Put sea bass fillet into a baking dish, season with salt and pepper, add capers, dill and lemon slices on top.
2. Introduce in the oven at 350 degrees F and bake for 15 minutes
3. Divide between plates and serve

Nutritional Info: Calories: 150, Fat: 3, Carbs: 0.7g, Protein: 5g

Shrimp Stew Recipe

Prep time: 15 minutes, Cook time: 8 minutes, Servings: 6

Ingredients:

¼ cup roasted and chopped red pepper.
Black pepper
¼ cup chopped yellow onion.
1 minced garlic clove
1 cup coconut milk
1½ lbs. peeled and deveined shrimp
¼ cup olive oil
2 tbsps. lime juice
¼ cup chopped cilantro.
14 oz. chopped canned tomatoes.
2 tbsps. sriracha sauce
Salt

Instructions:

1. Heat up a pan with the oil over medium heat; add onion; stir and cook for 4 minutes
2. Add peppers and garlic; stir and cook for 4 minutes more
3. Add cilantro, tomatoes and shrimp; stir and cook until shrimp turn pink.
4. Add coconut milk and sriracha sauce; stir and bring to a gentle simmer.
5. Add salt, pepper and lime juice; stir, transfer to bowls and serve

Nutritional Info: Calories: 250, Fat: 12g, Carbs: 5g, Protein: 20g

Swordfish and Mango Salsa Recipe

Prep time: 10 minutes, Cook time: 6 minutes, Servings: 2

Ingredients:

1 pitted, peeled and chopped avocado.
¼ tsp. onion powder
Black pepper.
2 medium swordfish steaks
1 chopped mango.
1 tbsp. chopped cilantro.
2 tsps. avocado oil
¼ tsp. cumin
½ balsamic vinegar
¼ tsp. garlic powder
1 peeled and sliced orange
Salt

Instructions:

1. Season fish steaks with salt, pepper, garlic powder, onion powder and cumin.
2. Heat up a pan with half of the oil over medium high heat; add fish steaks and cook them for 3 minutes on each side
3. Meanwhile; in a bowl, mix avocado with mango, cilantro, balsamic vinegar, salt, pepper and the rest of the oil and stir well.
4. Divide fish on plates, top with mango salsa and serve with orange slices on the side

Nutritional Info: Calories: 160, Fat: 3g, Carbs: 4g, Protein: 8g

Cod Coconut Curry

Prep time: 35 minutes, Cook time: 25 minutes, Servings: 6

Ingredients:

1 chopped onion
2 pounds cod
1 cup chopped dry coconut
Salt
Black pepper
1 cup fresh lemon juice

Instructions:

1. Put the cod along with all other ingredients in a pressure cooker.
2. Add 2 cups of water and cover the lid.
3. Cook on High Pressure for about 25 minutes and naturally release the pressure.
4. Open the lid and dish out the curry to serve hot.

Nutritional Info: Calories: 223, Fat: 6.1g, Carbs: 4.6g, Protein: 35.5g

Grilled Salmon

Prep time: 28 minutes, Cook time: 8 minutes, Servings: 4

Ingredients:

1 tbsp. olive oil
4 salmon fillets
Salt
1 tsp. sweet paprika
½ tsp. ancho chili powder
1 tsp. onion powder
1 tsp. ground cumin
Black pepper

For the salsa:

Black pepper.
1 chopped small red onion.
Juice from 2 limes
2 tbsps. chopped cilantro.
1 pitted, peeled and chopped avocado.

Salt

Instructions:

1. In a bowl, mix salt, pepper, chili powder, onion powder, paprika and cumin.
2. Rub salmon with this mix, drizzle the oil and rub again and cook on preheated grill for 4 minutes on each side
3. Meanwhile; in a bowl, mix avocado with red onion, salt, pepper, cilantro and lime juice and stir.
4. Divide salmon between plates and top each fillet with avocado salsa.

Nutritional Info: Calories: 300, Fat: 14, Carbs: 5g, Protein: 20g

Tasty Cod

Prep time: 10 minutes, Cook time: 20 minutes, Servings: 4

Ingredients:

1 tsp. grated ginger
Black pepper.
½ tsp. crushed chili pepper.
3 minced garlic cloves
1 lb. sliced cod
3 tbsps. soy sauce
2 chopped green onions.
1 cup fish stock
1 tbsp. balsamic vinegar
Salt

Instructions:

1. Heat up a pan over medium high heat; add fish pieces and brown it a few minutes on each side
2. Add garlic, green onions, salt, pepper, soy sauce, fish stock, vinegar, chili pepper and ginger; stir, cover, reduce heat and cook for 20 minutes
3. Divide between plates and serve

Nutritional Info: Calories: 154, Fat: 3, Carbs: 4g, Protein: 24g

Grain Free Salmon Bread

Prep time: 35 minutes, Cook time: 20 minutes, Servings: 6

Ingredients:

½ cup olive oil
¼ tsp. baking soda
2 lbs. steamed and shredded salmon
2 pastured eggs

Instructions:

1. Preheat the oven to 375⁰ F and grease a baking dish with olive oil.
2. Mix together eggs, baking soda and salmon in a bowl.
3. Pour the batter of salmon bread in the baking dish and transfer into the oven.
4. Bake for about 20 minutes and remove from the oven to serve hot.

Nutritional Info: Calories: 413, Fat: 32.4g, Carbs: 1.5g, Protein: 31.8g

Energetic Cod Platter

Prep time: 40 minutes, Cook time: 30 minutes, Servings: 6

Ingredients:

3 minced garlic cloves
1 lb. halved cherry tomatoes
24 oz. cod fillets
Salt
2 tbsps. olive oil
Black pepper

Instructions:

1. Preheat the oven to 375⁰ F and grease a baking dish.

2. Put half the cherry tomatoes in the baking dish and layer with cod fillets.

3. Season with garlic, salt and black pepper and drizzle with olive oil.

4. Arrange remaining tomatoes on the cod fillets and transfer to the oven.

5. Bake for about 30 minutes and dish out to serve hot.

Nutritional Info: Calories: 147, Fat: 5.8g, Carbs: 3.5g, Protein: 21g

Keto Dinner Mussels

Prep time: 20 minutes, Cook time: 11 minutes, Servings: 6

Ingredients:

4 tbsps. olive oil
2 lbs. cleaned and debearded mussels
2 minced garlic cloves
Salt
Black pepper
1 cup homemade chicken broth

Instructions:

1. Heat olive oil in a skillet over medium heat and add garlic.

2. Sauté for about 1 minute and add mussels.

3. Cook for about 5 minutes and stir in the broth, salt and black pepper.

4. Cover with lid and cook for about 5 minutes on low heat.

5. Dish out to a bowl and serve hot.

Nutritional Info: Calories: 218, Fat: 13g, Carbs: 6.1g, Protein: 18.9g

Prosciutto Wrapped Salmon Skewers

Prep time: 10 minutes, Cook time: 10 minutes, Servings: 4

Ingredients:

3 oz. sliced prosciutto
Black pepper
1 lb. frozen salmon pieces
1 tbsp. olive oil
¼ cup finely chopped fresh basil

Instructions:

1. Soak 4 skewers in water and season the salmon fillets with black pepper.

2. Mount the salmon fillets lengthwise on the skewers.

3. Roll the skewers in the chopped basil and wrap with prosciutto slices.

4. Drizzle with olive oil and fry in a nonstick pan for about 5-10 minutes on all sides.

5. Dish out and immediately serve.

Nutritional Info: Calories: 211, Fat: 11.7g, Carbs: 0.4g, Protein: 26.5g

Clam Chowder

Prep time: 10 minutes, Cook time: 20 minutes, Servings: 6

Ingredients:

2½ cups unsweetened almond milk
1½ cups chicken broth
13 oz. finely chopped and liquid retained clams
Sea salt
1 lb. sliced cauliflower florets
Black pepper

Instructions:

1. Put cauliflower florets, clams, almond milk, chicken broth, sea salt and black pepper in a skillet and mix well.

2. Bring to a boil and lower the heat.
3. Allow to simmer for about 20 minutes and dish out in a bowl to serve hot.

Nutritional Info: Calories: 311, Fat: 25.6g, Carbs: 12.1g, Protein: 12.3g

Lemon Herbed Salmon

Prep time: 10 minutes, Cook time: 10 minutes, Servings: 4

Ingredients:

¾ cup water
3 sprigs fresh dill
3 sprigs fresh tarragon
2 sprigs fresh basil
1 lb. salmon fillet
3 tsp. ghee
Salt
Black pepper
4 slices lemon
1 sliced zucchini
1 sliced red bell pepper
1 sliced carrot

Instructions:

1. Pour the water into the Instant Pot.
2. Add the sprigs of herbs. Place a steamer inside the pot.
3. Put the salmon on top of the rack with the skin down.
4. Brush the top of the salmon with ghee.
5. Season with the salt and pepper. Arrange lemon slices on top.
6. Cover the pot. Press the steam setting. Cook for 3 minutes.
7. Release the pressure quickly.
8. Take the salmon out of the pot and transfer to a plate.
9. Cover with foil. Discard the water and herbs. Add the vegetables to the pot. Press the sauté setting. Cook for 2 minutes.
10. Serve the salmon with the vegetables.

Nutritional Info: Calories: 206, Fat: 10.4g, Carbs: 6.4g, Protein: 23.3g

Teriyaki Salmon

Prep time: 10 minutes, Cook time: 10 minutes, Servings: 2
Preparation time: 50 minutes

Ingredients:

1¼ cup water
¼ cup soy sauce
1 tbsp. sesame oil
¼ cup mirin
1 minced garlic clove
1 tbsp. grated ginger
4 chopped green onions
2 tbsps. brown sugar
2 tsps. sesame seeds
2 salmon fillets

Instructions:

1. Mix all the ingredients except the 1 cup water, salmon fillets, sesame seeds and 2 green onions.
2. Place the salmon in a small baking sheet.
3. Pour the sauce on top.
4. Let sit for 30 minutes in the refrigerator.
5. Add 1 cup water into the pot.
6. Place a steamer rack inside.
7. Put the baking sheet with the salmon on top of the rack.
8. Seal the pot.
9. Choose manual mode.
10. Cook at high pressure for 8 minutes.
11. Sprinkle sesame seeds and remaining green onion on top before serving.

Nutritional Info: Calories: 452, Fat: 19.5g, Carbs: 33g, Protein: 40g

Chapter 8 Poultry

Creamy and Cheesy Chicken Salad

Prep time: 20 minutes, Cook time: 15 minutes, Servings: 6

Ingredients:

¼ cup finely grated parmesan
2 chicken breasts
1/3 tsp. dried basil
2 romaine hearts
½ tsp. coarse salt
¼ tsp. ground black pepper
2 sliced medium-sized cucumbers
¼ tsp. chili pepper flakes
½ tsp. dried oregano

For the dressing:

1 tsp. mustard
2 large egg yolks
1 tbsp. fresh lime juice
¼ cup olive oil

2 minced garlic cloves

Instructions:

1. Grill the chicken breast until done and cube them.
2. Toss cucumbers and chicken with black pepper, salt, oregano, chili pepper and basil then put the romaine leaves in a salad bowl.
3. Add cucumber and chicken mixture and prepare the dressing through whisking all the dressing ingredients.
4. Dress the salad and top with parmesan and serve to enjoy.

Nutritional Info: Calories: 183, Fat: 12.5g, Carbs: 1.7g, Protein: 16.3g

The Best Ever Chicken Stew

Prep time: 1 hour, Cook time: 15 minutes, Servings: 6

Ingredients:

2 finely chopped medium-sized shallots
1 tsp. dried marjoram
½ tsp. ground black pepper
1-quart chicken broth
2 tbsps. room temperature tallow
1 lb. chicken drumsticks
1 chopped celery
2 chopped ripe tomatoes
½ lb. chopped carrots
2 sliced garlic cloves
1 tsp. dried marjoram
1 chopped bell pepper
1 tsp. salt
½ tsp. smoked paprika
1 chopped poblano pepper

1 sprig rosemary

Instructions:

1. Set up a preheated large heavy pot and melt the tallow over modern flame.
2. Sweat the garlic and shallots until aromatic and tender.
3. Turn the heat to medium-high and stir in rosemary, chicken broth, chicken drumsticks and marjoram then bring to a boil.
4. Add rest of ingredients, lower the heat to medium-low to simmer for 15 minutes.
5. Remove the bones and chop the chicken into small chunks and serve.

Nutritional Info: Calories: 239, Fat: 14.7g, Carbs: 2.5g, Protein: 25.6g

Rutabaga, Taro Leaf and Chicken Soup

Prep time: 10 minutes, Cook time: 35 minutes, Servings: 4

Ingredients:

1 cup canned chicken consommé
Black pepper.
1 tbsp. chopped fresh parsley
½ cup roughly chopped taro leaves

1 lb. chicken thighs
2 peeled carrots
1 tsp. cayenne pepper
½ cup chopped leek

2 celery stalks
½ cup cubed rutabaga
¼ tsp. ground cloves
Salt
3 cups water
¼ tsp. granulated garlic

Instructions:

1. In a large stock pot, add all the ingredients with the exception of cayenne pepper.
2. Reduce the heat to medium low and simmer partially covered for about 35 minutes.
3. Discard the vegetables and chicken then add cayenne pepper to the broth to simmer for 8 more minutes.
4. Let the chicken thighs cool and cut off meat from the bones.
5. Add the meat back to the soup and serve warm.
6. Enjoy.

Nutritional Info: Calories: 256, Fat: 12.9g, Carbs: 3.2g, Protein: 35.1g

Chicken Liver Pâté with Keto Flatbread

Prep time: 30 minutes, Cook time: 2 hours, Servings: 4

Ingredients:
1 finely chopped white onion
10 oz. chicken livers
4 tbsps. olive oil
1 tsp. granulated garlic
½ tsp. Italian seasoning blend

For Flatbread:
½ tsp. minced fresh ginger
1 cup lukewarm water
½ tsp. turmeric powder
½ cup flax meal
1 ½ tbsps. psyllium husks
Salt
½ stick butter
1 ¼ cups almond flour

Instructions:

1. Blend granulated garlic, chicken livers, olive oil, Italian seasoning and onion and combine well before reserving.
2. Make the flatbread by combining all dry ingredients in a bowl.
3. Combine all wet ingredients and add them to the dry mixture and mix well.
4. Let the dough rest for about 2 hours at room temperature.
5. Divide the dough into eight balls and roll out each ball until it is very thin.
6. Cook in a slightly greased skillet that is preheated over medium-high heat.
7. Cook for 1 minute per side and serve the chicken with liver pâté.
8. Enjoy.

Nutritional Info: Calories: 395, Fat: 30.2g, Carbs: 3.6g, Protein: 17.9g

Chicken Nuggets

Prep time: 10 minutes, Cook time: 15 minutes, Servings: 2

Ingredients:
2 cubed chicken breasts
1 egg
Ground black pepper.
½ cup butter
½ cup coconut flour
Salt
2 tbsps. garlic powder

Instructions:

1. Set up a small bowl to combine garlic powder with salt, pepper, garlic powder and stir.
2. Set up another medium bowl and whisk the egg well.
3. Pass the chicken cubes through the egg mixture then the flour mixture.
4. Set a pan on fire over medium heat and drop chicken nuggets to cook for 5 minutes per side.
5. Transfer to paper towels and grease before serving.
6. Enjoy!

Nutritional Info: Calories: 1171, Fat: 74.9g, Carbs: 26.3g, Protein: 94.1g

Chinese-Style Turkey Meatballs

Prep time: 10 minutes, Cook time: 15 minutes, Servings: 4
Ingredients:
For the meatballs:
1/3 tsp. Five-spice powder
1/3 cup freshly grated cheddar cheese
¾ lb. ground turkey
1 egg
1/3 tsp. black pepper
For the sauce:
½ tsp. cayenne pepper
¾ cup erythritol
1 1/3 cups water
½ cup sugar-free tomato puree
1/3 tsp. guar gum
2 tbsps. Worcestershire sauce
1/3 cup red wine vinegar
Instructions:
1. In a mixing bowl, thoroughly combine egg, ground turkey, black pepper, Five-spice powder and cheese then form about 28 meatballs out of the mixture.
2. Preheat a nonstick skillet over medium heat and brown the meatballs on all sides before setting aside.
3. To the skillet, add vinegar, cayenne pepper, Worcestershire sauce, water, erythritol and cayenne pepper and whisk until mixed.
4. Gradually add the guar gum and whisk until the sauce is thickened.
5. Reduce the temperature and bring the sauce to simmer while stirring periodically.
6. Add meatballs to the sauce and simmer for 12 more minutes until the meatballs are thoroughly cooked. Serve with lettuce and enjoy.

Nutritional Info: Calories: 244, Fat: 13.7g, Carbs: 5g, Protein: 27.6g

Chicken Meatballs

Prep time: 10 minutes, Cook time: 15 minutes, Servings: 3
Ingredients:
3 tsps. cayenne pepper powder
1 egg
1 lb. ground chicken
Salt
½ cup almond flour
¼ cup tomato paste
Ground black pepper.
Instructions:
1. Stir together chicken meat, salt, pepper, tomato paste, flour, egg and cayenne pepper in a mixing bowl.
2. Mold 9 meatballs and put them on a lined baking sheet to bake for 15 minutes at 500⁰F.
3. Serve the chicken meatballs alongside hot sauce.

Nutritional Info: Calories: 461, Fat: 19.2g, Carbs: 18.7g, Protein: 52.2g

Grilled Chicken Wings

Prep time: 2 hours 10 minutes, Cook time: 15 minutes, Servings: 5
Ingredients:
Lime wedges.
1 chopped jalapeño pepper
Ground black pepper.
2 lbs. wings
3 tbsps. coconut oil
Salt
2 peeled and minced garlic cloves
½ cup chopped fresh cilantro
Juice from 1 lime
Instructions:
1. In a large bowl, combine lime juice with cilantro, coconut oil, jalapeño, garlic, salt, and pepper and whisk well.
2. Add chicken wings and toss to coat then refrigerate for 2 hours.
3. Put the chicken wings in the preheated grill pan over medium-high heat to cook for 7 minutes on each of the sides.
4. Serve the chicken wings with lime wedges.

Nutritional Info: Calories: 723, Fat: 51.8g, Carbs: 0.6g, Protein: 60.3g

Bacon Wrapped Chicken with Grilled Asparagus

Prep time: 10 minutes, Cook time: 40 minutes, Servings: 4

Ingredients:

1 lb. asparagus spears
1 tbsp. olive oil
3 tbsps. olive oil
2 tbsps. fresh lemon juice
Black pepper.
8 bacon slices
6 chicken breasts
Pink salt

Instructions:

1. Preheat the oven to 400°F.
2. Add seasonings to chicken breasts and wrap 2 slices of bacon around each chicken breast.
3. Arrange them on a baking sheet lined with parchment paper.
4. Drizzle with oil to bake for 30 minutes until bacon is brown and crispy.
5. Preheat the grill over high heat.
6. Rub asparagus spears with olive oil and season with salt.
7. Grill for 10 minutes turning frequently until charred.
8. Set on a plate and drizzle with lemon juice.

Nutritional Info: Calories: 468, Fat: 38g, Carbs: 2g, Protein: 26g

Cilantro Chicken Breasts with Mayo-Avocado Sauce

Prep time: 10 minutes, Cook time: 12 minutes, Servings: 4

Ingredients:

For the sauce:
½ cup mayonnaise
Salt
1 pitted avocado
For the chicken:
½ cup chicken broth
Black pepper.
3 tbsps. ghee
1 cup chopped cilantro leaves
Pink salt
4 chicken breasts

Instructions:

1. In a small food processor, spoon the avocado, salt and mayonnaise and puree until a smooth sauce is formed.
2. Pour the sauce into a jar and refrigerate while making the chicken.
3. In a large skillet, melt ghee and season with pepper and salt to fry for 4 minutes per side until golden brown then set the chicken on a plate.
4. Pour the broth in the same skillet, add cilantro and bring to simmer covered for 3 minutes and add the chicken.
5. Cover to cook for 5 minutes on low until the chicken is fragrant and the liquid has reduced.
6. Dish the chicken into serving plates and spoon mayo sauce over.

Nutritional Info: Calories: 398, Fat: 32g, Carbs: 4g, Protein: 24g

Chicken Enchiladas

Prep time: 5 minutes, Cook time: 25 minutes, Servings: 2

Ingredients:

2 oz. chopped shiitake mushrooms
½ tbsp. olive oil
Sea salt
2 oz. shredded chicken
½ tsp. apple cider vinegar
Black pepper.

Instructions:

1. Heat olive oil in a skillet and add mushrooms.
2. Sauté for about 30 seconds and stir in chicken.
3. Cook for about 2 minutes and pour in apple cider vinegar.
4. Season with sea salt and black pepper and cover the lid.
5. Cook for about 20 minutes on medium low heat.
6. Dish out and serve hot.

Nutritional Info: Calories: 88, Fat: 4.4g, Carbs: 3.9g, Protein: 8.7g

Lemon Threaded Chicken Skewers

Prep time: 17 minutes, Cook time: 2 hours, Servings: 4

Ingredients:

1 tsp. rosemary leaves

4 lemon wedges

2/3 jar peeled and drained preserved lemon

2 minced garlic cloves

½ cup lemon juice

Salt

3 cubed chicken breasts

Black pepper

2 tbsps. divided olive oil

Instructions:

1. First, thread the chicken onto skewers and set aside.
2. In a wide bowl, mix half of the oil, garlic, salt, pepper, and lemon juice, and add the chicken skewers, and lemon rind. Cover the bowl and let the chicken marinate for at least 2 hours in the refrigerator.
3. When the marinating time is almost over, preheat a grill to 350ºF, and remove the chicken onto the grill. Cook for 6 minutes on each side.
4. Remove and serve warm with a drizzle of tomato sauce. Garnish with rosemary leaves and lemons wedges, and serve with braised asparagus.

Nutritional Info: Calories: 350, Fat: 11g, Carbs: 3.5g, Protein: 34g

Healthy Chicken Salad

Prep time: 10 minutes, Cook time: 10 minutes, Servings: 4

Ingredients:

½ tsp. mustard powder

1/3 cup olive oil

2 egg yolks

1 tbsp. lime juice

2 chicken breasts

½ tsp. sea salt

1 large pitted and sliced avocado

¼ tsp. dried thyme

1 tbsp. Worcestershire sauce

1/3 tsp. sea salt

1/3 tsp. crushed red pepper flakes

Instructions:

1. Put your grill on high. Season the chicken breasts with pepper, salt and thyme. Cook each side of the chicken for 3 – 5 minutes until browned.
2. Cut the grilled chicken into strips.
3. Put the sliced avocado onto 4 plates.
4. Make the dressing. Combine the egg yolks, Worcestershire sauce, olive oil, lime juice, mustard powder and sea salt.
5. Put the chicken strips on top of the avocado and then pour the dressing over them. Enjoy!

Nutritional Info: Calories: 400, Protein: 22.7g, Fat: 34.2g, Carbs: 4.8g

Delicious and Easy Chicken Drumettes

Prep time: 4 minutes, Cook time: 26 minutes, Servings: 4

Ingredients:

1 tsp. dried marjoram

1 tbsp. Worcestershire sauce

4 chicken drumettes

½ cups chopped leeks

1 sliced carrot

½ tsp. mustard seeds

1 rosemary sprig

2 minced garlic cloves

1 thyme sprig

2 crushed tomatoes

2 tbsps. tallow

Salt

1 tsp. cayenne pepper

1 tsp. mixed peppercorns

1 cup turkey stock

Instructions:

1. Put a saucepan on a moderate-high heat and melt the tallow, Put the salt on the chicken drumettes.

2. Fry the chicken drumettes until they are brown on all sides. Put to one side.
3. In the pan drippings cook the garlic, carrots and leeks over a moderate heat for 6 minutes.
4. Add the remaining ingredients and the chicken and simmer for 15 – 20 minutes

partially covered. Serve hot with mashed potatoes.

Nutritional Info: Calories: 165, Protein: 12.4g, Fat: 9.8g, Carbs: 4.7g

Salsa Chicken Sausage

Prep time: 10 minutes, Cook time: 6 minutes, Servings: 4

Ingredients:

1 cup diced onion
2 tbsps. minced fresh cilantro
2 deveined and chopped bell peppers
1 cup pureed tomato
2 tsps. lard at room temperature
1 tsp. granulated garlic
¼ cup Sauvignon Blanc
3 tsps. lime juice
4 sliced chicken sausage
1 minced jalapeno pepper

Directions:

1. Put a skillet on a medium-high heat and warm the lard.
2. Fry the chicken sausage until browned. Pour in the wine and cook for 3 minutes. Put to one side.
3. Make the salsa by mixing together the lime juice, cilantro, onion, jalapeno pepper, tomato, garlic and bell peppers.
4. Place the sausage on 4 plates and put the salsa on the side. Serve!!

Nutritional Info: Calories: 156, Protein: 16.2g, Fat: 4.2g, Carbs: 4.1g

Chicken Thighs with a Rum Glaze

Prep time: 5 minutes, Cook time: 55 minutes, Servings: 4

Ingredients:

2 lbs. chicken thighs
2 tbsps. olive oil
Sea salt
Ground black pepper
1 tsp. dried marjoram
1 tsp. paprika
1 tsp. dried oregano
2 minced habanero chili peppers
1 tbsp. minced fresh ginger
1 tsp. ground allspice
2 tbsps. Swerve
3 tbsps. soy sauce
¾ cup dark rum
2 pureed ripe tomatoes
2 tbsps. fresh lime juice

Instructions:

1. Put your oven on at 420 degrees F.
2. Mix together the olive oil, salt, pepper, marjoram, paprika and oregano. Toss the chicken thighs in this mixture.
3. In another bowl mix together the habanero chili peppers, fresh ginger, allspice, Swerve, soy sauce, dark rum, tomatoes and lime juice.
4. Pour this mixture over the chicken thighs and marinate in the fridge for 2 hours. Make sure you cover the bowl.
5. Pour the marinade into a bowl and put the chicken thighs on a baking sheet. Cook for about 50 minutes.
6. While they are baking, heat the marinade over a moderate heat. Cook until the liquid has reduced by half.
7. Pour the marinade over the chicken and cook under the broiler on high for 4 minutes. Serve hot.

Nutritional Info: Calories: 307, Protein: 33.6g, Fat 12.1g, Carbs 2.7g

Turkey Balls

Prep time: 15 minutes, Cook time: 20 minutes, Servings: 6

Ingredients:

2 tsps. ginger-garlic paste
Salt
1 cup chopped broccoli
Lemon pepper seasoning.
1 lb. boiled and chopped turkey
½ cup olive oil

Instructions:

1. Preheat the oven to 360^0 F and grease a baking tray.

2. Mix together turkey, olive oil, broccoli, ginger-garlic paste, salt and lemon pepper seasoning in a bowl.
3. Make small balls out of this mixture and arrange on the baking tray.
4. Transfer to the oven and bake for about 20 minutes.
5. Remove from the oven and serve with the dip of your choice.

Nutritional Info: Calories: 275, Fat: 20.1g, Carbs: 1.5g, Protein: 22.4g

Chicken Zucchini Cutlets

Prep time: 15 minutes, Cook time: 5 minutes, Servings: 6

Ingredients:

½ lb. boiled and chopped chicken
Black pepper.
3 boiled and mashed zucchinis
½ cup avocado oil
Salt
3 tbsps. lemon pepper seasoning

Instructions:

1. Mix together chicken, zucchinis, lemon pepper seasoning, salt and black pepper in a bowl.

2. Make cutlets out of this mixture and set aside.
3. Heat avocado oil in a pan and put the cutlets in it.
4. Fry for about 2-3 minutes on each side and dish out to serve.

Nutritional Info: Calories: 106, Fat 3.8g, Carbs: 6.4g, Protein: 12.7g

Air Fried Chicken

Prep time: 10 minutes, Cook time: 10 minutes, Servings: 2

Ingredients:

1 tablespoon olive oil
4 skinless, boneless chicken tenderloins
1 egg
Salt
Black pepper.
½ tsp. turmeric powder

Instructions:

1. Preheat the air fryer to 370^0 F and coat the fryer basket with olive oil.

2. Beat the egg and dip the chicken tenderloins in it.
3. Mix together turmeric powder, salt and black pepper in a bowl and dredge chicken tenderloins.
4. Arrange the chicken tenderloins in the fryer basket and cook for about 10 minutes.
5. Dish out on a platter and serve with salsa.

Nutritional Info: Calories: 304, Fat: 15.2g, Carbs: 0.6g, Protein: 40.3g

Mediterranean Turkey Cutlets

Prep time: 15 minutes, Cook time: 20 minutes, Servings: 6

Ingredients:

1 cup almond flour
2 tsps. Greek seasoning
4 tbsps. olive oil
2 tsps. turmeric powder
2 lbs. turkey cutlets

Instructions:

1. Mix together almond flour, Greek seasoning and turmeric powder in a bowl.
2. Dredge the turkey cutlets and set aside for about 15 minutes.
3. Heat olive oil in a skillet and transfer half of the turkey cutlets.
4. Cover the lid and cook on medium low heat for about 20 minutes.
5. Dish out in a serving platter and repeat with the remaining batch.

Nutritional Info: Calories: 454, Fat: 25.9g, Carbs: 5g, Protein: 48.4g

Chicken Coconut Curry

Prep time: 10 minutes, Cook time: 30 minutes, Servings: 6

Ingredients:

1 tbsp. grated fresh ginger
13 oz. coconut milk
6 skinless and boneless chicken thighs
1 tbsp. curry powder
1 tsp. salt
1 tbsp. chopped garlic
1 chopped jalapeno
1 lime juice
15 fresh basil leaves
1 sliced onion

Instructions:

1. Add all ingredients except basil and lime juice into the instant pot and stir well.
2. Seal pot with lid and select soup button, it takes 30 minutes.
3. Allow to releasing pressure naturally then open the lid.
4. Stir well and using fork lightly shred the chicken.
5. Add basil and lime juice and stir well.
6. Serve hot and enjoy.

Nutritional Info: Calories: 437, Fat 25.7 g, Carbs: 7.6 g, Protein: 44.3 g

Tasty Chicken Fajitas

Prep time: 12 minutes, Cook time: 8 minutes, Servings:6

Ingredients:

3 sliced bell peppers
1 fresh lime juice
1 sliced onion
3 minced garlic cloves
1 packet taco seasoning
2 lbs. chicken tenderloins
10 oz. diced tomatoes

Instructions:

1. Place chicken into the instant pot then sprinkles taco seasoning over chicken.
2. Add lime juice, onion, peppers, garlic, and tomatoes over the chicken.
3. Seal instant pot with lid and cook on manual high pressure for 8 minutes.
4. Release pressure using quick release method than open the lid carefully.
5. Serve and enjoy.

Nutritional Info: Calories: 177, Fat: 1 g, Carbs: 11.2 g, Protein: 31.9 g

Simple Lime Chicken

Prep time: 14 minutes, Cook time: 6 minutes, Servings: 4

Ingredients:
¼ tsp. black pepper
1 ½ tsps. chili powder
1 tsp. onion powder
1 tsp. cumin
5 minced garlic cloves
2 fresh limes juice
1 tsp. kosher salt
2 lbs. skinless and boneless chicken breasts
½ tsp. liquid smoke

Instructions:
1. Place chicken into the instant pot.
2. Add lemon juice and sprinkle all seasoning over the chicken.
3. Add garlic and liquid smoke and rub all over the chicken.
4. Seal pot with lid and cook on high pressure for 6 minutes.
5. Allow releasing pressure naturally then open the lid.
6. Using fork shred the chicken.
7. Season chicken with pepper and salt.
8. Serve and enjoy.

Nutritional Info: Calories: 444, Fat: 17.1 g, Carbs: 2.6 g, Protein: 66.1 g

Olive Lemon Chicken

Prep time: 10 minutes, Cook time: 10 minutes, Servings: 4

Ingredients:
½ tsp. cumin
½ juiced lemon
½ cup sliced onion
1 cup chicken broth
1 can pitted green olives
¼ tsp. black pepper
1 tsp. sea salt
4 skinless and boneless chicken breasts

Instructions:
1. Season chicken with pepper and salt.
2. Set the instant pot on sauté mode then place season chicken into the pot and brown them on both the sides.
3. Add all remaining ingredients and seal pot with lid.
4. Cook on manual high pressure for 10 minutes.
5. Release pressure using quick release method than open the lid.
6. Serve and enjoy.

Nutritional Info: Calories: 499, Fat: 34.3 g, Carbs: 1.9 g, Protein: 44 g

Juicy and Tender Chicken Breasts

Prep time: 10 minutes, Cook time: 10 minutes, Servings: 3

Ingredients:
¼ tsp. garlic salt
1 cup water
1/8 tsp. dried basil
1 tbsp. extra virgin olive oil
¼ tsp. black pepper
3 skinless and boneless chicken breasts
1/8 tsp. dried oregano

Instructions:
1. Add oil into the instant pot and select sauté function.
2. Season chicken breasts from one side and place into the instant pot.
3. Sauté chickens for 3 minutes then turn to another side.
4. Season chicken with the second side and sauté for another 3 minutes.
5. Transfer chicken to a dish and pour 1 cup water into the pot.
6. Place trivet into the pot.
7. Place season chicken breasts over the trivet.
8. Seal pot with lid and cook on manual high pressure for 5 minutes.
9. Allow releasing pressure naturally then open the lid.
10. Serve and enjoy.

Nutritional Info: Calories: 319, Fat: 15.5 g, Carbs: 0.3 g, Protein 42.3 g

Yummy Chicken Soup

Prep time: 10 minutes, Cook time: 20 minutes, Servings: 4

Ingredients:

2 peeled and diced medium carrots
2 sliced celery ribs
1 ½ lbs. chicken drumsticks
2 bay leaves
1 peeled and diced rutabaga
1 peeled and diced parsnip
½ tsp. black pepper
4 cups chicken broth
1 diced small onion

Instructions:

1. Add all ingredients into the instant pot and stir well.
2. Seal pot with lid and select soup function.
3. Allow releasing pressure naturally then open the lid.
4. Remove meat from chicken drumsticks and discard bones.
5. Return meat to the pot and stir well.
6. Season with pepper and salt.
7. Serve and enjoy.

Nutritional Info: Calories 411, Fat: 11.4 g, Carbs: 20.7 g, Protein: 53.9 g

Easy Chicken Wings

Prep time: 10 minutes, Cook time: 20 minutes, Servings: 6

Ingredients:

1 1/3 lbs. chicken wings
1½ tsps. smoked salt
4 tbsps. taco seasoning

Instructions:

1. In a dish mix together taco seasoning and smoked salt.
2. Coat all chicken wings with seasoning mixture.
3. Pour 1 cup water into the pot then place trivet into the pot.
4. Place seasoned chicken wings over the trivet.
5. Seal pot with lid and cook on manual high pressure for 10 minutes.
6. Allow releasing pressure naturally then open the lid.
7. Transfer chicken wings to baking sheet and broil chicken wings for 10 minutes.
8. Serve hot and enjoy.

Nutritional Info: Calories: 207, Fat 7.5 g, Carbs: 3 g, Protein 29.2 g

Green Chicken Curry

Prep time: 10 minutes, Cook time: 20 minutes, Servings: 4

Ingredients:

1 tbsp. extra virgin olive oil
1 tsp. sea salt
14 oz. coconut milk
1 tbsp. coconut palm sugar
2 tbsps. green curry paste
1 sliced medium onion
¼ cup chopped fresh cilantro
1 peeled and diced large sweet potato
3 diced small zucchini
1¼ lbs. skinless, boneless and sliced chicken thighs

Instructions:

1. Add 1 tbsp. oil in instant pot and set the pot on sauté mode.
2. Add zucchini in a pot and sauté for 6 minutes then remove from pot and set aside. Add remaining oil to the pot. Add onion and sauté for 5 minutes.
3. Stir in coconut sugar, curry paste, and salt and cook for few minutes.
4. Add coconut milk and stir well.
5. Add sweet potatoes and chicken and stir well.
6. Seal pot with lid and cook on high pressure for 10 minutes.
7. Release pressure using quick release method than open the lid.
8. Stir in cilantro and zucchini. Serve and enjoy.

Nutritional Info: Calories: 583, Fat: 36.9 g, Carbs: 19.9 g, Protein: 45.3 g

Chicken Potato Curry

Prep time: 10 minutes, Cook time: 25 minutes, Servings: 8

Ingredients:

4 cups peeled and diced potatoes
1 tsp. kosher salt
2 tbsps. extra virgin olive oil
1 tsp. garlic powder
1 tbsp. coconut sugar
1 cup water
4 lbs. chicken thighs
2 tbsps. curry powder
1 tsp. onion powder

Instructions:

1. In a large bowl, combine together chicken, oil, 1 tbsp. curry powder, onion powder, garlic powder and salt and set aside for 1 hour.
2. Add marinated chicken into the instant pot.
3. Set the instant pot on sauté mode and brown the chicken on all sides.
4. Add coconut sugar, potatoes, and 1 tbsp. curry powder into the pot and stir well.
5. Seal pot with lid and cook on manual high pressure for 25 minutes.
6. Release pressure using quick release method than open the lid.
7. Stir well and serve.

Nutritional Info: Calories: 658, Fat: 34.9 g, Carbs: 16.5 g, Protein: 68.5 g

Tasty Chicken Enchilada Soup

Prep time: 10 minutes, Cook time: 20 minutes, Servings:6

Ingredients:

1 tbsp. chili powder
14 oz. crushed tomatoes
½ tsp. ground pepper
1 sliced bell pepper
½ tsp. smoked paprika
½ tsp. sea salt
1 tsp. oregano
1 tbsp. cumin
½ cup water
2 cups chicken broth
3 minced garlic cloves
1½ lbs. skinless and boneless chicken thighs

Instructions:

1. Add all ingredients into the instant pot and stir well.
2. Seal pot with lid and cook on manual high pressure for 20 minutes.
3. Allow releasing pressure naturally then open the lid.
4. Using fork shred the chicken.
5. Stir well and serve.

Nutritional Info: Calories: 268, Fat: 9.4 g, Carbs: 8.9 g, Protein: 35.9 g

Delicious Chicken Lettuce Wraps

Prep time: 10 minutes, Cook time: 10 minutes, Servings: 4

Ingredients:

5 tsps. minced garlic
1/8 tsp. allspice
2 tbsps. balsamic vinegar
¼ cup chicken broth
½ cup drained and sliced water chestnuts
½ tsp. ground ginger
¾ cup diced onion
1 lb. ground chicken
¼ cup coconut amino

Instructions:

1. Add all ingredients into the instant pot and stir well.
2. Seal pot with lid and select manual and set timer for 10 minutes.
3. Release pressure using quick release method than open the lid.
4. Add meat into lettuce leaves and serve.

Nutritional Info: Calories: 269, Fat: 8.6 g, Carbs: 10.5 g, Protein: 33.6 g

Simple Shredded Chicken

Prep time: 5 minutes, Cook time: 20 minutes, Servings: 8

Ingredients:
4 lbs. chicken breasts
½ cup chicken broth
½ tsp. black pepper
1 tsp. salt

Instructions:
1. Add all ingredients into the instant pot.
2. Seal pot with lid and cook on manual high pressure for 20 minutes.
3. Release pressure using quick release method than open the lid.
4. Using fork shred the chicken and serves.

Nutritional Info: Calories: 434, Fat: 16.9 g, Carbs: 0.1 g, Protein: 65.9 g

Flavorful Chicken Curry

Prep time: 15 minutes, Cook time: 6 minutes, Servings: 4

Ingredients:
2 tsps. garam masala
½ chopped yellow pepper
3 minced garlic cloves
1 chopped small onion
½ cup coconut milk
2 lbs. skinless and boneless chicken breast
½ tsp. turmeric
1 tsp. coriander
15 oz. diced tomatoes
1 tsp. cumin
¼ tsp. cayenne pepper
2 tbsps. extra virgin olive oil
1 tsp. grated fresh ginger

Ingredients:
1. Add oil, yellow peppers, and onion into the instant pot and select sauté and cook for 4 minutes.
2. Add spices, ginger, garlic, and salt and cook for another 2 minutes.
3. Add coconut milk and tomatoes and stir well.
4. Add chicken and seal pot with lid and select poultry function.
5. Open the lid and using fork shred the chicken.
6. Stir well and serve.

Nutritional Info: Calories: 428, Fat: 20.3 g, Carbs: 10.4 g, Protein: 50.5 g

Perfect Mexican Chicken

Prep time: 10 minutes, Cook time: 15 minutes, Servings: 6

Ingredients:
4 oz. diced jalapenos
1 tbsp. extra virgin olive oil
½ cup red bell pepper
2/3 cup chicken broth
2 tsps. cumin
2 tsps. garlic powder
10 oz. diced tomatoes
½ cup green bell pepper
¼ tsp. salt
1 fresh lime juice
2 lbs. chicken breasts
½ tsp. chili powder
½ cup diced onion

Instructions:
1. Add oil into the instant pot and select sauté.
2. Add onion, bell peppers and salt into the pot and sauté for 3 minutes.
3. Add remaining ingredients into the pot and stir well.
4. Seal pot with lid and cook on manual high pressure for 12 minutes.
5. Release pressure using quick release method than open the lid carefully.
6. Remove chicken from pot and using fork shred the chicken.
7. Return chicken to the instant pot and stir well. Serve and enjoy.

Nutritional Info: Calories: 341, Fat: 14.2 g, Carbs: 9.7 g, Protein: 46.1 g

Instant Pot Whole Chicken

Prep time: 10 minutes, Cook time: 20 minutes, Servings: 8

Ingredients:

1 chopped medium onion
1 tsp. thyme
Salt
3 cups water
2 chopped large carrots
1 tsp. oregano
5 smashed garlic cloves
Pepper
3 chopped celery stalks
5 lbs. whole chicken

Instructions:

1. Add garlic and vegetables into the instant pot.
2. Pour water into the instant pot then place a rack over the veggies.
3. Season chicken with herbs, pepper, and salt.
4. Place chicken into the instant pot rack.
5. Seal pot with lid and select meat setting.
6. Allow releasing pressure naturally then open the lid.
7. Cut chicken into the pieces and serve.

Nutritional Info: Calories: 556, Fat: 21.1 g, Carbs: 4.1 g, Protein: 82.5 g

Onion Garlic Chicken

Prep time: 8 minutes, Cook time: 12 minutes, Servings: 6

Ingredients:

½ tsp. salt
1 tbsp. chopped garlic
1 chopped small onion
1 cup chicken broth
2 lbs. skinless and boneless chicken breasts

Instructions:

1. Add all ingredients into the instant pot and stir well.
2. Seal pot with lid and cook on manual high pressure for 12 minutes.
3. Allow releasing pressure naturally then open the lid.
4. Remove chicken from pot and using fork shred the chicken.
5. Return chicken to the instant pot and stir well.
6. Serve and enjoy.

Nutritional Info: Calories: 300, Fat: 11.5 g, Carbs: 1.7 g, Protein: 44.8 g

Mushroom Leek Chicken

Prep time: 10 minutes, Cook time: 15 minutes, Servings: 6

Ingredients:

1¼ lbs. sliced mushrooms
3 lbs. sliced leeks
2 tbsps. arrowroot
½ tsp. pink Himalayan salt
6 skinless and boneless chicken breasts
½ cup chicken broth
¼ tsp. pepper

Instructions:

1. Season chicken with pepper and salt.
2. Add chicken to the pot and brown them on both the sides.
3. Remove chicken from pot and place on a plate.
4. Add chicken broth, mushrooms, leeks, and chicken to the pot and stir well.
5. Seal pot with lid and cook on manual high pressure for 8 minutes.
6. Allow releasing pressure naturally for 4 minutes then release pressure using quick release method than open the lid.
7. Transfer chicken from pot and place on a plate.
8. Stir arrowroot to the pot and select sauté. Stir for 2 minutes.
9. Serve chicken on top of mushrooms and leeks.

Nutritional Info: Calories: 555, Fat: 24.3 g, Carbs: 36.8 g, Protein: 49.7 g

Spicy Buffalo Chicken

Prep time: 13 minutes, Cook time: 12 minutes, Servings: 6

Ingredients:

½ cup buffalo wing sauce
½ cup chicken broth
2/3 cup chopped onion
2 lbs. chicken breasts
½ cup diced celery

Instructions:

1. Add all ingredients into the instant pot and stir well.
2. Seal pot with lid and cook on manual high pressure for 12 minutes.
3. Release pressure using quick release method than open the lid carefully.
4. Remove chicken from pot and using fork shred the chicken.
5. Return chicken to the instant pot and stir well.
6. Serve and enjoy.

Nutritional Info: Calories: 297, Fat: 11.3 g, Carbs: 1.6 g, Protein: 44.3 g

Onion Balsamic Chicken

Prep time: 13 minutes, Cook time: 12 minutes, Servings: 6

Ingredients:

1 tbsp. Dijon mustard
1/3 cup balsamic vinegar
2 lbs. chicken breasts
1 tsp. chopped garlic
1 chopped medium onion
½ tsp. dried thyme
½ cup chicken broth

Instructions:

1. Combine together Dijon, chicken broth, and vinegar and pour into the instant pot.
2. Add thyme, garlic, onion, and chicken to the pot and stir well.
3. Seal pot with lid and cook on manual high pressure for 12 minutes.
4. Release pressure using quick release method than open the lid.
5. Remove chicken from pot and using fork shred the chicken.
6. Return shredded chicken to the instant pot and stir well.
7. Serve and enjoy.

Nutritional Info: Calories: 303, Fat: 11.4 g, Carbs: 2.3 g, Protein: 44.5 g

Spicy Shredded Chicken

Prep time: 10 minutes, Cook time: 20 minutes, Servings: 8

Ingredients:

1 tbsp. extra virgin olive oil
2 lbs. chicken breasts
½ chopped onion
½ cup hot sauce
½ chopped red bell pepper

Instructions:

1. Add oil in instant pot and select sauté.
2. Add onion and bell peppers to the pot and sauté for 4 minutes.
3. Add chicken and hot sauce and stir well.
4. Seal pot with lid and cook on high pressure for 12 minutes.
5. Release pressure using quick release method than open the lid carefully.
6. Remove chicken from pot and using fork shred the chicken.
7. Return chicken to the instant pot and stir well.
8. Serve and enjoy.

Nutritional Info: Calories: 237, Fat: 10.2 g, Carbs: 1.5 g, Protein: 33 g

Yummy Chicken Tacos

Prep time: 10 minutes, Cook time: 15 minutes, Servings: 8

Ingredients:

½ cup chicken stock
14 oz. tomato paste
1 tsp. hot sauce
½ tsp. crushed red pepper
Pepper
½ tsp. cilantro
2 lbs. chicken breasts
1 tbsp. coriander
2 tbsps. cumin
1 tbsp. extra virgin olive oil
1 chopped onion
Salt

Instructions:

1. Add oil in instant pot and select sauté.
2. Add onion to the pot and sauté for 3 minutes.
3. Add chicken and brown the both sides.
4. Add remaining ingredients and mix well.
5. Seal pot with lid and select poultry function.
6. Release pressure using quick release method than open the lid carefully.
7. Remove chicken from pot and shred.
8. Return shredded chicken to the pot and stir well. Serve and enjoy.

Nutritional Info: Calories: 287, Fat: 10.9 g, Carbs: 12.3 g, Protein: 35.6 g

---

Lemon Garlic Chicken

Prep time: 10 minutes, Cook time: 25 minutes, Servings: 4

Ingredients:

2 lbs. boneless chicken thighs
½ cup chicken stock
1 lb. green beans
1 lb. potatoes
1 tsp. herb de Provence
1 lemon juice
5 crushed garlic cloves
3 tbsps. extra virgin olive oil
4 tbsps. ghee
¼ tsp. black pepper
½ tsp. salt

Ingredients:

1. Add ghee and oil in instant pot and select sauté.
2. Add garlic, lemon juice, pepper, and salt into the pot and stir well.
3. Add chicken and sauté for 10 minutes.
4. Add remaining all ingredients and stir well.
5. Seal pot with lid and cook on manual high pressure for 15 minutes.
6. Stir well and serve.

Nutritional Info: Calories: 504, Fat: 27g, Carbs: 18.4 g, Protein 46.7 g

---

Mediterranean Chicken Wings

Prep time: 10 minutes, Cook time: 10 minutes, Servings: 10

Ingredients:

6 tbsps. chicken broth
1 tbsp. chicken seasoning
12 chicken wings
1 tbsp. oregano
Pepper
3 tbsps. tarragon
1 tbsp. basil
3 tbsps. extra virgin olive oil
1 tbsp. garlic puree
Salt

Instructions:

1. Add all ingredients into the large bowl and mix well.
2. Pour 1 cup water into the instant pot and place rack in the pot.
3. Place marinated chicken on the rack.
4. Seal pot with lid and cook on manual high pressure for 10 minutes.
5. Release pressure using quick release method than open the lid carefully.
6. Serve and enjoy.

Nutritional Info: Calories: 161, Fat: 12.6 g, Carbs: 0.6 g, Protein: 11.3 g

Delicious Slow Cooked Chicken

Prep time: 10 minutes, Cook time: 6 hours, Servings: 4

Ingredients:

1½ lbs. boneless chicken thighs
½ cup coconut milk
1 tbsp. water
¼ cup lime juice
1 cup chicken broth
2 sliced bell peppers
½ tsp. cayenne pepper
1 tsp. sea salt
1 tsp. garlic powder
1 tsp. ground coriander
1 tsp. ground cumin
2 tsps. paprika
1 tbsp. chili powder

Instructions:

1. Spray large pan with cooking spray and heat over medium-high heat.
2. In a small bowl, combine together all spices.
3. Rub spice mixture over chicken thigh on both sides.
4. Place chicken on hot pan and cook for 2 minutes on each side.
5. Now place seared chicken into the slow cooker and pour lime juice and coconut milk over chicken.
6. Place sliced bell pepper over chicken.
7. Seal slow cooker with lid and cook on low for 6 hours.
8. Now add coconut milk and cook on low for another 10 minutes.
9. Stir well and serve hot.

Nutritional Info: Calories: 435, Fat: 20.9g, Carbs: 8.9g, Protein: 52.3g

Yummy Butter Chicken

Prep time: 10 minutes, Cook time: 3 hours, Servings: 4

Ingredients:

1 lb. skinless chicken thighs
1 lime juice
6 oz. tomato paste
¼ cayenne pepper
1 tsp. cardamom
1 tsp. cumin
1 tsp. coriander
1 tsp. ginger, minced
4 minced garlic cloves
2 tsps. coconut oil
1 diced onion
½ tsp. salt

Instructions:

1. Heat coconut oil in pan over medium heat.
2. Add diced onion in hot pan and sauté until onion is soften.
3. Add ginger, garlic, and spices and sauté for 1 minute.
4. Add tomato paste and stir well to combined.
5. Place chicken into the slow cooker and pour pan mixture over the chicken.
6. Cook chicken on high heat for 3 hours.
7. Using fork shred the chicken add lime juice and mix well.
8. Serve hot and enjoy.

Nutritional Info: Calories: 519, Fat: 34.8g, Carbs: 18.1g, Protein: 37.6g

Spicy and Juicy Pepperoncini Chicken

Prep time: 10 minutes, Cook time: 4 hours, Servings: 6

Ingredients:

2 lbs. skinless chicken breast
1½ tbsps. Italian seasoning
6 oz. pepperoncini with liquid
¾ cup low sodium chicken broth

Instructions:

1. Add all ingredients into the slow cooker and mix well.
2. Cook chicken on low for 4 hours.
3. Using fork shred the chicken.
4. Serve hot and enjoy.

Nutritional Info: Calories: 79, Fat: 3.4g, Carbs: 1.5g, Protein: 9.5g

Chicken Chili

Prep time: 10 minutes, Cook time: 4 hours, Servings: 6
Ingredients:
2½ lbs. skinless chicken breast
6 cups low sodium chicken broth
1 tsp. oregano
2 tsps. cumin
½ cup chopped cilantro
2 diced poblano peppers
2 diced jalapeno peppers
4 minced garlic cloves
1 minced onion
Pepper
Salt

Instructions:
1. Add 2 cups chicken broth, oregano, cumin, cilantro, poblanos, jalapeno, garlic, and onion in blender and blend until smooth.
2. Add chicken, chicken broth mixture and remaining chicken broth into the slow cooker.
3. Cook on low for 4 hours.
4. Once it done then shred chicken using fork.
5. Serve hot and enjoy.

Nutritional Info: Calories: 130, Fat: 4.5g, Carbs: 5.6g, Protein: 16.2g

Tomato Spinach Chicken

Prep time: 10 minutes, Cook time: 4 hours, Servings: 6
Ingredients:
2 lbs. skinless chicken breast
6 cups fresh spinach
1 tbsp. Italian seasoning
3 tbsps. balsamic vinegar
4 minced garlic cloves
1 sliced onion
28 oz. diced tomatoes
Pepper
Salt
Instructions:

1. Season chicken with pepper and salt.
2. Place seasoned chicken into the slow cooker.
3. Now add all remaining ingredients except spinach into the slow cooker and stir well.
4. Cook chicken on low for 4 hours.
5. Add spinach into the chicken just before 30 minutes of cooking.
6. Stir well and serve.

Nutritional Info: Calories: 110, Fat: 3.1g, Carbs: 10.6g, Protein: 10.7g

Chicken Green Chili Soup

Prep time: 10 minutes, Cook time: 5 hours, Servings: 6
Ingredients:
2 lbs. chicken breasts
1 cup coconut milk
2 tbsps. coconut flour
¼ tsp. pepper
½ tsp. coriander powder
½ tsp. cumin powder
1 tsp. granulated garlic
4 cups chicken stock
1 cup mild green chilies, diced
1 diced onion
6 chopped carrots

1 tsp. salt
Instructions:
1. Add all ingredients except coconut milk and coconut flour into the slow cooker and stir well.
2. Cover with lid and cook on low for 5 hours.
3. Just before 10 minutes serving add coconut flour and coconut milk and stir well.
4. Serve hot and enjoy.

Nutritional Info: Calories: 461, Fat: 22.2g, Carbs: 17.9g, Protein: 47.3g

Chicken Vegetable Curry

Prep time: 10 minutes, Cook time: 4 hours, Servings: 6

Ingredients:

2 lbs. skinless chicken breast
4 cups spinach
1 chopped zucchini
2 cups broccoli
1 cup snow peas
2 cups chopped butternut squash
14 oz. coconut milk
½ cup chicken broth, low sodium
2 tbsps. curry powder
1 diced onion
2 tbsps. minced ginger
3 minced garlic cloves
2 tsps. olive oil

Instructions:

1. Heat olive oil in small saucepan over medium high heat.
2. Add onion, ginger, and garlic in pan and cook for 5 minutes.
3. Add curry powder in pan and stir for 1 minute.
4. Turn off the heat and add coconut milk and chicken broth and stir well.
5. Place vegetables and chicken into the slow cooker.
6. Pour saucepan mixture over vegetables and chicken.
7. Cook on high for 4 hours.
8. Using fork shred the chicken.
9. Season with pepper and salt.
10. Serve hot and enjoy.

Nutritional Info: Calories: 299, Fat: 20.4g, Carbs: 19.6g, Protein: 14.1g

Turmeric Garlic Coconut Chicken

Prep time: 10 minutes, Cook time: 4 hours, Servings: 6

Ingredients:

1 whole chicken
4 grated garlic cloves
2 grated ginger
2 fresh grated turmeric
½ cup coconut milk
Pepper
Salt

Instructions:

1. Season chicken with pepper and salt.
2. Add turmeric, ginger, garlic, and coconut milk into the slow cooker and mix well.
3. Place season chicken into the slow cooker.
4. Seal slow cooker with lid and cook on high for 4 hours.
5. Remove chicken from slow cooker and pull meat from bone.
6. Using fork shred the chicken and returns in slow cooker.
7. Stir chicken well with sauce.
8. Serve and enjoy.

Nutritional Info: Calories: 334, Fat: 23.7g, Carbs: 2g, Protein: 27.6g

Delicious Lemon Thyme Chicken

Prep time: 15 minutes, Cook time: 4 hours, Servings: 6

Ingredients:

1 whole chicken
3 garlic cloves
2 bay leaves
1 tsp. dried thyme
¼ cup lemon juice
¼ tsp. pepper
1 tsp. sea salt

Instructions:

1. Place chicken into the slow cooker.
2. Pour lemon juice over chicken.
3. Sprinkle thyme, pepper, and salt over chicken.
4. Add bay leaves and garlic around the chicken.
5. Cover slow cooker with lid and cook on high for 4 hours.
6. Serve and enjoy.

Nutritional Info: Calories: 436, Fat: 16.9g, Carbs: 0.9g, Protein: 65.8g

Tasty Herb Chicken

Prep time: 10 minutes, Cook time: 4 hours, Servings: 6

Ingredients:

4 lbs. whole chicken
1 tbsp. diced thyme
1 tbsp. diced sage
1 tbsp. diced rosemary
3 tbsps. oil
2 minced garlic cloves
6 whole garlic cloves
¾ cup chicken broth
1 chopped onion
1 chopped carrot
Pepper
Salt

Instructions:

1. Add onion and carrot into the slow cooker.
2. Add chicken broth and whole garlic cloves in slow cooker.
3. Rub oil over whole chicken then season chicken with pepper and salt.
4. Rub minced garlic and spices over chicken.
5. Place chicken into the slow cooker and cook on low for 4 hours.
6. Serve and enjoy.

Nutritional Info: Calories: 661, Fat: 29.6 g, Carbs: 5g, Protein: 88.7g

Chicken and Potatoes

Prep time: 10 minutes, Cook time: 4 hours, Servings: 4

Ingredients:

4 skinless chicken breasts
1 tsp. garlic powder
1 tbsp. Italian seasoning
3 tbsps. oil
3 cups chopped potatoes
Pepper
Salt

Instructions:

1. Add all ingredients into the large bowl and toss well.
2. Add bowl mixture into the slow cooker and cook on low for 4 hours.
3. Serve hot and enjoy.

Nutritional Info: Calories: 396, Fat: 19.8g, Carbs: 18.6g, Protein: 34.8g

Tomato Chicken Soup

Prep time: 10 minutes, Cook time: 4 hours minutes, Servings: 4

Ingredients:

1½ lbs. boneless chicken breasts
1 tsp. garlic powder
1 tbsp. Italian seasoning
8 oz. tomato sauce
14 oz. diced tomatoes
1 cup chicken broth
1 chopped onion
½ tsp. salt

Instructions:

1. Add all ingredients into the slow cooker and mix well.
2. Cook on low for 4 hours.
3. Using fork shred the chicken.
4. Stir well and serve.

Nutritional Info: Calories: 588, Fat: 35.5 g, Carbs: 14.3 g, Protein 54.6 g

Chicken Kale Sweet Potato Stew

Prep time: 15 minutes, Cook time: 4 hours, Servings: 6

Ingredients:

1 lb. chicken breasts
1 bunch kale
3 bay leaves
2 tsps. Gluten free yellow mustard
3 tbsps. Balsamic vinegar
1/3 cup tomato paste
1 cup low sodium chicken broth
3 minced garlic cloves
1 diced sweet potato
3 diced carrots
1 diced onion
Pepper

Salt

Instructions:

1. Add chicken, onion, carrots, sweet potatoes, garlic, chicken broth, tomato paste, vinegar, mustard, and bay leaves into the slow cooker and mix well.
2. Cover slow cooker and cook on high for 4 hours.
3. In the last hour add kale into the slow cooker and mix well.
4. Using fork shred the chicken.
5. Season stew with pepper and salt.
6. Serve hot and enjoy.

Nutritional Info: Calories: 218, Fat: 6 g, Carbs: 15.6 g, Protein: 24.8 g

Easy Salsa Chicken

Prep time: 8 minutes, Cook time: 12 minutes, Servings: 8

Ingredients:

¾ cup chopped onion
2 lbs. chicken breasts
1 cup salsa

Instructions:

1. Add all ingredients into the slow cooker and stir well.
2. Seal pot with lid and cook on manual high pressure for 12 minutes.
3. Release pressure using quick release method than open the lid carefully.
4. Remove chicken from pot and using fork shred the chicken.
5. Return chicken to the instant pot and stir well.

Nutritional Info: Calories: 229, Fat: 8.5 g, Carbs: 3 g, Protein: 33.4 g

Garlic Lemon Dump Chicken

Prep time: 10 minutes, Cook time: 10 minutes, Servings: 4

Ingredients:

¼ cup extra virgin olive oil
1 tbsp. chopped fresh parsley
2 tsp. minced garlic
4 skinless and boneless chicken breasts
2 tbsps. fresh lemon juice

Instructions:

1. Add all ingredients into the large zip lock bag and mix well.
2. Place bag in the refrigerator for 2 hours.
3. Remove marinated chicken from refrigerator and pour into the instant pot.
4. Add little water to the pot until you have one cup liquid in the pot.
5. Seal pot with lid and cook on manual high pressure for 10 minutes.
6. Release pressure using quick release method than open the lid carefully.
7. Serve and enjoy.

Nutritional Info: Calories: 390, Fat: 23.5 g, Carbs: 0.7 g, Protein: 42.4 g

Chicken Salad with Walnuts and Grapes

Prep time: 10 minutes, Cook time: 25 minutes, Servings: 2

Ingredients:

2 tbsps. fresh lemon juice
2 tbsps. Minced shallot
¼ cup olive oil
1 cup halved grapes
Black pepper
Sea salt
2 cups diced and cooked chicken
½ cup diced celery
½ cup chopped walnuts

2 tbsps. fresh parsley

Instructions:

1. Combine the lemon juice and shallots, and blend the oil in slowly. Flavor them with some pepper and salt.
2. Toss in the rest of the ingredients and enjoy!

Nutritional Info: Calories: 133.3. Fat: 6.6g, Carbs: 10.1g, Protein: 10.2g

Chapter 9 Beef, Lamb and Pork

Pork Belly with Homey Barbecue Sauce

Prep time: 10 minutes, Cook time: 2 hours, Servings: 8

Ingredients:

2 halved garlic cloves
½ tsp. freshly ground black pepper
2 lbs. pork belly
1 tsp. salt
2 tbsps. vegetable oil

For the barbecue sauce:

1/3 tsp. ground cumin
½ cup tomato puree
Liquid smoke drops
1/3 tsp. smoked paprika
1 tsp. hot sauce
1 tsp. Dijon mustard

Instructions:

1. Preheat the oven to 420 degrees F.
2. Rub the pork belly with vegetable oil and garlic and season with salt and pepper.
3. Roast the pork for 22 minutes and lower the heat to 330^0F.
4. Roast the pork for further 1 hour 30 minutes.
5. In the meantime, whisk all the ingredients for the barbecue sauce and blend everything.
6. Remove the pot belly and slice the pot belly.
7. Serve with the sauce and enjoy.

Nutritional Info: Calories: 561, Fat: 34g, Carbs: 1.7g, Protein: 52.7g

Oxtail Stew

Prep time: 10 minutes, Cook time: 6 hours, Servings: 8

Ingredients:

5 lbs. chopped oxtail
2 chopped celery stick
2 chopped leeks
Salt
Black pepper
2 tbsps. avocado oil
3 thyme springs
4 chopped carrots
3 rosemary springs
2 tbsps. coconut flour
4 cloves
4 bay leaves
28 oz. chopped tomatoes
1-quart beef stock

Instructions:

1. Place oxtail in a roasting pan, season with a pinch of salt and black pepper, drizzle half of the avocado oil, rub well, place in the oven at 425 °F and roast for 20 minutes.
2. Heat up a pan with the rest of the oil over medium heat, add leeks, carrots, celery, thyme, rosemary and bay leaf, stir and cook for 20 minutes.
3. Add coconut flour, cloves, tomatoes and stock and stir.
4. Add oxtail, stir; cover pan and cook on low heat for 5 hours. Take oxtail out of the pot, discard bones, return them to the pot, stir; divide into bowls and serve.

Nutritional Info: Calories: 435, Fat: 23g, Carbs: 7g, Protein: 30g

Oven-Roasted Pork Cutlets with Veggies

Prep time: 30 minutes, Cook time: 25 minutes, Servings: 4

Ingredients:

2 tbsps. melted lard
1 diced celery stalk
2 sliced carrots
1 tsp. garlic paste
1 tbsp. yellow mustard
4 pork cutlets

½ tsp. sea salt
1 cup sliced leeks
2 tbsps. cider vinegar
½ tsp. freshly ground black pepper

Instructions:

1. Combine salt, garlic paste, black pepper, cider vinegar, and mustard in a mixing bowl.
2. Add the pork cutlets to marinate for 2 hours.
3. Melt the lard in an oven-safe moderate heat and brown the pork cutlets for 5 minutes per side.
4. Add carrots, celery and leeks and cook for 5 more minutes stirring occasionally.
5. Transfer the pan to the oven and roast the pork with vegetables for 13 minutes.
6. Serve the meat and vegetables alongside pan juices.

Nutritional Info: Calories: 452, Fat: 34.8g, Carbs: 4.7g, Protein: 26.3g

Juicy Pork Medallions with Scallions

Prep time: 10 minutes, Cook time: 10 minutes, Servings: 4

Ingredients:

½ tsp. crushed red pepper flakes
1 tsp. crushed dried sage
2 minced rosemary sprigs
Coarse salt
½ tsp. garlic powder
1 tbsp. butter
Ground black pepper.
Roughly chopped scallion bunch
1 minced thyme sprig
1 lb. cut pork tenderloin

Instructions:

1. Season each of the pork medallion with salt, garlic powder, black pepper and red pepper flakes.
2. Melt the butter in a saucepan over medium high heat and cook pork tenderloin for about 3 minutes on each side.
3. Add rosemary, thyme and scallions to cook until heated through for 3 more minutes.
4. Serve sprinkled with dried sage and enjoy.

Nutritional Info: Calories: 192, Fat: 6.9g, Carbs: 0.9g, Protein: 29.8g

Crock Pot Peppery Pork Ribs

Prep time: 15 minutes, Cook time: 8 hours, Servings: 4

Ingredients:

1 crushed garlic clove
½ tsp. ground oregano
1 tsp. minced Ancho chiles
1 lb. pork ribs
½ tsp. smoked cayenne pepper
1 thinly sliced bell pepper
1 tbsp. lard
¼ cup dry red wine
½ tsp. ground cloves
1 tsp. grated orange peel
¼ cup Worcestershire sauce

Instructions:

1. Rub the sides and bottom of the Crock pot with melted lard and arrange peppers and pork chops on the bottom.
2. Drizzle wine and Worcestershire sauce over the peppers and pork chops.
3. Sprinkle garlic, ground cloves, cayenne pepper and oregano on top.
4. Cook on low for about 8 hours.
5. Serve garnished with grated orange peel.
6. Enjoy!

Nutritional Info: Calories: 192, Fat: 6.9g, Carbs: 0.9g, Protein: 29.8g

Beef and Veggie Stew

Prep time: 15 minutes, Cook time: 2 hours, Servings: 4

Ingredients:

2 lbs. cubed beef steak
1 tbsp. coconut oil
Salt
Black pepper
1 chopped red chili pepper

1 chopped yellow onion
1 tbsp. coconut aminos
1 tbsp. lemon juice
¼ tsp. ground nutmeg
2 minced garlic cloves

1 tsp. dried thyme
¼ tsp. fennel seeds
1 tsp. dried rosemary
4 cups beef stock
2 chopped carrots
2 chopped celery sticks
1 chopped sweet potato
6 chopped white mushrooms

Instructions:

1. Heat up a large saucepan with the oil over medium heat, add the onion, stir and cook for 5 minutes.
2. Add salt, pepper and the chili pepper, stir and cook for 1-2 minutes more.
3. Add the beef, stir and cook for 5 minutes.
4. Add coconut aminos, lemon juice, garlic, thyme, rosemary, fennel, nutmeg, and stock, stir, bring to a boil, cover the saucepan and cook the stew for 1 hour and 20 minutes.
5. Add celery, sweet potato, carrots, and mushrooms, stir, cover saucepan again and cook for 20 minutes more.
6. Divide into bowls and serve.
7. Enjoy!

Nutritional Info: Calories: 533, Fat: 18.4g, Carbs: 14.4g, Protein: 73.9g

The Best Sloppy Joes Ever

Prep time: 10 minutes, Cook time: 20 minutes, Servings: 6

Ingredients:

2 finely chopped shallots
1 tsp. deli mustard
1 tsp. minced garlic
Ground pepper.
1 tsp. cayenne pepper
½ cup pureed tomatoes
1 tbsp. coconut vinegar
2 tsps. tallow
Salt
1 tsp. chipotle powder
1 ½ lbs. ground chuck
1 tsp. celery seeds

Instructions:

1. In a heavy-bottomed skillet, melt 1 tablespoon tallow over a moderately high flame.
2. Sauté the shallots and garlic until aromatic and tender then reserve.
3. Melt another tablespoon of tallow in the same skillet then brown ground chuck, crumbling with spatula.
4. Add the vegetables to the skillet and stir in the rest of ingredients.
5. Reduce the heat to medium low and simmer for 20 minutes as you stir periodically.
6. Serve over the keto buns and enjoy.

Nutritional Info: Calories: 313, Fat: 20.6g, Carbs: 3.5g, Protein: 26.6g

Grilled Rib Eye Steak

Prep time: 10 minutes, Cook time: 10 minutes, Servings: 6

Ingredients:

1 tsp. crushed dried sage
2 chopped rosemary sprigs
2 tbsps. dry red wine
1 tbsp. oyster sauce
2 lbs. rib eye steaks
2 smashed garlic cloves
1 chopped thyme sprig
½ tsp. chipotle powder
1 tbsp. Worcestershire sauce
Celery salt
Ground black pepper.
2 tbsps. Swerve sweetener
2 tbsps. olive oil

Instructions:

1. Thoroughly combine chipotle powder, garlic, oyster sauce, rosemary, olive oil, Worcestershire sauce, sage, swerve, wine, salt and pepper, olive oil and wine in a mixing bowl.
2. Marinate the rib eye steaks in the refrigerator overnight.
3. Preheat the previously lightly greased grill.
4. Grill rib eye steaks over direct heat for 5 minutes per side.

Nutritional Info: Calories: 314, Fat: 11.4g, Carbs: 1g, Protein: 48.2g

Beef Sausage with Mayo Sauce

Prep time: 10 minutes, Cook time: 5 minutes, Servings: 4

Ingredients:

1/3 tsp. red pepper flakes

1 lb. crumbled beef sausage

2 tbsps. minced cilantro

1 tbsp. lard

½ tsp. salt

1 chopped red onion

½ tsp. dried marjoram

1 finely minced garlic clove

For the sauce:

1 ½ tsps. mustard

1 tsp. cayenne pepper

1 tbsp. tomato puree

¼ tsp. salt

¼ cup mayonnaise

Instructions:

1. Melt the lard over medium-high heat.
2. Add garlic and onions to cook for 2 minutes until fragrant and tender.
3. Add beef and stir to cook for 3 more minutes,
4. Add marjoram, salt, cilantro and red pepper to cook for another minute.
5. Whisk all the sauce ingredients to make the sauce.
6. Serve over the low-carb flat bread and enjoy.

Nutritional Info: Calories: 549, Fat: 49.3g, Carbs: 4.7g, Protein: 16.2g

Slow Cooker Beef Chuck Roast

Prep time: 15 minutes, Cook time: 6 hours, Servings: 8

Ingredients:

1/3 cup dry red wine

2 tbsps. chopped fresh parsley

1 wedged large-sized white onion

½ cup beef broth

2 tbsps. olive oil

3 minced garlic cloves

2 rosemary springs

1 thyme sprig

Salt

2 tbsps. Worcestershire sauce

1 cup sliced provolone

Pepper.

2 lbs. beef chuck roast

Instructions:

1. Add the garlic, olive oil, onion, beef, thyme and rosemary to the Crock pot.
2. Add Worcestershire sauce, dry red wine, pepper, salt and beef broth.
3. Cover to cook for about 6 hours on High settings until the meat is tender.
4. Garnish with sliced Provolone cheese and fresh parsley.
5. Serve and enjoy.

Nutritional Info: Calories: 519, Fat: 39.6g, Carbs: 2.7g, Protein: 34.4g

Baked Juicy Pork Chunks with Mushrooms

Prep time: 10 minutes, Cook time: 45 minutes, Servings: 8

Ingredients:

½ cup bone broth

Ground black pepper.

8 pork chunks

Salt

1 cup white wine

4 oz. mushrooms

Instructions:

1. Preheat the oven to 425⁰F.
2. Add salt and pepper to the pork chunks.
3. Put the pork chunks in a large baking sheet.
4. Sprinkle mushrooms over the pork.
5. Pour bone broth and white wine over pork and mushrooms.
6. Put in oven to bake for about 45 minutes.
7. Remove the pork chunks once the internal temperature reaches 160⁰F.

Nutritional Info: Calories: 173, Carbs: 1.2g, Proteins: 26g, Fat: 4g

Finger-Licking Good Beef Brisket

Prep time: 1 hour, Cook time: 2 hours 30 minutes, Servings: 8

Ingredients:

1 tsp. shallot powder
1 tsp. dried rosemary
2 lbs. trimmed beef brisket
1 tbsp. Dijon mustard
1 tsp. dried marjoram
¼ cup dry red wine
2 halved garlic cloves
½ tsp. freshly ground black pepper
1 tsp. sea salt

Instructions:

1. Preheat the oven to 375⁰ F.
2. Rub the raw brisket with Dijon mustard and garlic.
3. Mix the rest of ingredients to make a dry rub and season it on both sides of the brisket.
4. Pour the wine into the pan and lay in beef brisket.
5. Roast in the oven for 1 hour.
6. Reduce the temperature of the oven to 300^0F and roast for 2 hours 30 minutes.
7. Slice the meat and serve with juice from the baking pan.
8. Enjoy.

Nutritional Info: Calories: 219, Fat: 7.2g, Carbs: 0.6g, Protein: 34.6g

Baked Pork Chops with Mozzarella and Bacon Gravy

Prep time: 10 minutes, Cook time: 40 minutes, Servings: 4

Ingredients:

1 cup shredded mozzarella
1 tsp. nutmeg
1 cup cream
4 bacon slices
Salt
2 tbsps. olive oil
4 pork chops
1 beaten egg
Ground pepper.

Instructions:

1. Preheat the oven to 350^0F.
2. Rub the pork chops with oil and put them into a baking dish.
3. Add salt and ground pepper to the pork chops and grill them for 30 minutes turning once.
4. Meanwhile, fry bacon in a skillet strip until crisp.
5. Add shredded mozzarella, pepper, cream and nutmeg and stir continuously for 5 minutes.
6. Remove the skillet from heat when the mozzarella melts.
7. Stir in beaten egg for 3 minutes.
8. Remove pork chops from the oven and transfer to a serving platter.
9. Pour with bacon or mozzarella gravy and serve.

Nutritional Info: Calories: 581, Carbs: 3.2g, Proteins: 36g, Fat: 56g

Keto Barbecue Pork Skillet

Prep time: 5 minutes, Cook time: 15 minutes, Servings: 4

Ingredients:

1 tsp. smoked paprika
1 tsp. sesame oil
6 pork chops
¼ cup Italian dressing
¼ cup Worcestershire sauce
1 tsp. apple cider vinegar

Instructions:

1. Combine together Worcestershire sauce, Italian dressing, smoked paprika, vinegar and sesame oil in a large skillet for 2 minutes over medium heat.
2. Add pork chops with the sauce and simmer for 10 minutes.
3. Serve hot and enjoy.

Nutritional Info: Calories: 246, Carbs: 5g, Proteins: 31g, Fat: 10g

Pork with Celery in Egg-Lemon Sauce

Prep time: 10 minutes, Cook time: 35 minutes, Servings: 6

Ingredients:

3 cups warm water

2 free-range eggs

1 lb. fresh celery root and leaves

2 finely chopped scallions

Salt

2 lbs. boneless and cubed pork

Ground white pepper.

½ cup olive oil

1 lemon

Instructions:

1. Rinse the celery root and cut it into pieces.
2. Wash the celery leaves and chop them.
3. Set up a large pot and bring water and salt to a boil before adding celery roots and leaves.
4. Lower the temperature to medium-low and cook for 30 minutes until soft and tender.
5. Drain and discard the cooking liquid.
6. Rinse the meat to dry on the kitchen pepper towel.
7. Ina large skillet, heat the olive oil and sauté the pork with chopped scallions.
8. Add 3 cups of warm water and cover to cook until meat is softened.
9. Add cooked celery and shake the pot.
10. Whisk the eggs with lemon juice in a small bowl.
11. Gently stir the lemon-egg mixture in the pot.
12. Set aside for 5 minutes to serve while hot.

Nutritional Info: Calories: 699, Carbs: 4.3g, Proteins: 19.5g, Fat: 79g

Breaded Triple Pork Rolls

Prep time: 15 minutes, Cook time: 35 minutes, Servings: 4

Ingredients:

Extra virgin olive oil

Almond flour

6 slices pork loin

6 cheese slices

6 bacon slices

2 beaten large eggs

Instructions:

1. Put a slice of cheese and bacon on top of each pork loin slice.
2. Roll up into a cylinder and secure with toothpicks.
3. Pass bacon through the bitten egg mixture then almond flour.
4. Fry in a large skillet for 7 minutes until golden brown.
5. Drain to serve while hot.
6. Enjoy.

Nutritional Info: Calories: 674, Carbs: 1g, Proteins: 53g, Fat: 50g

Keto Beef Roast

Prep time: 10 minutes, Cook time: 1 hour 25 minutes, Servings: 4

Ingredients:

12 oz. beef stock

1 oz. onion soup mix

4 oz. sliced mushrooms

3½ lbs. beef roast

½ cup Italian dressing

Instructions:

1. Combine stock, Italian dressing and onion soup in a bowl and stir.
2. Put beef roast in a medium pan and add stock mix, mushrooms then cover with foil.
3. Introduce in the oven to bake for 1 hour 15 minutes at 300^0F.
4. Let the roast cool down then slice and serve topped with gravy.

Nutritional Info: Calories: 700, Fat: 56g, Carbs: 10g, Protein: 70g

Thai Beef Recipe

Prep time: 10 minutes, Cook time: 10 minutes, Servings: 6

Ingredients:

1 tbsp. coconut aminos

3 chopped green onions.

1 cup beef stock

Salt

1½ tsps. lemon pepper

1 lb. sliced beef steak

¼ tsp. garlic powder

1 chopped green bell pepper

¼ tsp. onion powder

4 tbsps. Peanut butter

Black pepper.

Instructions:

1. Set up a bowl to combine peanut butter with stock, lemon pepper and aminos then stir well to set aside.
2. Set a pan over medium high heat and add beef then season with salt, pepper, garlic powder and onions then cook for 7 minutes.
3. Stir in green pepper to cook for 3 more minutes.
4. Add the premade peanut sauce and green onions then stir to cook for 1 minute.
5. Divide between plates and serve.

Nutritional Info: Calories: 224, Fat: 15g, Carbs: 3g, Protein: 19g

Lavender Lamb Chops

Prep time: 20 minutes, Cook time: 15 minutes, Servings: 4

Ingredients:

3 halved red oranges

2 small orange peel pieces

Olive oil

Salt

1½ lbs. lamb chops

1 tbsp. chopped lavender.

1 tsp. ghee

2 minced garlic cloves

2 tbsps. Chopped rosemary.

Black pepper.

Instructions:

1. Set up a mixing bowl to combine lavender, rosemary, salt, pepper, orange peel and garlic and toss to coat then reserve for some hours.
2. Rub the chicken grill with ghee and heat up over medium high heat.
3. Add lamb chops on the grill to cook for 3 minutes and flip.
4. Squeeze 1 orange half over the lamb chops to cook for 3 more minutes and flip and then do the same for the third time.
5. Put the lamb chops on plates and keep them warm.
6. Add the rest of orange halves on preheated grill and cook for 3 minutes then flip to cook for 3 more minutes.
7. Divide the lamb chops into plates and add orange halves on the sides drizzled with some olive oil.
8. Serve and enjoy.

Nutritional Info: Calories: 250, Fat: 5g, Carbs: 5g, Protein: 8g

Beef and Tomato Stuffed Squash

Prep time: 10 minutes, Cook time: 1 hour, Servings: 2

Ingredients:

1 chopped yellow onion.

1 tsp. dried oregano

Black pepper.

28 oz. chopped tomatoes.

½ tsp. dried thyme

¼ tsp. cayenne pepper

1 lb. ground beef

3 minced garlic cloves

1 sliced Portobello mushroom

Salt

1 chopped green bell pepper.

2 lbs. pricked spaghetti squash

Instructions:

1. Put spaghetti on a lined baking sheet and set in an oven to bake for 40 minutes at 400⁰F.

2. Place spaghetti squash on a lined baking sheet, introduce in the oven at 400 degrees F and bake for 40 minutes
3. Half the squash and deseed to set aside.
4. Set a pan on fire to heat over medium high heat and add mushroom, garlic, meat, mushroom and onions and stir to combine until meat browns.

5. Add thyme, pepper, salt, cayenne, oregano, green pepper and tomato then stir to cook for 10 minutes.
6. Stuff the beef mix into the squash halves and set in an oven to bake for 10 minutes at 400°F.
7. Divide into 2 plates and serve.

Nutritional Info: Calories: 260, Fat: 7g, Carbs: 4g, Protein: 10g

Keto Goulash

Prep time: 15 minutes, Cook time: 15 minutes, Servings: 5

Ingredients:
14 oz. canned tomatoes and their juice
2 oz. chopped bell pepper.
¼ tsp. garlic powder
2 cups cauliflower florets
1½ lbs. ground beef
Salt
14 oz. water
¼ cup chopped onion.
1 tbsp. tomato paste
Black pepper.

Instructions:
1. Set a pan on fire over medium heat and stir in beef to brown for 5 minutes.

2. Add bell pepper and onion then stir well to cook for 4 more minutes.
3. Add cauliflower, water and tomatoes with their juices.
4. Stir to bring to a simmer and cover the pan to cook for 5 minutes.
5. Stir in garlic powder, tomato paste, salt and pepper then set aside.
6. Divide into bowls and serve.

Nutritional Info: Calories: 275, Fat: 7g, Carbs: 4g; Protein: 10g

Yummy Ground Beef Casserole

Prep time: 15 minutes, Cook time: 30 minutes, Servings: 6

Ingredients:
2 minced garlic cloves
1 torn romaine lettuce head
2 tbsps. toasted sesame seeds
1 tbsp. gluten free Worcestershire sauce
2 lbs. ground beef
2 tsps. onion flakes
Salt
1 cup Russian dressing
20 dill pickle slices
Black pepper.

Instructions:
1. Heat a pan with onion flakes, beef, salt, pepper, Worcestershire sauce and garlic over medium heat.
2. Transfer the mixture to a baking tray

3. Heat up a pan over medium heat; add beef, onion flakes, Worcestershire sauce, salt, pepper and garlic; stir and cook for 5 minutes
4. Transfer this to a baking dish and add half of the Russian dressing.
5. Stir and spread evenly.
6. Arrange pickle slices on top, sprinkle the sesame seeds.
7. Introduce in an oven to bake for 20 minutes at 350°F.
8. Turn over to broil the casserole for 5 more minutes.
9. Divide lettuce on plates and serve topped with the remaining Russian dressing and beef casserole.

Nutritional Info: Calories: 554, Fat: 51g, Carbs: 5g, Protein: 45g

Healthy Beef Roast

Prep time: 10 minutes, Cook time: 55 minutes, Servings: 6

Ingredients:

4 tbsps. balsamic vinegar
1 tbsp. extra virgin olive oil
¼ tsps. dried thyme
1 tsp. salt
3 lbs. chuck roast
½ tsp. pepper
1 cup chicken stock
1 tbsp. melted butter
1 tsp. rosemary

Instructions:

1. In a small bowl, mix together thyme, rosemary, pepper, and salt and rub across roast.
2. Add oil in instant pot and select sauté.
3. Once the oil is hot then place roast in pot and brown them on both the sides, about 5 minutes on both sides.
4. Mix together broth, butter, and vinegar and pour over roast.
5. Seal pot with lid and select MANUAL button as well as set the timer for 40 minutes.
6. Allow to release steam on a unique then open and serve.

Nutritional Info: Calories: 532, Fat: 23.2 g, Protein: 75.1 g, Carbs: 0.5 g

Apple Pork and Sweet Potatoes

Prep time: 15 minutes, Cook time: 8 hours, Servings: 6

Ingredients:

2 peeled and chopped medium apples
¼ tsp. cinnamon
2 tbsps. brown sugar
3 lbs. boneless pork loin roast
¼ cup white wine
4 peeled and chopped sweet potatoes
¼ tsp. nutmeg
¼ tsp. cloves
1 tsp. organic olive oil

Instructions:

1. Cut the pork into 1-inch cubes and brown in skillet with extra virgin olive oil.
2. Place apple slices into bottom of instant cooker.
3. Layer sweet potatoes ahead, then pork cubes.
4. Stir together juice, brown sugar, and seasonings and after that pour into instant pot.
5. Choose the slow cooker setting on your instant pot.
6. Cover and turn the steam release handle to venting position.
7. Cook on medium for 8-12 hours or high for 4-5 hours until done.

Nutritional Info: Calories: 464, Fat: 15 g, Protein: 51 g, Carbs: 29 g

Savory Barbecue Pork Sandwiches

Prep time: 5 minutes, Cook time: 4 hours, Servings: 8

Ingredients:

½ tsp. fresh ground pepper
1 tsp. Worcestershire sauce
3 lbs. boneless pork loin roast
2 tsps. yellow mustard
1 can tomato sauce
½ cup brown sugar
¼ cup soy sauce

Instructions:

1. Set roast in instant pot.
2. Mix remaining ingredients and pour on the top of roast.
3. Choose the slow cooker setting on your instant pot.
4. Cover and turn the steam release handle to venting position.
5. Cook on medium for 6-8 hours or high for 3-4 hours until tender.
6. Slice thin and serve on rolls.

Nutritional Info: Calories: 323, Fat: 11 g, Protein: 38 g, Carbs: 15 g

Beef Zucchini Cups

Prep time: 45 minutes, Cook time: Servings: 4

Ingredients:

2 minced garlic cloves
1½ cups keto enchilada sauce
1 tsp. ground cumin
Black pepper and salt
1 tsp. smoked paprika
1 lb. ground beef
Chopped tomatoes.
1 tbsp. coconut oil
½ cup chopped red onion.
Chopped avocado
3 halved zucchinis
½ cup shredded cheddar cheese
¼ cup chopped cilantro.
Chopped green onions

Instructions:

1. Set a pan with olive oil on fire to heat up over medium high heat and stir in red onions to cook for 2 minutes.
2. Stir in beef and brown for a couple of minutes and add garlic, cumin, paprika, salt and pepper and stir to cook for 2 minutes.
3. Put zucchini halves in a baking pan and stuff each with beef and top with enchilada sauce sprinkled with cheddar cheese.
4. Set in an oven to bake covered for 20 minutes at 350⁰F.
5. Open the pan and sprinkle with cilantro to bake for 5 more minutes.
6. Top up with green onions, avocado and tomatoes and serve.

Nutritional Info: Calories: 222; Fat: 10g, Carbs: 8g, Protein: 21g

Beef Patties

Prep time: 45 minutes, Cook time: 30 minutes Servings: 6

Ingredients:

½ cup bread crumbs
3 tsps. Worcestershire sauce
10 oz. canned onion soup
¼ cup water
1 tbsp. coconut flour
½ tsp. mustard powder
¼ cup ketchup
Salt
1 egg
1½ lbs. ground beef
Black pepper.

Instructions:

1. In a bowl, mix 1/3 cup onion soup with beef, salt, pepper, egg and bread crumbs and stir well.
2. Heat up a pan over medium high heat; shape 6 patties from the beef mix, place them into the pan and brown on both sides
3. Meanwhile; in a bowl, mix the rest of the soup with coconut flour, water, mustard powder, Worcestershire sauce and ketchup and stir well.
4. Pour this over beef patties, cover pan and cook for 20 minutes stirring from time to time
5. Divide between plates and serve

Nutritional Info: Calories: 332, Fat: 18g, Carbs: 7, Protein: 25

Beef and Eggplant Casserole

Prep time: 30 minutes, Cook time: 4 hours, Servings: 12

Ingredients:

1 tbsp. olive oil
2 tsps. gluten free Worcestershire sauce
2 lbs. ground beef
2 cups grated mozzarella
Black pepper.

2 tbsps. chopped parsley.
28 oz. chopped canned tomatoes.
2 cups chopped eggplant.
1 tsp. dried oregano
2 tsps. Mustard

16 oz. tomato sauce

Salt

Instructions:

1. Add salt and pepper to eggplant slices and set them aside for 30 minutes.
2. Drain them and put in a bowl then add olive oil and toss to coat.
3. Set up another bowl to combine salt, pepper, beef, Worcestershire sauce and mustard and stir well.
4. Press the mixture on the bottom of a Crock pot.
5. Add eggplant and spread then add tomatoes, oregano, parsley, mozzarella and tomato sauce.
6. Cover the Crock pot to cook on Low for 4 hours.
7. Divide casserole between plates and serve hot.
8. Enjoy!

Nutritional Info: Calories: 200, Fat: 12g, Carbs: 6g, Protein: 15g

Gluten-Free Beef Rice

Prep time: 5 minutes, Cook time: 10 minutes, Servings: 4

Ingredients:

¾ cup chicken broth

½ tbsps. essential olive oil

½ tsp. salt

½ lb. ground beef

¾ cup rinsed and drained rice

2 minced garlic cloves

1 diced onion

2 cups shredded cabbage

Instructions:

1. Add oil in instant pot and select sauté.
2. Once the oil is hot you can add garlic and stir for thirty seconds.
3. Add onion and meat and stir for minutes.
4. Add cabbage, rice, stock, and salt and stir well.
5. Seal pot with lid and cook on HIGH pressure for 5 minutes.
6. Allow releasing steam on its very own then open.
7. Stir well and serve.

Nutritional Info: Calories: 276, Fat: 5.9 g, Protein 21.4 g, Carbs 33 g

Lentil Beef Stew

Prep time: 10 minutes, Cook time: 20 minutes, Servings: 4

Ingredients:

2 tbsps. curry powder

3 peeled and diced potatoes

Pepper

28 oz. can diced tomatoes

4 minced garlic cloves

2 diced carrots

1 diced onion

1 cup dry lentils

Salt

1 lb. sliced beef

4 cups chicken stock

Instructions:

1. Add all ingredients in the instant pot and stir well.
2. Seal pot with lid and select manual button and hang the timer for twenty or so minutes.
3. Allow to discharge steam on its then open and stir well.
4. Serve warm and revel in.

Nutritional Info: Calories: 581, Fat: 8.8 g, Protein: 53.1 g, Carbs: 73.2 g

Classic Garlic Herb Pot Roast

Prep time: 10 minutes, Cook time: 55 minutes, Servings: 6

Ingredients:

1 tsp. black pepper

3 lbs. beef chuck roast

1 tbsp. Italian seasoning

2 cups chicken stock

2 tbsps. butter

2 minced garlic cloves

5 peeled large carrots
1 tsp. salt
1 diced onion

Instructions:
1. Place beef chunks inside a large dish and sprinkle with spices.
2. Add butter in instant pot and select sauté.
3. Add onion inside a pot and stir fry until brown, about 5 minutes.
4. Add roast chunks in the onions then pour chicken stock.
5. Seal pot with lid and select MANUAL button and hang the timer for 40 minutes.
6. Release steam quickly than open lid carefully.
7. Add carrots and stir well.
8. Again, Seal pot with lid and select MANUAL button and hang up the timer for one more 10 minutes.
9. Release steam quickly than open the lid.
10. Stir well and serve.

Nutritional Info: Calories: 902, Fat: 67.9 g, Protein 60.4 g, Carbs: 8.7 g

Hot Beef Shred

Prep time: 10 minutes, Cook time: 60 minutes, Servings: 4

Ingredients:
½ cup bone broth
1 sliced large onion
2 lbs. boneless beef chuck roast
1 tsp. oregano
1 tbsp. lime juice
1 tsp. garlic powder
1 tbsp. chili powder
1 tsp. salt
1 tsp. maple syrup

Instructions:
1. In a tiny bowl, mix together, chili powder, oregano, garlic powder, and salt.
2. Rub bowl mixture around chuck roast.
3. Add sliced onion in instant pot then place chuck roast over the onion.
4. Pour broth, maple syrup and lime juice over roast.
5. Seal pot with lid and select MANUAL button and hang up the timer for an hour.
6. Allow releasing steam on its very own then open.
7. Using fork shred the chuck roast and serves.

Nutritional Info: Calories: 863, Fat: 63.5 g, Protein: 62.6 g, Carbs: 6.7 g

Apple Pork Tenderloin

Prep time: 10 minutes, Cook time: 26 minutes, Servings: 4

Ingredients:
2 tbsps. olive oil
2 cored and chopped apples
Pepper
1 pork tenderloin
2 cups apple cider
1 chopped large onion
Salt
½ cup brown sugar

Instructions:
1. Add olive oil in instant pot and select sauté mode.
2. Add pork tenderloin in the pot and brown them on both the perimeters, about 2 minutes on either side.
3. Transfer pork tenderloin on the dish.
4. Add apple cider, onion, and apples in a very pot and stir well.
5. Season tenderloin with pepper and salt and rub 4 tbsps. brown sugar over tenderloin.
6. Return tenderloin towards the pot and add remaining sugar.
7. Seal pot with lid and select MANUAL HIGH pressure for 2 minutes.
8. Allow releasing steam on its own then open.
9. Serve and get.

Nutritional Info: Calories: 422, Fat: 11.4 g, Protein: 30.5 g, Carbs: 51.2 g

Jalapeno Beef

Prep time: 10 minutes, Cook time: 15 minutes, Servings: 6

Ingredients:
½ cup brown sugar
1 cup low sodium soy sauce
2 lbs. thinly sliced flank steak
2 minced garlic cloves
5 chopped green onion
2 tbsps. olive oil
½ cup water
1 tbsp. cornstarch
1 seeded and sliced jalapeno peppers

Instructions:
1. Add sliced steak, jalapenos, and garlic in instant pot and select sauté and sauté for 5 minutes.
2. Add water, soy sauce, and brown sugar. Stir well.
3. Seal pot with lid and cook on MANUAL HIGH pressure for ten minutes.
4. Release steam quickly than open.
5. Remove half cup broth from pot and mix with cornstarch.
6. Return broth mixture on the pot and stir well and select sauté for just two minutes.
7. Garnish with green onions and serve.

Nutritional Info: Calories: 413, Fat: 17.3 g, Protein: 45.1 g, Carbs: 17.7 g

Simple Beef Tacos

Prep time: 5 minutes, Cook time: 2 hours, Servings: 6

Ingredients:
4 tbsps. taco seasoning
2/3 cup chicken stock
3 lbs. beef roast

Instructions:
1. Place beef roast in instant pot.
2. Pour stock over the roast and sprinkle roast with taco seasoning.
3. Seal pot with lid and select MANUAL button and hang up the timer for 2 hours.
4. Allow releasing steam on a unique then open.
5. Using a fork and shred the roast and serve.

Nutritional Info: Calories: 427, Fat: 14.2 g, Protein: 68.9 g, Carbs: 1.1 g

Spicy Beef with Tomato Sauce

Prep time: 10 minutes, Cook time: 1 hour 20 minutes, Servings: 4

Ingredients:
2 tbsps. chipotle sauce
2 tsps. cumin
8 oz. tomato sauce
½ tsp. pepper
2 lbs. halved chuck roast
1 tsp. garlic powder
2 tsps. chili powder
1 tbsp. organic olive oil
1 tbsp. lime juice
½ cup chicken broth
1 tsp. salt
¼ cup fresh cilantro

Instructions:
1. Season roast with garlic powder, pepper, cumin, chili powder, and salt.
2. Add oil in instant pot and select sauté.
3. Once the oil is hot then place seasoned roast in pot and sauté for 5 minutes on either side.
4. Now add remaining ingredients and stir well.
5. Seal pot with lid and select MANUAL button and set the timer for 70 minutes.
6. Allow releasing steam on its own then open.
7. Using fork shred the beef and serves.

Nutritional Info: Calories: 557, Fat: 23.1 g, Protein: 76.8 g, Carbs: 6.6 g

Apple Cider Pork

Prep time: 10 minutes, Cook time: 25 minutes, Servings: 4

Ingredients:

Black pepper

1 tbsp. minced dry onion

2 lbs. pork loin

2 chopped apples

2 tbsps. extra virgin organic olive oil

Salt

1 chopped yellow onion

2 cups apple cider

Instructions:

1. Set your instant pot on Sauté mode, add the oil and warmth
2. Add pork loin, salt, pepper and dried onion, stir and brown meat on all sides and transfer to some plate.
3. Add onion to pot, stir and cook for 2 minutes.
4. Return meat to pot, add cider, apples, more salt and pepper, stir, cover and cook on High for 20 minutes.
5. Release pressure, uncover, transfer pork to some cutting board, slice it and divide among plates.
6. Add sauce and mixture through the pot quietly and serve.

Nutritional Info: Calories: 450, Fat: 22 g, Protein: 37.2 g, Carbs: 29 g

Pork Chops with Lime

Prep time: 10 minutes, Cook time: 15 minutes, Servings: 4

Ingredients:

2 tbsps. extra virgin olive oil

½ cup white wine

4 pork chops

1 minced garlic herb

2 tbsps. lime juice

2 tbsps. cornstarch combined with 3 tbsps. water

2 tbsps. chopped parsley

1 lb. sliced onions

½ cup milk

Salt

2 tbsps. butter

Black pepper

1 tbsp. white flour

Instructions:

1. Set your instant pot on Sauté mode, add the oil and butter and also heat
2. Add pork chops, salt and pepper, brown on all sides and transfer with a bowl.
3. Add garlic and onion to pot, stir and cook for two main minutes.
4. Add wine, lime juice, milk, parsley and return pork chops to pot.
5. Stir, cover and cook on High for 15 minutes.
6. Release the stress, uncover, add cornstarch and flour, stir well and cook on Simmer mode for 3 minutes.
7. Divide pork chops and onions on plates, drizzle cooking sauce across and enjoy!

Nutritional Info: Calories 222, Fat: 7 g, Protein: 22.2 g, Carbs: 9 g

Creamy Mushroom Pork Chops

Prep time: 10 minutes, Cook time: 20 minutes, Servings: 4

Ingredients:

2 tbsps. extra virgin essential olive oil

½ small bunch chopped parsley

4 boneless pork chops

Black pepper

1 cup water

10 oz. canned mushroom soup cream

1 cup sour cream

Salt

2 tsps. chicken bouillon powder

Instructions:

1. Set your instant pot on Sauté mode, add oil and also heat
2. Add pork chops, salt and pepper, brown them on every side, transfer to a plate and set aside.

3. Add water and chicken bouillon powder towards the pot and stir well.
4. Return pork chops, stir, cover and cook on High for 9 minutes.
5. Release the pressure naturally, transfer pork chops to your platter whilst warm.
6. Set the pot on Simmer mode and heat up the cooking liquid.
7. Add mushroom soup, stir, cook for 2 minutes and take off heat.
8. Add parsley and sour cream, stir and pour over pork chops.

Nutritional Info: Calories: 284, Fat: 16 g, Protein: 23.2 g, Carbs: 10.5 g

Pork Roast with Fennel

Prep time: 10 minutes, Cook time: 1 hour 20 minutes, Servings: 4

Ingredients:
Black pepper
1 lb. sliced fennel bulbs
2 lbs. pork meat, boneless
1 chopped yellow onion
Salt
2 minced garlic cloves
2 tbsps. extra virgin organic olive oil
5 oz. chicken stock
5 oz. white wine

Instructions:
1. Set your instant pot on Sauté mode, add oil and heat
2. Add pork, salt and pepper, stir, brown on every side and transfer with a plate.
3. Add garlic, wine and stock on the pot, stir and cook for just two minutes.
4. Return pork to pot, cover and cook on High for 40 minutes.
5. Release the pressure, uncover and add onion and fennel, stir, cover and cook on High for fifteen minutes.
6. Release the pressure again, stir your mixture, transfer pork to a cutting board, slice and portion out among plates.
7. Serve with onion and fennel privately with cooking sauce drizzled over. Delicious!

Nutritional Info: Calories: 428, Fat: 16 g, Protein: 38 g, Carbs: 29 g

Chinese BBQ Pork

Prep time: 10 minutes, Cook time: 50 minutes, Servings: 86

Ingredients:
8 tbsps. Char Siu sauce
1 tsp. peanut oil
2 tsps. sesame oil
2 lbs. pork belly
2 tbsps. dry sherry
2 tbsps. honey
4 tbsps. soy sauce
1-quart chicken stock

Instructions:
1. Set your instant pot on Simmer mode, add sherry, stock, soy sauce and 1 / 2 of Char Siu sauce, stir and cook for 8 minutes.
2. Add pork, stir, cover and hang on High for 30 minutes.
3. Release pressure naturally, transfer pork to your cutting board, leave for cooling down and chop in small pieces.
4. Heat up a pan using the peanut oil over medium high heat, add pork, stir and cook for a couple minutes.
5. Meanwhile, in a very bowl, mix sesame oil using the rest of the Char Siu sauce and honey.
6. Brush pork from your pan with this mix, stir and cook for ten mins.
7. Heat up another pan over medium high heat, add cooking liquid in the instant pot and provide to some boil.
8. Simmer for 3 minutes and remove from heat.
9. Divide pork on plates, drizzle the delicious sticky sauce over it and serve.

Nutritional Info: Calories: 400, Fat: 23 g, Protein: 41 g, Carbs: 15 g

Classic Tex-Mex Steak

Prep time: 10 minutes, Cook time: 8 hours, Servings: 6

Ingredients:

2 tbsps. Mexican seasoning
¼ cup salsa
Nonstick cooking spray
14 oz. diced tomatoes
4 oz. canned diced green chilies
2 lbs. sliced beef round steak
Salt
8 oz. tomato sauce

Instructions:

1. Grease the insert of the Instant Pot with nonstick cooking spray.
2. In the insert of Instant Pot, place all ingredients and stir to combine.
3. Cover and lock lid, then turn the steam release handle to venting position.
4. Select the "Slow Cooker" setting and hang up to "Medium".
5. Cook for about 6-8 hours, checking meat occasionally. (If meat looks dry, stir in about 1 cup of water).
6. Enjoy this steak alongside green peppers and sautéed onion with the topping of avocado slices.

Nutritional Info: Calories: 418, Fat: 14.7 g, Protein: 51.4 g, Carbs: 20 g

Mushroom Steak

Prep time: 15 minutes, Cook time: 5 hours 5 minutes, Servings: 6

Ingredients:

2 tbsps. butter
10 oz. mushroom soup
1 cup seeded and sliced green bell pepper
Nonstick cooking spray
1½ lbs. sliced beef round steak
Freshly ground black pepper
¼ cup flour
1½ cups thickly sliced onions
Salt

Instructions:

1. In a large bowl, mix together flour, salt and black pepper.
2. Add steak pieces and toss to coat well.
3. In a skillet, melt butter and sear steak pieces until browned completely.
4. Grease the insert of your Instant Pot with nonstick cooking spray.
5. In the insert of Instant Pot, place steak pieces and top with onion and bell pepper.
6. Place mushroom soup on the top.
7. Cover and lock lid, then turn the steam release handle to venting position.
8. Select the "Slow Cooker" setting and set to "Medium".
9. Cook for about 4-5 hours.
10. Serve hot.

Nutritional Info: Calories: 339, Fat: 14.8 g, Protein: 37.6 g, Carbs: 12 g

Braised Pork with Paprika

Prep time: 10 minutes, Cook time: 1 hour, Servings: 6

Ingredients:

1 tbsp. paprika
4 lbs. chopped pork butt
16 oz. chicken stock
Salt
4 oz. lemon juice
2 tbsps. extra virgin olive oil
16 oz. merlot wine
¼ cup chopped onion
¼ cup garlic powder
Black pepper

Instructions:

1. In your instant pot, mix pork with stock, wine, fresh lemon juice, onion, garlic powder, oil, paprika, salt and pepper, stir, cover and cook on High for 45 minutes.
2. Leave the pot aside for 15 minutes, release the stress quickly, divide braised pork into bowls and serve.

Nutritional Info: Calories: 454, Fat: 45 g, Protein: 8 g, Carbs: 2 g

Tender Salsa Steak

Prep time: 10 minutes, Cook time: 10 hours, Servings: 6

Ingredients:

Hot pepper sauce
Salt
¼ tsp. garlic powder
2 cups salsa
2 lbs. flank steak
8 oz. tomato sauce
Freshly ground black pepper
Nonstick cooking spray

Instructions:

1. With a meat mallet, pound the beef steak into even thickness.
2. Season steak with garlic powder, salt and black pepper.
3. In a bowl, mix together salsa, tomato sauce and hot pepper sauce.
4. Grease the insert of your respective Instant Pot with nonstick cooking spray.
5. In the insert of Instant Pot, place steak and top with salsa mixture.
6. Select the "Slow Cooker" setting as well as set to "Medium".
7. Cook for around 8-10 hours.
8. Serve hot.

Nutritional Info: Calories: 344, Fat: 14.2 g, Protein: 45.1 g, Carbs: 7.6 g

Kalua Pork

Prep time: 2 hours 2 minutes, Cook time: 1 hour 30 minutes Servings: 2

Ingredients:

2 tbsps. hickory liquid smoke
6 lbs. sliced pork shoulder
1 cup water
Salt
3 tbsps. olive oil

Instructions:

1. Heat oil on Sauté, brown the pork each side for 8 minutes. Press Cancel and remove to a platter. Add in water and hickory smoke liquid. Stir and add the roasts with juices.
2. Sprinkle salt on top of the pork roasts. Seal the lid and cook on High Pressure 90 minutes. Once done, do a natural pressure release for 20 minutes. Remove the pork and shred it.
3. Discard fats that come off the meat while shredding.

Nutritional Info: Calories: 260, Protein: 24g, Carbs: 0g, Fat: 18g

Pork Shoulder

Prep time: 15 minutes, Cook time: 20 minutes, Servings: 2

Ingredients:

½ chopped onion
2 tbsps. coconut oil
¼ cup toasted and chopped almonds
1 lb. halved brussels sprouts
¼ tsp. black pepper
1 tsp. flax seed powder
1 lemon zest
¼ tsp. salt
¼ lb. cubed pork shoulder
½ cup coconut milk

Instructions:

1. Set on Sauté mode and heated the oil; add the pork and cook for 5 minutes. Add the onions, flax seed, Brussels sprouts, ½ cup of coconut milk and seal the lid.
2. Cook to Manual on High pressure for 15 minutes. When ready, do a quick pressure release. Season with pepper and salt. Serve with almonds and lemon zest.

Nutritional Info: Calories: 457, Protein: 24.1g, Carbs: 7.3g, Fat: 30.4g

Prosciutto Wrapped Asparagus Canes

Prep time: 5 minutes, Cook time: 5 minutes, Servings: 4

Ingredients:

1 lb. bacon strips
1 cup water
1 lb. asparagus

Instructions:

1. Pour in water and place a steamer basket. Wrap each asparagus with a bacon strip.
2. Arrange the canes in the basket.
3. Seal the lid, and cook on High Pressure for 5 minutes. Once done, quickly release the pressure.
4. Remove the canes and serve warm.

Nutritional Info: Calories: 242, Protein: 20g, Carbs: 1g, Fat: 18g

Hot Shredded Pork

Prep time: 30 minutes, Cook time: 16 minutes, Servings: 4

Ingredients:

½ tbsp. soy sauce
½ tbsp. garlic paste
2 tbsps. barbecue sauce
2 tbsps. lemon juice
2 tbsps. vinegar
½ tbsp. salt
½ cup chili garlic sauce
½ tbsp. chili powder
2 boiled and shredded pork fillets
2 tbsps. olive oil

Instructions:

1. Heat oil on Sauté, and cook garlic for 1 minute.
2. Add the pork and brown for 10 minutes per side.
3. Add soy sauce, chili sauce, vinegar, barbecue sauce, salt, and chili powder and cook for another 5 minutes.
4. Transfer to a serving dish and drizzle lemon juice.

Nutritional Info: Calories: 351, Protein: 45.1g, Carbs: 5.1g, Fat: 14.9g

Spicy Pork Chops

Prep time: 2 minutes, Cook time: 15 minutes, Servings: 3

Ingredients:

½ cup chicken broth
2 minced garlic cloves
2 julienned carrots
Salt
1 tbsp. coconut oil
1 sliced onion
3 tbsps. hot sauce
½ tsp. dried thyme
1 cup string beans
2 lbs. boneless pork chops

Instructions:

1. Heat oil on Sauté, add the chops, season with salt, and brown them on each side. Remove to a plate.
2. Add the onions, thyme, hot sauce, and garlic. Stir and cook for 5 minutes.
3. Add the pork chops back to the pot with the chicken broth, string beans and carrots. Seal the lid, and cook on High Pressure for 10 minutes.
4. Once ready, quickly release the pressure.

Nutritional Info: Calories: 320, Protein: 26g, Carbs: 5g, Fat: 19g

Sausage and Pepper Sauce

Prep time: 35 minutes, Cook time: 15 minutes, Servings: 3

Ingredients:

¼ cup tomato sauce
10 pork sausages
2 diced large green bell peppers
1 cup diced tomatoes
1 cup water
2 diced large red bell peppers

3 basil leaves
Salt
3 minced garlic cloves
1 tbsp. Italian seasoning
2 diced large yellow bell peppers
Instructions:
1. Place all ingredients in the pot with peppers arranged on top; don't stir.

2. Seal the lid and cook on High Pressure for 15 minutes.
3. Once ready, quickly release the pressure. Stir and serve.

Nutritional Info: Calories: 173, Protein: 9g, Carbs: 0g, Fat: 15g

Pork Roll Soup

Prep time: 45 minutes, Cook time: 30 minutes, Servings: 4
Ingredients:
½ cup coconut aminos
1 tsp. garlic powder
2 tbsps. olive oil
1 tsp. onion powder
1 chopped small cabbage
1 cup shredded carrots
Salt
1 diced onion
1 tsp. ginger paste
1 ½ lbs. minced pork

4 cups beef broth
Instructions:
1. Heat oil on Sauté, add the pork and brown for 10 minutes.
2. Stir in the remaining ingredients. Seal the lid, and cook on High Pressure for 25 minutes. Once ready, quickly release the pressure.

Nutritional Info: Calories: 101, Protein: 3.8g, Carbs: 0.5g, Fat: 10g

Bacon Onion Jam

Prep time: 6 hours 40 minutes, Cook time: 25 minutes, Servings: 6
Ingredients:
¼ cup monk fruit powder
¼ tsp. cayenne pepper
1/6 tsp. cinnamon powder
1 lb. sliced bacon strips
2 garlic cloves
¼ cup star fruit juice
4 chopped onions
¼ cup plain vinegar
1 tsp. fresh thyme leaves
Instructions:
1. Add bacon and fry until slightly cooked but not crispy, on Sauté. Remove to a paper-towel-lined plate and refrigerate.

2. Scoop out the grease from the pot leaving a tablespoon of oil.
3. Add the garlic and onion and cook for 5 minutes.
4. Stir in the remaining ingredients, seal the lid, and cook on Slow Cook mode for 5 hours. Once done, quickly release the pressure.
5. Stir in the bacon, and cook on Sauté for 10 minutes.
6. Scoop into an airtight container, refrigerate and use for up to a week.

Nutritional Info: Calories: 40, Protein: 22g, Carbs: 0g, Fat: 26g

Coconut Ginger Pork

Prep time: 55 minutes, Cook time: 45 minutes, Servings: 4
Ingredients:
¼ can coconut milk
1 tsp. coriander powder
1-inch grated ginger
1 tsp. cumin powder
Salt

2 minced garlic cloves
2 lbs. pork shoulder
Black pepper
1 sliced large onion
Lime wedges

1 tbsp. olive oil
Instructions:
1. Combine pepper, salt, cumin, and coriander and rub onto meat.
2. Heat oil on Sauté, add the meat, ginger, garlic, onion, and milk.
3. Seal the lid and cook on High Pressure for 45 minutes.
4. Once ready, quickly release the pressure.
5. Garnish with lemon wedges, to serve.

Nutritional Info: Calories: 78, Protein: 11g, Carbs: 0.8g, Fat: 3g

Pork Meatballs

Prep time: 55 minutes, Cook time: 15 minutes, Servings: 3
Ingredients:
1 cup beef broth
2 beaten eggs
2 minced garlic cloves
Salt
⅓ tsp. parsley flakes
Pepper
2 tsps. Grounded macadamia nuts
½ lb. ground pork
Instructions:
1. Combine all ingredients, except the meat and broth, in a bowl. Mix in the meat to the mixture. Shape 2-inch balls and press Sauté on the Instant Pot.
2. Pour in the broth and let boil.
3. Add the meatballs to the broth and simmer for 15 minutes, turning once.
4. Cook the meat until hardened and cooked through. Serve with tomato sauce.

Nutritional Info: Calories: 47, Protein: 5.5g, Carbs: 0.1g, Fat: 1.9g

No-Pressure Cumin Pork Chops

Prep time: 10 minutes, Cook time: 15 minutes, Servings: 4
Ingredients:
2 tbsps. Coconut Oil
Pepper
4 Pork Chops
1 tsp. Chili Powder
Salt
½ tbsp. Cumin
Instructions:
1. Combine the oil and all spies, in a bowl. Rub this mixture onto the meat.
2. Set the Instant Pot on Sauté and add in the pork.
3. Cook for about 15 minutes, flipping once halfway through cooking.
4. Serve the pork chops with steamed broccoli and keto mayo.

Nutritional Info: Calories: 305, Protein: 30g, Carbs: 0g, Fat: 19.5g

Creamy Ranch Pork Chops

Prep time: 20 minutes, Cook time: 10 minutes, Servings: 2
Ingredients:
1 oz. ranch dressing and seasoning mix
4 pork loin chops
½ cup chicken broth
Chopped parsley
15 oz. mushroom soup cream
Instructions:
1. Add pork, mushroom soup cream, ranch dressing and seasoning mix, and chicken broth. Seal the lid, select Meat/Stew mode on High pressure for 10 minutes.
2. Once ready, do a natural pressure release for 10 minutes, then a quick pressure release. Serve the pork and the sauce with well-seasoned sautéed cremini mushrooms.

Nutritional Info: Calories: 318, Protein: 26.1g, Carbs: 2g, Fat: 18.9g

Pork Roast with Mushroom Gravy

Prep time: 65 minutes, Cook time: 50 minutes, Servings: 3

Ingredients:

1 small head Cauliflower
1 tbsp. Olive oil
Black Pepper
3 minced garlic cloves
1 sliced Celery Rib
1 cup Chicken Broth
Salt
1 cup Portobello Mushrooms
1 cup Water
1 diced medium Onion
1 lb. Pork Roast

Instructions:

1. Place all vegetables and broth in the pot, add the pork roast on top and sprinkle with pepper and salt.
2. Seal the lid, secure the pressure valve and cook on High Pressure for 40 minutes.
3. Once done, quickly release the pressure.
4. Remove the pork to a baking dish. Preheat an oven to 400 F and bake the pork for 10 minutes.
5. Meanwhile, select Sauté on the pot and simmer the gravy until it boils down.
6. Place the pork roasts in a plate and dish the gravy over, to serve.

Nutritional Info: Calories: 364, Protein: 31.9g, Carbs: 5g, Fat: 30.9g

Tandoori BBQ Pork Ribs

Prep time: 40 minutes, Cook time: 20 minutes, Servings: 6

Ingredients:

¼ cup BBQ Sauce
Salt
1 ½ lbs. Pork Ribs
1-inch grated Ginger
1 cup Water
3 Garlic cloves
1 Bay Leaf
2 tbsps. Tandoori Spice Mix

Instructions:

1. Line ribs flat in the Instant Pot, add water, ginger, garlic, bay leaf, one tbsp. of Tandoori spice mix and salt.
2. Seal the lid, select Manual and cook on High Pressure for 20 minutes.
3. Once done, do a natural pressure release for 10 minutes. Carefully remove the ribs and place on a flat surface.
4. Wrap the bony sides with foil, pat dry the meaty sides and coat with the BBQ sauce.
5. Sear with a torch or broil for 5 minutes per side. Serve immediately.

Nutritional Info: Calories: 296, Protein: 22g, Carbs: 0g, Fat: 23g

Meatballs Stuffed with Brie

Prep time: 15 minutes, Cook time: 20 minutes, Servings: 5

Ingredients:

2 beaten eggs
1 tbsp. fresh cilantro
1 lb. ground pork
10 cubes of brie
1 tsp. kosher salt
2 minced garlic cloves
1 tsp. dried thyme
2 tbsps. minced shallots
½ tsp. ground black pepper

Instructions:

1. Combine the pork, thyme, pepper, salt, garlic, shallots, cilantro, and eggs.
2. Shape the mixture into 10 balls using oiled hands. Put a cube of brie in the center of each ball and roll.
3. Put your oven on at 390 degrees F. Put the meatballs on a baking pan and bake for 20 minutes.
4. Serve with mustard or salsa. Enjoy!

Nutritional Info: Calories: 302, Protein: 33.4g, Fat: 17.3g, Carbs: 1.9g

Pork North Carolina Style

Prep time: 4 hours 30 minutes, Cook time: 3 hours, Servings: 4

Ingredients:

Water
2 wedged onions
1 tsp. chipotle powder
1½ lbs. pork butt
1 tbsp. liquid smoke sauce
Freshly ground black pepper
1 tsp. onion powder
Kosher salt
1 tsp. ground cumin
1 tsp. garlic powder
½ tbsp. paprika

Instructions:

1. Combine the liquid smoke sauce, cumin, salt, pepper, onion powder, garlic powder, paprika and chipotle powder.

2. Rub this mixture all over the pork butt. Cover with plastic wrap and marinate in the fridge for 3 hours.

3. Put your oven on to 325 degrees F. Wrap the pork in foil and roast for 3 hours. Turn the oven heat up to 375 degrees F.

4. Unwrap the pork and roast for 90 minutes at the higher temperature.

5. Put the pork in a pot with the onion wedges and water. Cook over a medium heat until the pork is completely cooked.

6. Shred the pork with meat claws and check the seasonings. Serve with a keto salad on the side.

Nutritional Info: Calories: 350, Protein: 53.6g, Fat: 11g, Carbs: 5g

Pork Gumbo for Entertaining

Prep time: 35 minutes, Cook time: 30 minutes, Servings: 6

Ingredients:

2 roughly chopped shallots
2 deveined and thinly sliced bell peppers
¾ lb. okra
2 tbsps. olive oil
2 chopped celery stalks
Salt
8 oz. sliced pork sausage
1 tbsp. Cajun spice
1 tsp. crushed red pepper
1 tsp. gumbo file
1 lb. cubed pork shoulder
Freshly cracked black pepper
1 cup water
¼ cup flaxseed meal
1 tsp. beef bouillon granules
4 cups bone broth

Instructions:

1. Preheat a pot over a medium-high flame and heat the oil. Cook the pork until it is brown. Put to one side.

2. Put in the sausage and cook for 5 minutes. Put to one side.

3. Put in the shallots and cook until they are translucent. Add the bone broth, Cajun spice, red pepper, gumbo file, beef bouillon granules, salt and pepper. Bring to the boil.

4. Add the water, celery and bell pepper. Reduce the heat to moderate-low and cook for around 20 minutes.

5. Put in the flaxseed and okra and cook for another 5 minutes.

Nutritional Info: Calories: 427, Protein: 35.2g, Fat 26.2g, Carbs: 3.6g

Meatloaf Muffins

Prep time: 35 minutes, Cook time: 30 minutes, Servings: 6

Ingredients:

2 minced garlic cloves
Ground black pepper
½ lb. ground pork
1 tsp. dry oregano

1 cup shredded carrots
1 tbsp. Worcestershire sauce
1 lb. ground turkey
1 tbsp. Dijon mustard

½ tsp. dry basil
2 pureed ripe tomatoes
Kosher salt
1 oz. envelope onion soup mix
1 whisked egg
Instructions:
1. Put your oven on at 350 degrees F.
2. Mix together all the ingredients until they are combined well.

3. Spray a muffin tin with nonstick cooking spray and put in the mixture.
4. Cook them in the oven for half an hour. Let them cool a little before removing from the tin. Serve!!

Nutritional Info: Calories: 220, Protein: 33.8g, Fat: 6.3g, Carbs: 2.9g

A Mug of Breakfast Pork

Prep time: 10 minutes, Cook time: 7 minutes, Servings: 2
Ingredients:
½ tsp. onion powder
Ground black pepper
½ cup tomato sauce
1 tsp. garlic paste
Salt
½ lb. ground pork
½ tsp. cayenne pepper
Instructions:

1. Mix together the pork, tomato sauce, cheese, cayenne pepper, onion powder, garlic paste, salt and pepper.
2. Split the mixture in two and put it in 2 microwave-safe mugs.
3. Put in the microwave on high and cook for 7 minutes. It tastes good hot and served with pickles. Serve!!

Nutritional Info: Calories: 327, Protein: 40g, Fat: 16.6g, Carbs: 5.8g

Pork and Veggie Skewers

Prep time: 20 minutes, Cook time: 13 minutes, Servings: 6
Ingredients:
1 thickly sliced green bell pepper
1 tbsp. Italian spice mix
1 thickly sliced red bell pepper
1 wedged onion
2 tbsps. fresh lime juice
3 tbsps. olive oil
1½ lbs. cubed pork shoulder
1 lb. small button mushrooms
1 cubed zucchini
3 tbsps. tamari sauce
Soaked wooden skewers
2 crushed garlic cloves

Instructions:
1. First make the marinade. Combine the garlic, Italian spice mix, fresh lime juice, tamari sauce and olive oil.
2. Pour the marinade over the pork and marinate for 2 hours. Then thread the pork cubes, peppers, mushrooms, onions and zucchini onto skewers.
3. Preheat your grill and cook the skewers for about 13 minutes turning often. Enjoy!

Nutritional Info: Calories: 428, Protein: 28.9g, Fat: 31.6g, Carbs: 7.7g

Pork with Bamboo Shoots and Cauliflower

Prep time: 20 minutes, Cook time: 15minutes, Servings: 6
Ingredients:
2 tbsps. oyster sauce
Celery salt
1 ½ lbs. boneless pork loin
½ cup vodka
½ tsp. garlic powder

8 oz. can bamboo shoots
¼ tsp. dried thyme
1½ tbsps. olive oil
Ground black pepper
1 chopped yellow onion

½ tsp. dried marjoram
1 head cauliflower florets

Instructions:

1. Put the pork loin in a bowl. Add the olive oil, vodka, oyster sauce, marjoram, garlic powder, thyme, salt and ground pepper. Combine thoroughly. Add the pork loin to a mixing dish.
2. In a skillet heat 1 tablespoon of olive oil over a moderate-high heat. Sauté the onion until soft.
3. Put in the cauliflower florets and cook for 3 – 4 minutes until they are tender. Put this to one side.
4. Put another tablespoon of olive oil in the pan and heat with a high flame. Put the marinade to one side and brown the pork for 3 minutes on each side.
5. Put in the marinade, the cauliflower and bamboo shoots.
6. Cook for another 4 minutes until the sauce has thickened. Serve hot. Enjoy!

Nutritional Info: Calories: 356, Protein 33.1g, Fat 19.5g, Carbs 6.4g

Frittata with Spicy Sausage

Prep time: 35 minutes, Cook time: 25 minutes, Servings: 4

Ingredients:
½ lb. thinly sliced pork sausage
8 beaten eggs
1 tsp. salt
3 tbsps. olive oil
1 tsp. finely minced jalapeno pepper
2 minced garlic cloves
¼ tsp. cayenne pepper
½ tsp. ground black pepper
1 cup chopped onion
1 tsp. crushed dried sage

Instructions:

1. Preheat a skillet over a moderate-high flame and heat the oil. Sauté the garlic, onion and jalapeno pepper until the onion is translucent.
2. Sprinkle in the cayenne pepper, salt and black pepper. Then add the sausage and cook until it has slightly browned. Stir often.
3. Put the mixture into a greased baking dish. Beat the eggs and pour over the sausage mixture. Scatter the dried sage on top.
4. Preheat the oven to 420 degrees F and cook for 25 minutes. Serve!!

Nutritional Info: Calories: 423, Protein: 22.6g, Fat: 35.4g, Carbs: 4.1g

Pork Chops with Mushroom

Prep time: 10 minutes, Cook time: 30 minutes, Servings: 4

Ingredients:
Pepper
1 tsp. garlic powder
½ chopped onion
10 oz. low sodium mushroom soup cream
1 cup bone broth
8 oz. sliced mushrooms
1 tbsp. extra virgin olive oil
3 minced garlic cloves
Salt
4 pork chops
1 fresh thyme sprig

Instructions:

1. Add oil in instant pot and select sauté.
2. Add garlic and onion and sauté for 2 minutes.
3. Season pork chops with pepper and salt.
4. Add thyme, broth, and pork chops in a pot.
5. Seal pot with lid and cook on manual high pressure for 20 minutes.
6. Allow releasing pressure naturally then open the lid.
7. Remove pork chops from pot and place on a serving plate.
8. Add mushroom soup in a pot and stir well.
9. Pour gravy over pork chops and serve.

Nutritional Info: Calories: 360, Fat: 25.6 g, Carbs: 6.7 g, Protein 25.7 g

Pork Chops with Brussels sprouts

Prep time: 10 minutes Cook time: 35 minutes, Servings: 4

Ingredients:

1 tbsp. coconut oil
1 cup sliced onion
1 tbsp. arrowroot powder
1 cup chopped carrot
2 cups halved Brussels sprouts
1 cup chicken stock
½ tsp. dried thyme
2 tsps. minced garlic
1 tsp. salt
1 lb. boneless pork chops

Instructions:

1. Season pork chops with salt.
2. Add oil in instant pot and select sauté.
3. Add pork chops to the pot and cook until brown.
4. Remove pork chops from pot and place on a plate.
5. Add thyme, garlic, and onion and sauté for 2 minutes. Add broth and pork chops.
6. Seal pot with lid and select manual and set timer for 15 minutes.
7. Release pressure using quick release method than open the lid.
8. Add carrots and Brussels sprouts and stir well.
9. Seal pot again and select a manual and set timer for 3 minutes.
10. Release pressure using quick release method than open the lid.
11. Remove vegetables and pork chops from pot and place on a serving plate.
12. Add arrowroot powder and stir until thickened.
13. Pour gravy over vegetables and pork chops.
14. Serve and enjoy.

Nutritional Info: Calories: 439, Fat: 31.9 g, Carbs: 12.1 g, Protein: 27.8 g

Smoked Pulled Pork

Prep time: 15 minutes, Cook time: 1 hour 20 minutes, Servings: 12

Ingredients:

2 tbsps. coconut amino
3½ lbs. pork shoulder
2 tbsps. liquid smoke
1 cup chicken broth
2 minced garlic cloves

Instructions:

1. Place pork into the instant pot.
2. Pour remaining ingredients over the pork.
3. Seal pot with lid and select manual button and set timer for 70 minutes.
4. Allow releasing pressure naturally then open the lid.
5. Remove pork from pot and place on cutting board.
6. Using fork shred the meat and serves.

Nutritional Info: Calories: 390, Fat: 28.4 g, Carbs: 0.8 g, Protein: 31.2 g

Tomato Pulled Pork

Prep time: 10 minutes, Cook time: 1 hour 30 minutes, Servings: 8

Ingredients:

1 tsp. garlic powder
½ cup water
1 tbsp. onion powder
4 lbs. Pork
½ tsp. black pepper
2 tsp. salt
½ cup diced tomatoes
1 tbsp. mustard powder

Instructions:

1. Mix together all dry ingredients and rub over pork.
2. Place pork in instant pot and pour remaining ingredients over pork.
3. Seal pot with lid and cook on high for 1 hour.
4. Allow releasing pressure naturally then open the lid.
5. Using fork shred the pork and stir well in pot juices.
6. Serve and enjoy.

Nutritional Info: Calories: 345, Fat: 24.7 g, Carbs: 2.3 g, Protein: 27 g

Perfect Cuban Pork

Prep time: 10 minutes, Cook time: 8 hours 10 minutes, Servings: 6

Ingredients:

1 tsp. dried oregano
2 tbsps. extra virgin olive oil
1 bay leaf
1 sliced small onion
¼ tsp. red pepper flakes
1 tsp. cumin
½ cup lime juice
6 smashed garlic cloves
½ cup orange juice
1½ tsps. salt
3 lbs. pork shoulder roast
1/8 tsp. black pepper

Instructions:

1. In a bowl, whisk together garlic, pepper, red pepper flakes, oregano, cumin, salt, lime juice, orange juice and oil.
2. Rub bowl mixture over pork and place pork in instant pot.
3. Add remaining bowl juice over pork with onion and bay leaf.
4. Seal pot with lid and select slow cooker setting and set the timer for 8 hours.
5. Using fork shred the pork and serves.

Nutritional Info: Calories: 652, Fat: 51.1 g, Carbs: 7.4 g, Protein: 38.8 g

Green Chile Pork Stew

Prep time: 15 minutes, Cook time: 35 minutes, Servings: 6

Ingredients:

1 tbsp. extra virgin olive oil
3 cups chicken stock
½ tsp. kosher salt
½ tsp. black pepper
3 ½ cups salsa Verde
¾ cup chopped roasted green Chile
3 chopped large onion
1 lb. sliced lean pork stew meat
4 cups diced potatoes
½ tsp. garlic powder
¼ cup arrowroot powder

Instructions:

1. Add pork, arrowroot powder, pepper, and garlic powder in a large zip lock bag.
2. Seal bag and shake well and set aside.
3. Add oil in instant pot and select sauté.
4. Add pork pieces in a pot and cook until browned, about 5 minutes.
5. Add remaining all ingredients into the pot and stir well.
6. Seal pot with lid and cook on manual high pressure for 20 minutes.
7. Allow releasing pressure naturally then open the lid.
8. Stir well and serve.

Nutritional Info: Calories: 305, Fat 8.5 g, Carbs: 36.5 g, Protein: 19.8 g

Simple Pork Ribs

Prep time: 15 minutes, Cook time: 35 minutes, Servings: 4

Ingredients:

3½ cups apple juice
2 lbs. rack pork back ribs
½ cup apple cider vinegar

Instructions:

1. Pour apple cider vinegar and apple juice in instant pot.
2. Place trivet into the instant pot.
3. Place pork ribs on a trivet.
4. Seal pot with lid and select manual and set timer for 30 minutes.
5. Allow releasing pressure naturally then open the lid.
6. Serve and enjoy.

Nutritional Info: Calories: 504, Fat: 27.5 g, Carbs: 25 g, Protein: 38.7 g

Tender and Juicy Shredded Pork

Prep time: Cook time: 1 hour 10 minutes, Servings: 8

Ingredients:
4 lbs. trimmed pork shoulder
3 tbsps. extra virgin olive oil
2 tbsps. lime juice
2 tbsps. dried oregano
1 small dried hot chili
1 mild chili
1 quartered medium onion
4 peeled garlic cloves
2 tsps. black pepper
1 tbsp. salt

Instructions:
1. Add 2 tbsps. oil, pepper, lime juice, oregano, chilies, onion, garlic and salt into the blender and blend until smooth.
2. Rub marinade over pork and cover and place in refrigerator for 30 minutes.
3. Add remaining oil in instant pot and place marinated pork in the pot.
4. Seal pot with lid and cook on manual high pressure for 60 minutes.
5. Allow releasing pressure naturally then open the lid.
6. Using fork shred the pork and serves.

Nutritional Info: Calories: 721, Fat: 53.9 g, Carbs: 3.1 g, Protein: 53.2 g

Apple Cider Shredded Pork

Prep time: Cook time: 8 hours 10 minutes, Servings: 8

Ingredients:
4 lbs. boneless pork butt
1½ cups unsweetened apple cider
1 sliced large onion
For the rub:
1½ tsps. smoked paprika
½ tsp. chili powder
½ tsp. black pepper
1 tbsp. sea salt
½ tsp. ground ginger
1½ tsps. garlic powder

Instructions:
1. In a small bowl, mix together all spice ingredients.
2. Rub spice mixture all over the pork.
3. Add onion sliced into the instant pot then place season pork over onions.
4. Pour apple cider over the pork.
5. Seal pot with lid and select slow cooker setting and set the timer for 8 hours.
6. Remove pork from pot and using fork shred the pork.
7. Serve and enjoy.

Nutritional Info: Calories: 471, Fat: 15.3 g, Carbs: 8 g, Protein: 71 g

Jerk Pork Roast

Prep time: 10 minutes, Cook time: 55 minutes, Servings: 8

Ingredients:
½ cup bone broth
¼ cup Jamaican jerk spice blend
4 lbs. pork shoulder
1 tbsp. extra virgin olive oil

Instructions:
1. Rub oil and jerk spice blend over pork and place pork in instant pot.
2. Select sauté and brown the meat on all sides.
3. Add broth into the pot.
4. Seal pot with lid and cook manual high pressure for 45 minutes,
5. Allow releasing pressure naturally then open the lid.
6. Using fork shred the meat and serve.

Nutritional Info: Calories: 455, Fat: 33.5 g, Carbs: 0 g, Protein: 36 g

Tasty Pork Carnitas

Prep time: 10 minutes, Cook time: 45 minutes, Servings: 6

Ingredients:

2 tsps. ground cumin
1 grapefruit juice
1 bay leaf
1 tsp. chili powder
1 tsp. dried oregano
¼ tsp. ground cinnamon
4 minced garlic cloves
½ sliced onion
4 lbs. sliced pork shoulder
3 tsps. kosher salt

Instructions:

1. Add all ingredients into the instant pot and stir well.
2. Seal pot with lid and select manual and set timer for 35 minutes.
3. Allow releasing pressure naturally then open the lid.
4. Using slotted spoon remove meat from pot and place on a baking dish.
5. Using fork shred the meat and broil shredded meat in hot broiler until crisp.
6. Serve and enjoy.

Nutritional Info: Calories: 901, Fat: 65 g, Carbs: 4 g, Protein 71 g

Delicious Pork Stew

Prep time: 10 minutes, Cook time: 55 minutes, Servings: 6

Ingredients:

1 sliced large leek
8 oz. sliced mushrooms
1 ½ cups chicken broth
1 lemon juice
1 diced small onion
2 tbsps. extra virgin olive oil
1 tsp. sea salt
4 lbs. sliced pork cheeks
6 peeled garlic cloves

Instructions:

1. Add oil in instant pot and select sauté.
2. Add meat into the pot and cook until browned.
3. Add remaining ingredients and stir well.
4. Seal pot with lid and select meat/stew, it takes 45 minutes.
5. Release pressure using quick release method than open the lid carefully.
6. Remove meat from pot and place on a plate.
7. Using fork shred the meat.
8. Add pot vegetable and juices into the blender and blend until smooth.
9. Add shredded meat in blended liquid and stir well.
10. Serve and enjoy.

Nutritional Info: Calories: 510, Fat: 15.9 g, Carbs: 5.8 g, Protein: 82.1 g

Simple Pulled Pork

Prep time: 15 minutes, Cook time: 1 hour 50 minutes, Servings: 8

Ingredients:

2 tsps. mustard powder
2 tsps. sea salt
2 tbsps. apple cider vinegar
1 tbsp. coconut oil
1 tsp. garlic powder
1 tsp. paprika
1 tbsp. chili powder
4 lbs. sliced pork shoulder
1 ½ cups chicken stock

Instructions:

1. Add oil in instant pot and select sauté.
2. In a bowl, mix together mustard powder, garlic powder, paprika, chili powder, and salt.
3. Rub spice mixture all over the pork.
4. Add seasoned pork pieces into the pot and cook until browned.
5. Add vinegar and chicken stock in a pot.
6. Seal pot with lid and set the timer for 1 hour 40 minutes.
7. Release pressure using quick release method than open the lid carefully.
8. Stir well and serve.

Nutritional Info: Calories: 688, Fat: 50.8 g, Carbs: 1.4 g, Protein: 53.4 g

Chapter 10 Snacks, Sides and Appetizers

Pumpkin Muffins

Prep time: 10 minutes, Cook time: 15 minutes, Servings: 18

Ingredients:

¾ cup pumpkin puree
¼ cup sunflower seed butter
1 tsp. ground cinnamon
¼ cup coconut flour
1 egg
½ cup erythritol
2 tbsps. flaxseed meal
½ tsp. ground nutmeg
½ tsp. baking soda
½ tsp. baking powder
¼ tsp. salt

Instructions:

1. Mix sunflower seed butter with pumpkin puree and egg then blend well.
2. Add coconut flour, baking soda, flaxseed meal, erythritol, nutmeg, baking powder, cinnamon, salt and stir well.
3. Spoon into a greased muffin pan and set in an oven to bake for 15 minutes at 350⁰F.
4. Set the muffins aside to cool and serve.
5. Enjoy.

Nutritional Info: Calories: 42, Fat: 2.6g, Carbs: 4.9g, Protein: 1.6g

Baked Almond Crusted Zucchini Slices

Prep time: 15 minutes, Cook time: 15 minutes, Servings: 6

Ingredients:

1 tsp. garlic powder
Ground black pepper
2 sliced large zucchini
1 tsp. finely chopped fresh thyme
1 egg free range chickens
Sea salt
1 tsp. onion powder
1 cup almond flour

Instructions:

1. Preheat the oven to 450⁰F.
2. Line a parchment paper on a baking sheet and set aside.
3. Beat the egg in a large bowl.
4. Set up a separate bowl and combine onion powder, garlic, almond flour, salt and black pepper.
5. Pass the zucchini slices in the egg letting the excess drip off then drop in the almond flour mixture to coat.
6. Put the coated zucchinis onto the baking tray to bake for 15 minutes and flip once.
7. Serve while warm and enjoy.

Nutritional Info: Calories: 165, Carbs: 6g, Proteins: 8g, Fat: 13g

Chili Almond Coated Turkey Bites

Prep time: 15 minutes, Cook time: 15 minutes, Servings: 6

Ingredients:

1 lb. ground turkey meat
3 tbsps. Mayonnaise
2 tbsps. Grated onion
2 tbsps. Minced parsley
Salt
3 drops hot pepper sauce
4 tbsps. Ground almonds

Instructions:

1. In a medium bowl, stir all the ingredients except almonds until well combined.
2. Mold the mixture into small bite-size pieces and roll in ground nuts.
3. Cover and put in a refrigerator until serving.
4. Enjoy.

Nutritional Info: Calories: 177, Carbs: 4g, Proteins: 16.5g, Fat: 12g

Pancetta Muffins

Prep time: 15 minutes, Cook time: 3 hours, Servings: 12

Ingredients:

¾ cup unsweetened almond milk

1 ½ cup grated parmesan cheese

6 cubed pancetta

2 cups almond flour

2 tsps. baking soda

¼ tsp. salt

½ cup olive oil

2 tbsps. chopped spring onion

1 ½ tsps. ground allspice

1 cup water

2 free-range eggs

Instructions:

1. Grease the muffin cups and set aside.

2. In a medium mixing bowl, stir allspice powder, almond flour, salt, baking soda, parmesan cheese, spring onion and pancetta.

3. Set up a second bowl to whisk olive oil, almond milk, salt and eggs.

4. Combine the egg and almond mixture and stir well.

5. Pour butter in muffin cups.

6. Add water to the inner stainless-steel pot in the crock pot and place the trivet in it.

7. Put the muffin cups on the trivet and cover to cook on High for 3 hours.

8. Serve warm and enjoy.

Nutritional Info: Calories: 233, Carbs: 1.5g, Proteins: 8g, Fat: 22g

Spicy Keto Roasted Nuts

Prep time: 7 minutes, Cook time: 5 minutes, Servings: 2

Ingredients:

1/3 tsp. paprika powder or chili powder

1/3 tsp. salt

1/3 tbsps. olive oil

1/3 tsp. ground cumin

2 oz. pecans, almonds and walnuts

Instructions:

1. Combine all ingredients and transfer them into a medium frying pan.

2. Let them cook for about 5 minutes on medium heat until the nuts are warmed completely.

3. Let the nuts cook and serve immediately.

4. Enjoy.

Nutritional Info: Calories: 220, Carbs: 4.4g, Fat: 22.7g, Protein: 3.2g

Creamy Chicken Topped Cucumbers

Prep time: 15 minutes, Cook time: 20 minutes, Servings: 18

Ingredients:

4 tbsps. Mayonnaise

Ground black pepper

2 tbsps. Yellow mustard

1/8 tsp. garlic powder

3 sliced cucumbers

8 oz. finely chopped chicken breast

2 tbsps. Chopped green onions

Instructions:

1. Line a parchment paper on a shallow dish.

2. Cut cucumbers into thin slices and put on a dish.

3. Combine chicken, mustard, mayonnaise, ground powder, green onions and ground black pepper in a bowl.

4. Top each slice of cucumber with 1 ½ tablespoon chicken mixture.

5. Refrigerate for 2 hours before serving.

Nutritional Info: Calories: 28, Carbs: 2g, Proteins: 1.5g, Fat: 2g

Low Carb Broccoli and Cheese Fritters

Prep time: 15 minutes, Cook time: 20 minutes, Servings: 2

Ingredients:

For the fritters:
1 small egg
1 oz. mozzarella cheese
3 tbsps. flaxseed meal
Black pepper.
1 oz. fresh broccoli
Salt
4 tbsps. almond flour
¼ tsp. baking powder
For the sauce:
½ tsp. lemon juice
4 tbsps. fresh chopped dill
Black pepper.
4 tbsps. mayonnaise
Salt
Instructions:

1. In your food processor, add broccoli and process until completely chopped.
2. Put the broccoli in a bowl and add 2 tablespoons flaxseed meal, mozzarella cheese, almond flour, baking powder, salt and pepper.
3. Mix well and roll to form batter balls.
4. Coat the balls in a tablespoon of flaxseed meal and keep inside.
5. Drop the balls in the basket of a deep fat fryer heated to 375⁰F.
6. Fry the fritters for 5 minutes until golden brown and dish out in a platter.
7. Combine all the ingredients for the sauce and make a deep.
8. Serve the deep with fitters.

Nutritional Info: Calories: 428, Carbs: 11.4g, Fats: 38.6g, Proteins: 12.9g

Almond Jade Stir-Fry

Prep time: 5 minutes, Cook time: 20 minutes, Servings: 4

Ingredients:

2 tbsps. almond flour
1 lb. button mushrooms
Black pepper.
3 tsps. minced fresh ginger
1/3 cup water
3 tbsps. coconut aminos
2 halved garlic cloves
1 cup whole almonds
Salt
2 tbsps. olive oil

Instructions:

1. In a large skillet, heat olive oil over medium heat.
2. Add almonds and cook then stir for 8 minutes until lightly browned.
3. Remove almond from slotted spoon on a plate and set aside.
4. Add little oil on the same skillet and sauté garlic with salt for 3 minutes.
5. Add ginger and mushrooms and stir fry for 5 minutes.
6. Combine water, almond flour and coconut aminos in a small bowl and mix thoroughly.
7. Transfer the mixture to the skillet to cook and toss for 2 minutes.
8. Taste and adjust the pepper and salt.
9. Serve and enjoy.

Nutritional Info: Calories: 304, Carbs: 8g, Proteins: 17g, Fat: 27g

Low Carb Cauliflower Hummus

Prep time: 15 minutes, Cook time: 15 minutes, Servings: 2

Ingredients:

2 whole garlic cloves
1 cup raw cauliflower florets
1/3 tsp. kosher salt
¼ tsp. salt
¾ tbsp. water
¾ tbsp. avocado oil
¾ tbsp. lemon juice
½ tbsp. Tahini paste
¾ tbsp. extra-virgin olive oil
¼ tsp. smoked paprika

Instructions:
1. Mix together water, half of salt, 1 garlic clove, cauliflower, olive oil and avocado oil in a microwave safe dish.
2. Microwave for about 15 minutes and set the mixture into a food processor.
3. Add lemon juice, tahini paste, and the remaining avocado oil, garlic clove, kosher salt and olive oil in a blender and blend to smoothness.
4. Dish out hummus in a bowl sprinkled with paprika ready for serving.

Nutritional Info: Calories: 93, Carbs: 5g, Fats: 8.1g, Proteins: 2g

Cheesy Herb Muffins

Prep time: 28 minutes, Cook time: 20 minutes, Servings: 2

Ingredients:
1/8 cup unsweetened almond milk
1/8 tsp. xanthan gum
¾ tbsp. coconut flour
1/8 tsp. garlic powder
1/8 cup shredded sharp cheddar cheese
¼ tsp. granulated erythritol
½ tsp. baking powder
1½ tbsps. butter
¼ cup blanched almond flour
¼ tsp. kosher salt
1 egg
1/8 tsp. fresh thyme leaves

Instructions:
1. Preheat the oven to 375°F and grease 2 muffin cups.
2. Put butter in a microwave safe bowl and microwave uncovered, for 30 seconds on high.
3. Combine the butter, erythritol, coconut flour, almond flour, baking powder, xanthan gum, garlic powder, almond milk, fresh thyme, cheddar cheese and salt in a bowl.
4. Transfer the mixture into the muffin cups and place in the oven.
5. Bake for about 20 minutes and remove from the oven to serve.

Nutritional Info: Calories: 272, Carbs: 13.7g, Fat: 23.7g, Proteins: 8.

Roasted Caprese Tomatoes with Basil dressing

Prep time: 10 minutes, Cook time: 25 minutes, Servings: 2

Ingredients:
2 tbsps. balsamic vinegar
4 basil leaves
4 halved large ripe tomatoes
Salt
4 thin Mozzarella slices
1 tbsp. olive oil
Black pepper.

For the dressing:
2 tbsps. olive oil
1 garlic clove
½ tsp. lemon
Salt
Small handful fresh basil

Instructions:
1. Preheat the oven to 360°F then grease a baking tray.
2. Put the tomatoes on the baking tray with the cut side up.
3. Drizzle the balsamic vinegar, olive oil and add seasonings.
4. Roast for 20 minutes and top mozzarella cheese on the tomatoes.
5. Roast for 5 more minutes and remove from the oven.
6. Put a basil leaf on each bottom half and close it with the top half.
7. Combine all ingredients in a food processor until finely chopped to form a dressing.
8. Serve tomatoes with the dressing and enjoy.

Nutritional Info: Calories: 412, Carbs: 17g, Fat: 31.8g, Proteins: 19.4g

Caprese Grilled Eggplant Roll Ups

Prep time: 5 minutes, Cook time: 15 minutes, Servings: 2

Ingredients:

3 tbsps. olive oil

1 thinly shredded basil leaf

2 oz. thinly sliced mozzarella cheese

½ thinly sliced large tomato

¼ tsp. black pepper

½ thinly sliced eggplant

Instructions:

1. Rub the eggplant slices with olive oil and set aside.

2. Heat the griddle pan and put the egg slices in a pan.

3. Grill for about 3 minutes on each side topped with tomato slice, mozzarella slice, black pepper and basil leaf.

4. Grill for 1 more minute and roll the eggplant holding with a cocktail stick.

5. Dish out to serve warm.

Nutritional Info: Calories: 298, Carbs: 9.7g, Fat: 26.3g, Protein: 9.6g

---

Chicken Skewers

Prep time: 3 hours, Cook time: 15 minutes, Servings: 4

Ingredients:

Black pepper

4 cubed chicken breasts

¾ cup garlic powder

2 tbsps. Chopped parsley

Instructions:

1. Combine chicken with garlic powder, parsley, and black pepper and stir well then cover to refrigerate for 3 hours.

2. Arrange the chicken pieces on skewers and put them on preheated grill to cook for 15 minutes flipping once.

3. Arrange the skewers on a platter to serve as an appetizer.

4. Enjoy!

Nutritional Info: Calories: 485, Fat: 22.9g, Carbs: 18.6g, Protein 53.1g

---

Kale Chips

Prep time: 10 minutes, Cook time: 20 minutes, Servings: 6

Ingredients:

¼ tsp. sea salt

1 tbsp. avocado oil

Black pepper

1 bunch separated kale

Instructions:

1. Pat dry leaves of kale and arrange them on a lined baking tray.

2. Add oil and sprinkle with seasonings to taste before putting in an oven to bake for 20 minutes at 275⁰F.

3. Serve the chips cold and enjoy.

Nutritional Info: Calories: 9, Fat: 0.3g, Carbs: 1.3g, Protein 0.4g

---

Rosemary Crackers

Prep time: 10 minutes, Cook time: 14 minutes, Servings: 40

Ingredients:

½ tsp. chopped thyme

Black pepper

½ cup toasted and ground sesame seeds

1 cup almond flour

¼ tsp. sea salt

1 tsp. onion powder

2 tbsps. tapioca flour

1 tsp. chopped rosemary

2 eggs

3 tbsps. olive oil

¼ cup coconut flour

Instructions:

1. Combine coconut flour, almond flour, sesame seeds, thyme, salt, pepper onion powder and rosemary and stir well.

2. Whisk eggs with the oil in another bowl and stir well.
3. Add this to the flour mix and knead to form a dough.
4. Mold a disk out of the dough and flatten to cut 40 crackers out of it.
5. Arrange the crackers on a lined baking sheet and put in an oven to bake for 14 minutes at 375⁰F.
6. Let the crackers cool down and serve them as a snack.
7. Enjoy.

Nutritional Info: Calories: 37, Fat: 2.9, Carbs: 2.2g, Protein: 1.1g

Seed Crackers

Prep time: 10 minutes, Cook time: 3 hours, Servings: 40

Ingredients:

½ cup chia seeds
1 tsp. dried thyme
¼ tsp. sea salt
1 tsp. dried basil
1 cup ground flaxseed
1/3 cup sesame seeds
½ cup pumpkin seeds
1 ¼ cups water
½ tsp. garlic powder

Instructions:

1. In the food processor, add pumpkin seeds and pulse well before transferring them into a bowl.
2. Add sesame seeds, flaxseed, water, salt, chia, basil, thyme and garlic powder and stir well to combine.
3. Spread this on a lined baking sheet and spread to cut 40 pieces.
4. Put in an oven to bake for 3 hours at 200⁰F.
5. Let the crackers cool before serving them as a snack.
6. Enjoy.

Nutritional Info: Calories: 35, Fat: 2.5g, Carbs: 1.7g, Protein: 1.3g

Coconut Bars

Prep time: 30 minutes, Cook time: 0 minutes, Servings: 10

Ingredients:

¼ tsp. sea salt
1 tsp. vanilla extract
1 cup unsweetened coconut flakes
1 ¼ cups dried figs
1 cup cocoa powder
2 cups cashews

Instructions:

1. In your food processor, mix figs with vanilla, cashews, a pinch of salt, cocoa powder and coconut and blend them well.
2. Transfer this into a baking dish and press well.
3. Put cocoa powder and cocoa butter in a heatproof bowl, place in your microwave for 3 minutes until it melts.
4. Pour this over coconut mix, spread well, place in your freezer for 20 minutes, cut into bars and serve as a snack.
5. Enjoy!

Nutritional Info: Calories: 1504, Fat: 28.1g, Carbs: 331.5g, Protein: 22.1g

Oyster Spread

Prep time: 10 minutes, Cook time: 0 minutes, Servings: 4

Ingredients:

1 tbsp. chopped red onion
4 oz. cooked oysters
½ tsps. cayenne pepper
2 tsps. coconut cream

Instructions:

1. Put the oysters in a bowl, mash them well, add all the other ingredients, whisk well and serve as an appetizer!
2. Enjoy!

Nutritional Info: Calories: 146, Fat: 4.5g, Carbs: 8.9g, Protein: 16.2g

Almond Bowls

Prep time: 10 minutes, Cook time: 16 minutes, Servings: 4

Ingredients:

1 tsp. dried sage

1 tbsp. chopped rosemary

Black pepper

½ tsp. smoked paprika

1 tbsp. garlic powder

¼ tsp. sea salt

16 oz. almonds

Instructions:

1. Spread the almonds on a lined baking sheet, add all the other ingredients, toss, place in the oven at 300 degrees F and roast for 8 minutes.
2. Flip nuts and bake them for 8 minutes more.
3. Divide into bowls and serve as a snack.
4. Enjoy!

Nutritional Info: Calories: 667, Fat: 56.9g, Carbs: 26.6g, Protein: 24.4g

Wrapped Olives

Prep time: 10 minutes, Cook time: 35 minutes, Servings: 20

Ingredients:

12 thin turkey fillet slices

¼ tsp. black pepper

Olive oil

36 almond stuffed green olives

Instructions:

1. Wrap each olive with a turkey piece, secure them with a toothpick, sprinkle some black pepper and olive oil all over, place them on a lined baking sheet, place in the oven at 400 degrees F and bake for 35 minutes.
2. Arrange the wrapped olives on a platter and serve.
3. Enjoy!

Nutritional Info: Calories: 26, Fat: 0.7g, Carbs: 0.1g, Protein: 4.5g

Stuffed Mushrooms

Prep time: 10 minutes, Cook time: 20 minutes, Servings: 8

Ingredients:

¼ tsp. smoked paprika

3 tbsps. olive oil

¼ tsp. cayenne pepper

Onion dip

1 lb. cremini mushrooms caps

For the dip:

¼ tsp. white pepper

2 tbsps. chopped green onions

1 cup coconut cream

1 chopped yellow onion

¼ tsp. garlic powder

½ cup mayonnaise

2 tbsps. coconut oil

Instructions:

1. Heat up a pan with 2 tablespoons coconut oil over medium heat, add onion, garlic powder and white pepper, stir, cook for 10 minutes, take off heat and leave aside to cool down.
2. In a bowl, mix mayo with coconut cream, green onions and caramelized onions, stir well and keep in the fridge for now.
3. Season mushroom caps with a pinch of cayenne pepper and paprika and drizzle the olive oil over them.
4. Rub them, place on preheated grill over medium high heat and cook them for 10 minutes
5. Arrange them on a platter, stuff them with the onion dip and serve and enjoy!

Nutritional Info: Calories: 244, Fat: 20.7g, Carbs: 12.2g, Protein: 16.6g

Apricot Bites

Prep time: 2 hours, Cook time: 40 minutes, Servings: 4

Ingredients:

2 tsps. chopped lemongrass

10 cooked and halved turkey fillet strips

4 tbsps. minced garlic

½ cup coconut aminos

10 dried apricots

10 oz. shelled, peeled and cooked chestnuts

Instructions:

1. Cut an "X" shape into the flat side of each chestnut. Place the chestnuts in a microwave and bake for 5 minutes on max, then peel. Wrap a chestnut and an apricot in turkey strip and secure with a toothpick.
2. Repeat this with the rest of the ingredients.
3. Heat up a pan over medium-low heat, add garlic, stir and sauté it for 20 minutes.
4. Transfer garlic to a bowl, cool down, add lemongrass, coconut aminos and the apricot bites, cover and leave them aside for 2 hours.
5. Spread apricot bites on a lined baking sheet, place in the oven at 350 degrees F and bake for 20 minutes.
6. Arrange them on a platter and serve as an appetizer.
7. Enjoy!

Nutritional Info: Calories: 380, Fat: 2.4g, Carbs: 46.1g, Protein: 41.3g

Zucchini Rolls

Prep time: 10 minutes, Cook time: 5 minutes, Servings: 4

Ingredients:

Black pepper

½ cup chopped basil

10 oz. cooked and sliced turkey meat

4 tbsps. raspberry vinegar

¼ tsp. sea salt

3 thinly sliced zucchinis

½ cup drained and chopped sun-dried tomatoes

Instructions:

1. Place zucchini slices in a bowl, sprinkle a pinch of sea salt and vinegar over them and leave aside for 10 minutes.
2. Drain well and season with black pepper to taste.
3. Divide turkey slices, chopped sun dried tomatoes and basil over zucchini ones, roll each and secure with a toothpick and arrange them on a lined baking sheet.
4. Place in the oven at 400 degrees F for 5 minutes, then arrange them on a platter and serve as an appetizer.
5. Enjoy!

Nutritional Info: Calories: 152, Fat: 3.9g, Carbs: 6g, Protein: 22.8g

Watermelon Wraps

Prep time: 10 minutes, Cook time: 0 minutes, Servings: 20

Ingredients:

1 tsp. coconut aminos

1 peeled, pitted and chopped avocado

¼ cup chopped red onion

1 tsp. lime juice

4 watermelon slices

½ cup chopped cucumber

Instructions:

1. Cut 20 circles of watermelon using a cookie cutter.
2. In a bowl, mix onion with avocado, aminos, cucumber and lime juice and stir well.
3. Divide this into watermelon circles, place them on a platter and serve.
4. Enjoy!

Nutritional Info: Calories: 27, Fat: 2g, Carbs: 2.5g, Protein: 0.3g

Mini Hot Dogs

Prep time: 10 minutes, Cook time: 25 minutes, Servings: 6

Ingredients:

½ tsp. mustard powder
2 whisked eggs
¼ tsp. smoked paprika
¼ cup coconut flour
1 cup rice cauliflower
½ tsp. baking soda
1 tsp. apple cider vinegar
1 tsp. red pepper sauce
¼ tsp. sea salt
¼ tsp. chili powder
1½ tbsps. coconut oil
2 tsps. chopped jalapenos
20 oz. ground turkey

Instructions:

1. In a bowl, mix the cauliflower rice with the coconut flour, eggs, oil, red pepper sauce, mustard, salt, chili powder, paprika and jalapenos and stir.
2. Add the baking soda and the vinegar and stir well again.
3. Place 12 spoonful of this mix on a lined baking sheet, put 1 teaspoon of turkey mince on each cauliflower circle, and top with other 12 spoonful of cauliflower mix.
4. Seal edges, place in the oven at 400 degrees F and bake for 30 minutes.
5. Arrange on a platter and serve them.
6. Enjoy!

Nutritional Info: Calories: 240, Fat: 15g, Carbs: 1.6g, Protein: 28.2g

Cucumber Rolls

Prep time: 10 minutes, Cook time: 0 minutes, Servings: 3

Ingredients:

1 tsp. chopped dill
6 ham slices
3 tsps. mayonnaise
6 chopped green onions
1 thinly sliced cucumber
1 chopped jalapeno

Instructions:

1. Arrange ham slices on a working surface.
2. In a bowl, mix mayo with jalapeno, green onions and dill and stir well.
3. Spread some of this mix over 1 ham slice, add a cucumber slice at the end, roll cucumber around ham and secure with a toothpick.
4. Repeat with the remaining ingredients and serve as an appetizer.
5. Enjoy!

Nutritional Info: Calories: 137, Fat 6.7g, Carbs: 9.6g, Protein: 10.7g

Chicken Bites

Prep time: 10 minutes, Cook time: 20 minutes, Servings: 2

Ingredients:

3 skinless, boneless and sliced chicken breasts
1 cup coconut flour
1 tbsp. cumin powder
1 tbsp. garlic powder
Black pepper
3 tbsps. curry powder
2 tsps. ground turmeric

Instructions:

1. In a bowl, mix curry powder with flour, turmeric, cumin, garlic powder and black pepper and stir well.
2. Add chicken strips, toss well to coat, arrange them on a lined baking sheet, and bake at 350 degrees F for 20 minutes.
3. Transfer chicken strips to a bowls and serve them cold.
4. Enjoy!

Nutritional Info: Calories: 905, Fat: 31.3g, Carbs: 58.5g, Protein: 96.4g

Fried Peppers

Prep time: 10 minutes, Cook time: 13 minutes, Servings: 4
Ingredients:
1 minced garlic clove
Juice of ½ lemon
2 tsps. olive oil
¼ tsp. sea salt
10 shishito peppers
Black pepper
Instructions:
1. Heat up a pan with the oil over medium high heat, add peppers, lemon juice, garlic, a pinch of salt and black pepper, stir and cook for 10 minutes.
2. Drain excess grease on paper towels, arrange on a small platter and serve.
3. Enjoy!
Nutritional Info: Calories: 62, Fat: 2.4g, Carbs: 8.8g, Protein: 2.6g

Spanish Potato Cakes

Prep time: 10 minutes, Cook time: 25 minutes, Servings: 18
Ingredients:
¼ tsp. cayenne pepper
2 minced garlic cloves
¼ tsp. sea salt
Juice of 2 limes
2 tbsps. nutritional yeast
4 tbsps. chopped cilantro
2 cups peeled, cubed and boiled sweet potatoes
1 tsp. black pepper
Instructions:
1. In a bowl, mix sweet potatoes with a pinch of salt and pepper and mash well.
2. Add garlic, cilantro, a black pepper, lime juice, cayenne and nutritional yeast and stir very well.
3. Shape small cakes out of this mix, arrange them on a baking sheet, place in the oven at 350 degrees F and bake for 25 minutes.
4. Arrange cakes on a platter and serve them cold.
5. Enjoy!
Nutritional Info: Calories: 25, Fat: 0.1g, Carbs: 5.7g, Protein: 0.8g

Tomato Chicken Bites

Prep time: 10 minutes, Cook time: 45 minutes, Servings: 13
Ingredients:
¼ cup tomato sauce
1 chopped adobo chili pepper
2 lbs. skinless, boneless and cubed chicken breasts
Instructions:
1. Put the tomato sauce in a large saucepan, heat up over medium heat, add the chili, stir and bring to a boil.
2. Add the chicken cubes, toss, spread on a lined baking sheet, and bake at 375 degrees F and bake for 45 minutes.
3. Leave chicken bites to cool down, arrange them on a platter and serve.
4. Enjoy!
Nutritional Info: Calories: 135, Fat: 5.2g, Carbs: 0.6g, Protein: 20.3g

Paprika Mushrooms with Coconut Flour Naan

Prep time: 20 minutes, Cook time: 10 minutes, Servings: 6
Ingredients:
8 tbsps. melted coconut oil
1 lb. thinly sliced cremini mushrooms
¾ cup coconut flour
2 tbsps. psyllium powder
1 egg
1 tsp. smoked paprika
¼ tsp. salt
1 beaten egg yolk
1 tsp. kosher salt
½ tsp. baking powder

Instructions:
1. In a mixing bowl, combine coconut flour with baking powder, psyllium and salt; mix to combine well.
2. Add 6 tablespoons of coconut oil, egg and egg yolk; add the hot water to form a dough; let it rest for 10 minutes at room temperature.
3. Now, divide the dough into 6 balls; flatten the balls on a working surface.
4. Heat up a pan with 1 tablespoon of coconut oil over a medium-high flame. Fry naan breads until they are golden.
5. Then, heat the remaining 1 tablespoon of coconut oil in a nonstick skillet. Sauté the mushrooms until tender and fragrant; season with kosher salt and paprika.
6. Serve with naan and enjoy!

Nutritional Info: Calories: 281, Fat: 21.4g, Carbs: 6.1g, Protein: 6.4g

Cabbage Chips

Prep time: 10 minutes, Cook time: 2 hours, Servings: 8
Ingredients:
½ separated and halved green cabbage head
Black pepper
Olive oil
¼ tsp. sea salt
½ separated and halved red cabbage head
Instructions:
1. Spread cabbage leaves on a lined baking sheet, place in the oven at 200 degrees F and bake for 2 hours.
2. Drizzle the oil over them, sprinkle salt and black pepper, rub well, transfer to a bowl and serve as a snack.
3. Enjoy!

Nutritional Info: Calories: 39, Fat: 0.2g, Carbs: 9.1g, Protein: 2g

Kohlrabi with Thick Mushroom Sauce

Prep time: 25 minutes, Cook time: 0 minutes, Servings: 4
Ingredients:
1 ½ cups double cream
½ tsp. ground black pepper
3 tbsps. butter
1 minced garlic clove
1 tsp. sea salt
½ cup chopped scallions
¼ tsp. red pepper flakes
¾ lb. trimmed and thinly sliced kohlrabi
½ lb. sliced mushrooms
Instructions:
1. Boil kohlrabi in a large pot of salted water for 7 to 9 minutes. Drain and set aside.
2. Warm the butter over medium-high heat. Sauté the mushrooms, scallions, and garlic until tender and fragrant.
3. Season with salt, black pepper, and red pepper flakes.
4. Slowly stir in double cream, whisking continuously until the sauce has thickened, about 8 to 12 minutes.
5. Pour the mushroom sauce over the kohlrabi and serve warm.

Nutritional Info: Calories: 220, Fat: 20g, Carbs: 5.3g, Protein: 4g

Spinach and Strawberry Salad

Prep time: 10 minutes, Cook time: 15 minutes, Servings: 4
Ingredients:
2 tbsps. chopped fresh basil leaves
½ freshly squeezed lime
½ tsp. kosher salt
4 cups baby spinach
2 tbsps. olive oil
White pepper
1 cup pitted, peeled and sliced avocado
½ cup hulled and sliced strawberries
1/3 cup crumbled brie cheese
Instructions:
1. Pat the spinach leaves dry and transfer them to a salad bowl.

2. Add the slices of strawberries and avocado.
3. Now, make the dressing by whisking olive oil, lime juice, salt and white pepper. Dress the salad and top with crumbled cheese.

4. Serve garnished with fresh basil leaves. Bon appétit!

Nutritional Info: Calories: 190, Fat: 17.6g, Carbs: 4.6g, Protein: 4.3g

Simple Kimchi

Prep time: 1 hour 10 minutes, Cook time: 0 minutes, Servings: 6
Ingredients:
1 tbsp. fish sauce
3 peeled and minced garlic cloves
1 lb. chopped napa cabbage
3 chopped green onion stalks
3 tbsps. chili flakes
1 tbsp. sesame oil
½ inch peeled and grated fresh ginger
3 tbsps. salt
½ cup daikon radish
3 oz. julienned butternut squash
Instructions:

1. In a bowl, mix cabbage with salt, massage well for 10 minutes, cover, and set aside for 1 hour.
2. In a bowl, mix the chili flakes with fish sauce, garlic, sesame oil, ginger, and stir well.
3. Drain cabbage well, rinse under cold water, and transfer to a bowl.
4. Add squash, green onions, radish, and chili paste, and stir. Leave in a dark and cold place for at least 2 days before serving.

Nutritional Info: Calories: 43, Fat: 2.5, Carbs: 4.9g, Protein: 1.6g

Cauliflower Mash

Prep time: 10 minutes, Cook time: 10 minutes, Servings: 2
Ingredients:
2 tbsps. crumbled feta cheese
1 separated small cauliflower head
Salt
¼ cup sour cream
Ground black pepper
2 tbsps. pitted and sliced black olives
Instructions:
1. Put water in a saucepan, add some salt, bring to a boil over medium heat, add the florets, cook for 10 minutes, take off heat, and drain.

2. Return cauliflower to the saucepan, add salt, black pepper, and sour cream, and blend using an immersion blender.
3. Add black olives and feta cheese, stir, and serve.

Nutritional Info: Calories: 129, Fat: 9.1g, Carbs: 9.2g, Protein: 4.9g

Portobello Mushrooms

Prep time: 10 minutes, Cook time: 10 minutes, Servings: 4
Ingredients:
½ tsp. dried thyme
½ tsp. dried rosemary
Salt
2 tbsp. olive oil
½ tsp. dried tarragon
½ tsp. dried basil
Ground black pepper
2 tbsps. balsamic vinegar
12 oz. Portobello mushrooms
Instructions:

1. In a bowl, mix the oil with vinegar, salt, pepper, rosemary, tarragon, basil, and thyme, and whisk.
2. Add mushroom slices, toss to coat well, place them on a preheated grill over medium–high heat, cook for 5 minutes on both sides, and serve.

Nutritional Info: Calories: 85, Fat: 7g, Carbs: 2.5g, Protein: 2.5g

Broiled Brussels Sprouts

Prep time: 10 minutes, Cook time: 10 minutes, Servings: 4

Ingredients:

1 tbsp. sriracha
2 tbsps. sesame oil
Ground black pepper
1 tsp. sesame seeds
1½ tbsps. sukrin gold syrup
1 tbsp. coconut aminos
1 lb. trimmed, and halved Brussels sprouts
Salt
1 tbsp. chopped green onions

Instructions:

1. In a bowl, mix the sesame oil with coconut aminos, sriracha, syrup, salt, and black pepper, and whisk.
2. Heat a pan over medium–high heat, add the Brussels sprouts, and cook them for 5 minutes on each side.
3. Add the sesame oil mixture, toss to coat, sprinkle sesame seeds, green onions, stir again, and serve.

Nutritional Info: Calories: 192, Fat: 7.6g, Carbs: 30.3g, Protein: 4g

Brussels Sprouts and Bacon

Prep time: 10 minutes, Cook time: 30 minutes, Servings: 4

Ingredients:

1 lb. trimmed and halved Brussels sprouts
Salt
¼ tsp. crushed red pepper
2 tbsps. extra virgin olive oil
8 chopped bacon strips
¼ tsp. cumin
Ground black pepper

Instructions:

1. In a bowl, mix Brussels sprouts with salt, pepper, cumin, red pepper, and oil, and toss to coat.
2. Spread Brussels sprouts on a lined baking sheet, place in an oven at 375°F, and bake for 30 minutes.
3. Heat a pan over medium heat, add bacon pieces, and cook them until crispy. Divide the baked Brussels sprouts on plates, top with bacon, and serve.

Nutritional Info: Calories: 159, Fat: 11.9g, Carbs: 10.3g, Protein: 5.9g

Eggplant and Tomato Dish

Prep time: 10 minutes, Cook time: 15 minutes, Servings: 4

Ingredients:

Olive oil
Black pepper.
1 sliced tomato
¼ cup grated parmesan
Salt
1 sliced eggplant

Instructions:

1. Place eggplant slices on a lined baking dish, drizzle some oil and sprinkle half of the parmesan.
2. Top eggplant slices with tomato ones, season with salt and pepper to the taste. and sprinkle the rest of the cheese over them.
3. Introduce in the oven at 400 degrees F and bake for 15 minutes
4. Divide between plates and serve hot as a side dish.

Nutritional Info: Calories: 55, Fat: 1g, Carbs: 0.5g; Protein: 7g

Asian Coconut Chutney

Prep time: 10 minutes, Cook time: 3 minutes, Servings: 3

Ingredients:

1 spring curry leaves
¾ tbsp. avocado oil
2 tbsps. already fried chana dal
2 green chilies
½ cup grated coconut
½ tsp. urad dal
¼ tsp. mustard seeds
1 garlic clove
¼ tsp. hing
1 chopped red chili.
½ tsp. cumin
Salt.

Instructions:

1. In your food processor, mix coconut with salt to the taste., cumin, garlic, chana dal and green chilies and blend well.
2. Add a splash of water and blend again.
3. Heat up a pan with the oil over medium heat; add red chili, urad dal, mustard seeds, hing and curry leaves; stir and cook for 2-3 minutes
4. Add this to coconut chutney; stir gently and serve as a side

Nutritional Info: Calories: 90, Fat: 1g, Carbs: 1g, Protein: 6g

Easy Kimchi

Prep time: 1 hour 10 minutes, Cook time: Servings: 6

Ingredients:

1 tbsp. sesame oil
1 lb. chopped napa cabbage.
3 chopped green onion stalks.
3 tbsps. salt
½ cup daikon radish
1 julienned carrot
3 tbsps. chili flakes
1 tbsp. fish sauce
3 minced garlic cloves
½ inch grated ginger

Instructions:

1. In a bowl, mix cabbage with the salt, massage well for 10 minutes, cover and leave aside for 1 hour.
2. In a bowl, mix chili flakes with fish sauce, garlic, sesame oil and ginger and stir very well.
3. Drain cabbage well, rinses under cold water and transfer to a bowl.
4. Add carrots, green onions, radish and chili paste and stir everything.
5. Leave in a dark and cold place for at least 2 days before serving as a side for a keto steak.

Nutritional Info: Calories: 60, Fat: 3g, Carbs: 5g, Protein: 1g

Awesome Coleslaw

Prep time: 10 minutes, Cook time: 0 minutes, Servings: 4

Ingredients:

Juice of ½ lemon
Salt
1 tbsp. Dijon mustard
6 tbsps. mayonnaise
1 shredded small green cabbage head
¼ tsp. fennel seed
Black pepper.

Instructions:

1. In a bowl, mix cabbage with salt and lemon juice; stir well and leave aside for 10 minutes
2. Press well the cabbage, add more salt and pepper, fennel seed, mayo and mustard.
3. Toss to coat and serve

Nutritional Info: Calories: 150, Fat: 3g, Carbs: 2g, Protein: 7g

Spinach and Mushroom Side Dish

Prep time: 5 minutes, Cook time: 11 minutes, Servings: 4

Ingredients:

Chopped parsley.

14 oz. chopped mushrooms.

1 chopped yellow onion.

4 tbsps. olive oil

2 tbsps. balsamic vinegar

2 minced garlic cloves

Salt

10 oz. chopped spinach leaves.

Black pepper

Instructions:

1. Heat up a pan with the oil over medium high heat; add garlic and onion; stir and cook for 4 minutes
2. Add mushrooms; stir and cook for 3 minutes more
3. Add spinach; stir and cook for 3 minutes
4. Add vinegar, salt and pepper; stir and cook for 1 minute more
5. Add parsley; stir, divide between plates and serve hot as a side dish.

Nutritional Info: Calories: 200, Fat: 4g, Carbs: 2g, Protein: 12g

---

Keto Summer Salad

Prep time: 10 minutes, Cook time: 10 minutes, Servings: 6

Ingredients:

Black pepper.

½ cup extra virgin olive oil

1 bunch roughly chopped basil.

2 cubed baguettes

3 tbsps. balsamic vinegar

1 minced garlic clove

1 chopped red onion.

2 pints halved colored cherry tomatoes

1 chopped cucumber.

Salt

Instructions:

1. In a bowl, mix bread cubes with half of the oil and toss to coat.
2. Heat up a pan over medium high heat; add bread; stir, toast for 10 minutes, take off heat; drain and leave aside for now.
3. In a bowl, mix vinegar with salt, pepper and the rest of the oil and whisk very well.
4. In a salad bowl mix cucumber with tomatoes, onion, garlic and bread.
5. Add vinegar dressing, toss to coat, sprinkle basil, add more salt and pepper if needed, toss to coat and serve

Nutritional Info: Calories: 90, Fat: 0g, Carbs: 2g, Protein: 4g

---

Keto Brussels Sprouts And Bacon

Prep time: 10 minutes, Cook time: 30 minutes, Servings: 4

Ingredients:

Salt

1 lb. trimmed and halved Brussels sprouts

Black pepper.

¼ tsp. ground cumin

8 chopped bacon strips.

¼ tsp. crushed red pepper.

2 tbsps. extra virgin olive oil

Instructions:

1. In a bowl, mix Brussels sprouts with salt, pepper, cumin, red pepper and oil and toss to coat.
2. Spread Brussels sprouts on a lined baking sheet, introduce in the oven at 375 degrees F and bake for 30 minutes
3. Meanwhile; heat up a pan over medium heat; add bacon pieces and cook them until they become crispy.
4. Divide baked Brussels sprouts on plates, top with bacon and serve as a side dish right away.

Nutritional Info: Calories: 256, Fat: 20g, Carbs: 5g, Protein: 15g

Portobello Mushrooms

Prep time: 15 minutes, Cook time: 5 minutes, Servings: 4

Ingredients:

½ tsp. dried rosemary

Black pepper.

12 oz. sliced Portobello mushrooms

2 tbsps. balsamic vinegar

2 tbsps. olive oil

½ tsp. dried tarragon

½ tsp. thyme

½ tsp. dried basil

Salt

Instructions:

1. In a bowl, mix oil with vinegar, salt, pepper, rosemary, tarragon, basil and thyme and whisk well.
2. Add mushroom slices, toss to coat well, place them on your preheated grill over medium high heat; cook for 5 minutes on both sides and serve as a keto side dish.

Nutritional Info: Calories: 80, Fat: 4g, Carbs: 2g, Protein: 4g

Easy Okra and Tomatoes

Prep time: 15 minutes, Cook time: 5 minutes, Servings: 6

Ingredients:

2 chopped celery stalks.

Black pepper

1 lb. sliced okra

2 chopped bacon slices.

1 chopped small green bell peppers.

1 chopped yellow onion.

14 oz. chopped canned stewed tomatoes.

Salt

Instructions:

1. Heat up a pan over medium high heat; add bacon; stir, brown for a few minutes, transfer to paper towels and leave aside for now.
2. Heat up the pan again over medium heat; add okra, bell pepper, onion and celery; stir and cook for 2 minutes
3. Add tomatoes, salt and pepper; stir and cook for 3 minutes
4. Divide on plates, garnish with crispy bacon and serve

Nutritional Info: Calories: 100, Fat: 2g, Carbs: 2g, Protein: 6g

Special Broccoli with Lemon Almond Butter

Prep time: 12 minutes, Cook time: 8 minutes, Servings: 4

Ingredients:

¼ cup melted coconut butter

¼ cup blanched almonds

Black pepper.

2 tbsps. lemon juice

1 separated broccoli head

1 tsp. lemon zest

Salt

Instructions:

1. Put water in a pot, add salt and bring to a boil over medium high heat.
2. Place broccoli florets in a steamer basket, place into the pot, cover and steam for 8 minutes
3. Drain and transfer to a bowl.
4. Heat up a pan with the coconut butter over medium heat; add lemon juice, lemon zest and almonds; stir and take off heat.
5. Add broccoli, toss to coat, divide between plates and serve as a Ketogenic side dish.

Nutritional Info: Calories: 170, Fat: 15g, Carbs: 4g, Protein: 4g

Squash and Cranberries

Prep time: 12 minutes, Cook time: 28 minutes, Servings: 2

Ingredients:

12 oz. canned coconut milk
1 tsp. cinnamon powder
½ cup cranberries
1 tbsp. coconut oil
2 minced garlic cloves
1 chopped small yellow onion
1 peeled and cubed butternut squash
1 tsp. curry powder

Instructions:

1. Spread squash pieces on a lined baking sheet, place in the oven at 425 °F and bake for 15 minutes.
2. Take squash out of the oven and leave aside for now.
3. Heat up a pan with the oil over medium high heat, add garlic and onion, stir and cook for 5 minutes.
4. Add roasted squash, stir and cook for 3 minutes.
5. Add coconut milk, cranberries, cinnamon and curry powder, stir and cook for 5 minutes more. Divide between plates and serve as a side dish!

Nutritional Info: Calories: 100, Fat: 2g, Carbs: 8g, Protein: 2g

Spicy Sweet Potatoes

Prep time: 10 minutes, Cook time: 40 minutes, Servings: 4

Ingredients:

2 tbsps. melted coconut oil
2 tsps. nutmeg
Cayenne pepper
4 peeled and thinly sliced sweet potatoes

Instructions:

1. In a bowl; mix sweet potato slices with nutmeg, cayenne and oil and toss to coat really well.
2. Spread these on a lined baking sheet, place in the oven at 350 °F and bake for 25 minutes.
3. Take potatoes out of the oven, flip them, put them back into the oven and bake for 15 minutes more. Serve as a tasty side dish!

Nutritional Info: Calories: 140, Fat: 3g, Carbs: 4g, Protein: 10g

Chard Side Dish

Prep time: 10 minutes, Cook time: 11 minutes, Servings: 2

Ingredients:

¼ tsp. sea salt
½ cup chopped cashews
Black pepper
1 tbsp. coconut oil
1 bunch sliced chard

Instructions:

1. Heat up a pan with the oil over medium heat, add chard and cashews, stir and cook for 10 minutes.
2. Add a pinch of salt and pepper to the taste, stir; cook for 1 minute more, take off heat, transfer to plates and serve as a side dish.

Nutritional Info: Calories: 60, Fat: 0.3g, Carbs: 2g, Protein: 2g

Basil Zucchini Spaghetti

Prep time: 20 minutes, Cook time: 1 hour, Servings: 4

Ingredients:

2 minced garlic cloves
¼ tsp. sea salt
1/3 cup bacon grease
¼ cup chopped basil
Black pepper
4 sliced zucchinis
½ cup chopped walnuts

Instructions:

1. In a bowl; mix zucchini spaghetti with a pinch of salt and pepper, toss to coat, leave aside for 1 hour, drain well, rinse, drain again and put in a bowl.
2. Heat up a pan with the bacon grease over medium high heat, add zucchini spaghetti and garlic, stir and cook for 5 minutes.
3. Add basil and walnuts and some black pepper, stir and cook for 3 minutes more. Divide between plates and serve.

Nutritional Info: Calories: 240, Fat: 1g, Carbs: 7g, Protein: 13g

Turnips and Sauce

Prep time: 11 minutes, Cook time: 14 minutes, Servings: 4

Ingredients:

1 tbsp. chopped rosemary
Orange zest
3 tbsps. coconut oil
¼ tsp. sea salt
1 tbsp. lemon juice
16 oz. thinly sliced turnips
Black pepper

Instructions:

1. Heat up a pan with the oil over medium high heat, add turnips, stir and cook for 4 minutes.
2. Add lemon juice, a pinch of salt, black pepper and rosemary, stir and cook for 10 minutes more. Take off heat, add orange zest, stir; divide between plates and serve.

Nutritional Info: Calories: 90, Fat: 1g, Carbs: 3g, Protein: 4g

Eggplant and Mushrooms

Prep time: 20 minutes, Cook time: 23 minutes, Servings: 4

Ingredients:

3 chopped celery stalks
2 lbs. chopped oyster mushrooms
Black pepper
1 tbsp. dried savory
1 tbsp. chopped parsley
1 chopped yellow onion
3 tbsps. coconut oil
6 oz. chopped bacon
2 cubed eggplants
¼ tsp. sea salt

Instructions:

1. Put eggplant pieces in a bowl; add a pinch of salt and black pepper, toss a bit, leave aside for 1 hour, drain well and leave aside in a bowl.
2. Heat up a pan with the oil over medium high heat, add onion, stir and cook for 4 minutes.
3. Add bacon, stir and cook for 4 more minutes.
4. Add eggplant pieces, mushrooms, celery, savory and black pepper to the taste, stir and cook for 15 minutes. Add parsley, stir again, cook for a couple more minutes, divide between plates and serve.

Nutritional Info: Calories: 200, Fat: 3g, Carbs: 6g, Protein: 9g

Chapter 11 Desserts

Fruit Bowls

Prep time: 10 minutes, Cook time: 2 hours, Servings: 10
Ingredients:
1 tsp. ginger powder
1 tsp. lemon juice
1 tsp. grated lemon zest
2 cups sour apples
¼ cup erythritol
3 cored and chopped pears
Instructions:

1. Combine pears with apples, lemon juice and zest, erythritol and ginger in your Crockpot.
2. Cover to cook for 2 hours on High.
3. Divide between plates and serve cold.
4. Enjoy.
Nutritional Info: Calories: 140, Fat 3g, Carbs: 6g, Protein: 6g

Sweet Strawberry Cream

Prep time: 10 minutes, Cook time: 3 hours, Servings: 15
Ingredients:
½ cup stevia
1 tsp. vanilla extract
2 tbsps. lemon juice
1 tsp. cinnamon powder
2 lbs. chopped strawberries
Instructions:
1. Combine lemon juice, stevia, strawberries, vanilla and cinnamon in your Crockpot.

2. Cover to cook for 3 hours on Low.
3. Blend the mixture in your immersion blender.
4. Divide the mixture and refrigerate till serving.
5. Enjoy.
Nutritional Info: Calories: 100, Fat: 0g, Carbs: 2g, Protein: 2g

Sour Apple Stew

Prep time: 10 minutes, Cook time: 4 hours, Servings: 6
Ingredients:
3 tbsps. stevia
1 tbsp. cinnamon powder
¾ cup melted cashew butter
Cooking spray
6 cored, peeled and sliced apples
1 ½ cups almond flour
Instructions:

1. Rub the cooking pot with cooking spray and add stevia, apples, flour, coconut butter and cinnamon and stir gently.
2. Cover to cook for 4 hours and divide between bowls.
3. Serve cold and enjoy.
Nutritional Info: Calories: 180, Fat: 5g, Carbs: 8g, Protein: 4g

Berry Pie

Prep time: 10 minutes, Cook time: 2 hours, Servings: 6
Ingredients:
3 tbsps. melted coconut oil
1 tsp. grated lemon zest
1 lb. fresh blackberries
1/3 cup coconut milk
¾ cup water
1 lb. fresh blueberries
½ cup arrowroot powder

1 cup almond flour
1 tsp. baking powder
1 whisked egg
5 tbsps. stevia
Instructions:
1. Mix blackberries, blueberries, half of the almond flour, water and stevia in the Crockpot.

2. Cover and cook on High for 1 hour.
3. In the meantime, combine the remaining flour with arrowroot and baking powder and stir them in a mixing bowl.
4. Stir in lemon zest, oil, milk and egg then drop spoonful of this mix over the berries from the Crockpot.

5. Cover to cook on High for one more hour.
6. Set the pie aside to cool.
7. Divide into dessert bowls and serve.
8. Enjoy!

Nutritional Info: Calories: 240, Fat: 4g, Carbs: 6g, Protein: 6g

Simple Lemon Pudding

Prep time: 10 minutes, Cook time: 5 hours, Servings: 4
Ingredients:
3 tbsps. melted coconut oil
1 tsp. baking powder
¾ cup lemon juice
Cooking spray
¾ cup water
½ cup almond milk
1 cup almond flour
1/3 cup erythritol
½ cup chopped pecans
½ cup grated lemon peel
½ tsp. ground cinnamon
Instructions:
1. Stir together half of erythritol, flour, cinnamon and baking powder in a mixing bowl.

2. Stir in pecans, 2 tablespoons oil and almond milk.
3. Grease the Crock pot with cooking spray and pour in the mixture.
4. Heat up a small pan over medium-high heat and add lemon juice, water, lemon peel, the remaining erythritol and the remaining oil.
5. Stir and bring to a simmer and then pour in the crockpot.
6. Cover to cook on Low for 5 hours.
7. Divide to serve into dessert bowls.
8. Enjoy.

Nutritional Info: Calories: 182, Fat 3g, Carbs: 8g, Protein: 6g

Maple Pecans

Prep time: 10 minutes, Cook time: 1 hour, Servings: 3
Ingredients:
1 tbsp. coconut oil
¼ cup sugar-free maple syrup
2 tsps. vanilla extract
3 cups pecans
Instructions:
1. Put the pecans in the Crockpot and add sugar-free maple syrup, oil and vanilla extract.

2. Toss to coat and cook on High for 1 hour.
3. Divide into cups before serving.
4. Enjoy!

Nutritional Info: Calories: 200, Fat: 2g, Carbs: 4g, Protein: 7g

Plum and Cinnamon Mousse

Prep time: 10 minutes, Cook time: 2 hours, Servings: 20
Ingredients:
1 cup water
1 tsp. cinnamon powder
2 tbsps. erythritol
4 lbs. pitted and wedged plums
Instructions:
1. In your Crockpot, add cinnamon, erythritol and water.

2. Cover the Crockpot to cook on Low for 2 hours.
3. Divide into bowls and serve while cold.
4. Enjoy!

Nutritional Info: Calories: 103, Fat: 0g, Carbs: 2g, Protein: 4g

Stuffed Apples

Prep time: 10 minutes, Cook time: 2 hours, Servings: 4

Ingredients:

¼ tsp. ground nutmeg
1 tbsp. lemon juice
½ tsp. cinnamon powder
4 sliced and cored apples
¼ cup chopped pecans
2 tsps. grated lemon zest
1 tbsp. coconut oil
½ cup water
2 tbsps. stevia
1 tsp. ginger powder
4 figs

Instructions:

1. In a mixing bowl, combine pecans, ginger, lemon juice, oil, cinnamon, nutmeg, lemon zest, stevia and figs.
2. Whisk the mixture really well and stuff the apples with the mix.
3. Add water to the Crockpot and arrange apples in it.
4. Cover the pot to cook on High for 2 hours.
5. Divide in dessert plates before serving.
6. Enjoy.

Nutritional Info: Calories: 200, Fat: 1g, Carbs: 4g, Protein: 7g

Chocolate Cake

Prep time: 10 minutes, Cook time: 3 hours, Servings: 10

Ingredients:

1 ½ tsps. baking powder
1/3 cup keto chocolate chips
2/3 cup almond milk
1 cup almond flour
3 tbsps. swerve
Cooking spray
¾ tsp. vanilla extract
3 eggs
4 tbsps. melted coconut oil
½ cup cocoa powder

Instructions:

1. Set up a medium bowl and combine swerve with almond flour, almond milk, baking powder, cocoa powder, vanilla extract, chocolate chips, eggs and oil.
2. Whisk well and pour the mixture into the greased crockpot to cook on Low for 3 hours.
3. Set the cake aside to cool, slice and serve.
4. Enjoy.

Nutritional Info: Calories: 200, Fat: 12g, Carbs: 8g, Protein: 6g

Stewed Pears

Prep time: 10 minutes, Cook time: 4 hours, Servings: 4

Ingredients:

1 cinnamon stick
5 cardamom pods
1-inch grated ginger
4 peeled, chopped and cored pears
½ cup sugar-free maple syrup
2 cups water

Instructions:

1. Put the pears in the Crockpot and add water, cardamom pods, ginger, cinnamon, sugar-free maple syrup and ginger.
2. Cover to cook on Low for 4 hours.
3. Divide between bowls to serve topped with sauce.
4. Enjoy!

Nutritional Info: Calories: 200, Fat: 4g, Carbs: 3g, Protein: 4g

Passion Fruit Dessert Cream

Prep time: 10 minutes, Cook time: 4 hours, Servings: 6

Ingredients:

2 oz. melted coconut oil
3 eggs
1 cup water
½ cup almond flour
3 ½ oz. sugar-free maple syrup
3 ½ oz. coconut milk
½ tsp. baking powder
4 deseeded passion fruits

Instructions:

1. In your Crockpot, mix water with passion fruits pulp and seeds, sugar-free maple syrup, eggs, coconut, almond milk, almond flour and baking powder, whisk really well, cover and cook on Low for 4 hours.
2. Whisk really well, divide between bowls and serve cold.
3. Enjoy!

Nutritional Info: Calories: 230, Fat 12g, Carbs: 7g, Protein: 8g

Grapefruit and Mint Sauce

Prep time: 10 minutes, Cook time: 4 hours, Servings: 3

Ingredients:

2 peeled and chopped grapefruits
1 cup water
½ cup chopped mint
½ cup sugar-free maple syrup

Instructions:

1. In your Crockpot, mix grapefruit with water, sugar-free maple syrup, and mint, stir, cover and cook on Low for 4 hours.
2. Divide between bowls and serve cold.
3. Enjoy!

Nutritional Info: Calories: 120, Fat 1g, Carbs: 2g, Protein: 1g

Maple Figs Stew

Prep time: 10 minutes, Cook time: 1 hour, Servings: 4

Ingredients:

6 halved figs
2 tbsps. coconut butter
1 cup chopped almonds
¼ cup sugar-free maple syrup

Instructions:

1. In your Crockpot, mix coconut butter with sugar-free maple syrup, whisk well, add figs and almonds, toss, cover and cook on Low for 1 hour.
2. Divide between bowls and serve right away.
3. Enjoy!

Nutritional Info: Calories: 170, Fat: 6g, Carbs: 6g, Protein: 8g

Avocado Cake

Prep time: 10 minutes, Cook time: 4 hours, Servings: 6

Ingredients:

3 tbsps. avocado oil
2 tsps. baking powder
1 cup stoned and chopped avocados
4 tbsps. erythritol
3 eggs
¼ cup slice almonds
½ cup cocoa powder
1/8 tsp. almond extract
4 tbsps. coconut flour

Instructions:

1. In a bowl, mix almond extract with avocado, flour, cocoa, erythritol, oil, eggs, baking powder and almonds, whisk well, transfer to your Crockpot after you've greased it with cooking spray, cover and cook on Low for 4 hours.
2. Leave the cake to cool down, slice and serve.
3. Enjoy!

Nutritional Info: Calories: 164, Fat: 4g, Carbs: 8g, Protein: 4g

Ricotta and Dates Cake

Prep time: 30 minutes, Cook time: 4 hours, Servings: 6

Ingredients:

½ tsp. vanilla extract

2 oz.-soaked dates

Zest of grated ½ lemon

Cooking spray

2 tbsps. erythritol

1 lb. ricotta

4 eggs

Instructions:

1. In a bowl, whisk ricotta until it softens. Add eggs, erythritol, dates, vanilla and lemon zest, whisk well, pour into your Crockpot after you've greased it with cooking spray, cover and cook on Low for 4 hours. Leave the cake to cool down, slice and serve.
2. Enjoy!

Nutritional Info: Calories: 200, Fat 6g, Carbs: 8g, Protein: 10g

Chocolate Parfait

Prep time: 2 hours, Cook time: 0 minutes, Servings: 4

Ingredients:

½ tsp. vanilla extract

1 cup almond milk

¼ tsp. salt

2 tbsps. cocoa powder

1 tbsp. chia seeds

Instructions:

1. In a bowl, mix cocoa powder, almond milk, vanilla extract and chia seeds and stir well until they blend.
2. Transfer to a dessert glass, place in the fridge for 2 hours and then serve.
3. Enjoy!

Nutritional Info: Calories: 180, Fat: 16.8g, Carbs: 7.9g, Protein: 3g

Pomegranate Fudge

Prep time: 2 hours, Cook time: 5 minutes, Servings: 6

Ingredients:

½ cup chopped almonds

¼ cups cocoa butter

1 tsp. vanilla extract

½ cup coconut milk

½ cup pomegranate seeds

¾ cocoa powder

Instructions:

1. Put milk in a saucepan and heat up over medium-low heat.
2. Add cocoa butter, cocoa powder and stir for 5 minutes.
3. Take off heat, add vanilla extract, half of the pomegranate seeds and half the of the nuts and stir.
4. Pour this into a lined baking pan, spread, sprinkle a pinch of salt, the rest of the pomegranate arils and nuts, cover and keep in the fridge for a few hours.
5. Cut, arrange on a platter and serve.
6. Enjoy!

Nutritional Info: Calories: 215, Fat 19.2g, Carbs: 12.8g, Protein: 4.3g

Fruit Jelly

Prep time: 10 minutes, Cook time: 0 minutes, Servings: 2

Ingredients:

1 lbs. grapefruit jelly

½ lb. coconut cream

Fresh berries

Roughly chopped nuts

Instructions:

1. In a food processor, combine grapefruit jelly with coconut cream and blend well.
2. Add berries and nuts, toss gently, transfer to dessert cups and serve right away!
3. Enjoy!

Nutritional Info: Calories: 558, Fat 36.6g, Carbs 55.3g, Protein 7.8g

Avocado pops

Prep time: 5 minutes, Cook time: 0 minutes, Servings: 6

Ingredients:

14 oz. coconut milk

2 pitted avocados

2 frozen bananas

1 cup nut milk

Juice of 1 lime

Granola

Instructions:

1. Remove the coconut solids from the coconut milk can and place in the blender. Blend until creamy. Reserve the coconut water in the can.

2. Add the avocados, bananas, nut milk, coconut water, and lime juice.
3. Blend until creamy.
4. Pour into 4 to 6 ice pop molds filling each three-quarters full.
5. Sprinkle granola on the top
6. Cover and insert ice pop sticks.
7. Freeze overnight and serve.

Nutritional Info: Calories: 102, Fat: 6.0g, Carbs: 13.9g, Protein: 0.71g

Strawberry bliss bites

Prep time: 10 minutes, Cook time: 0 minutes, servings: 7

Ingredients:

1 tsp. vanilla extract

2 cups raw cashews

1 cup pitted dates

½ cup unsweetened shredded coconut

1 cup freeze-dried strawberries

½ cup oats

1 tsp. salt

Instructions:

1. In a food processor or high-powered blender, combine the cashews, dates, strawberries, coconut, oats, vanilla, and salt.

2. Pulse until the mixture forms into a sticky mass.
3. Transfer to a large bowl, and use clean hands to tightly form 14 bite-size balls.
4. Roll the balls in the remaining oats to coat.
5. Store in the refrigerator for up to 2 weeks or for 2 months in the freezer.

Nutritional Info: Calories: 55, Fat: 3g, Carbs: 5g, Protein: 1 g

Chapter 12 Sauces, Condiments and Dressings

Almond Oat Milk

Prep time: 5 minutes, Cook time: 0 minutes, Servings: 6

Ingredients:
6 pitted dates
1 tsp. vanilla extract
1 cup rolled oats
7 cups water
1 cup raw almonds

Instructions:
1. Set up a large container with almonds and oats, add enough water.
2. Cover the container and refrigerate to soak overnight.
3. Thoroughly drain and rinse the almonds and oats.
4. In a blender, add the soaked mixture, water, vanilla and dates.
5. Let the mixture blend for 2 minutes until well combined.
6. Put a cheesecloth over a large bowl and transfer the blended mixture into it.
7. Squeeze the mixture in the cheesecloth to drain the liquid in the bowl.
8. Set in container to refrigerate for one week.

Nutritional Info: Calories: 120, Fat: 5 g, Carbs: 16g, Protein: 2 g

Spicy avocado dressing

Prep time: 5 minutes, cook time: 0 minutes, Servings: 10

Ingredients:
4 garlic cloves
Juice of 1 lime
¼ cup avocado oil
½ peeled and pitted avocado
Water
1 cup chopped fresh cilantro
2 chopped scallions
Salt
1 jalapeño pepper
1 cup chopped fresh parsley

Instructions:
1. Combine avocado, cilantro, scallions, salt, garlic, jalapeño, lime juice, parsley and avocado oil in a blender in a blender.
2. Blend to the desired consistency adding water where necessary.
3. Refrigerate for up to one week.

Nutritional Info: Calories: 15, Fat: 1g, Carbs: 2g, Protein: 0 g

Green Caesar Dressing

Prep time: 5 minutes, Cook time: 0 minutes, Servings: 10

Ingredients:
Water
½ cup raw almonds
¼ cup chopped fresh parsley
½ tsp. salt
7 garlic cloves
1 shallot
½ cup avocado oil
Juice of 1 lemon
½ tsp. hemp seeds
½ tsp. freshly ground black pepper
3 chopped scallions
¼ cup white balsamic vinegar

Instructions:
1. In a blender, combine avocado oil, hemp seeds, shallot, scallions, lemon juice, garlic, hemp seeds, parsley, vinegar and seasonings.
2. Blend to the desired consistency adding water where necessary.
3. Refrigerate for one week.

Nutritional Info: Calories: 41, Fat: 3 g, Carbs: 2 g, Protein: 2g

Creamy Balsamic Dressing

Prep time: 5 minutes, cook time: 0 minutes, Servings: 10

Ingredients:

Water
1 tbsp. fresh rosemary
½ cup walnut oil
2 garlic cloves
Salt
½ cup balsamic vinegar
Freshly ground black pepper
2 tbsps. tahini

Instructions:

1. Combine rosemary, walnut oil, tahini, vinegar and garlic in a blender.
2. Blend till the dressing is thick and creamy.
3. Add water to the blender for a thinner consistency.
4. Use immediately or refrigerate for one week.
5. Shake well before using.

Nutritional Info: Calories: 155, Fat: 5 g, Carbs: 3 g, Protein: 0 g

Peppery Pesto

Prep time: 5 minutes, Cook time: 0 minutes, Servings: 4

Ingredients:

½ cup arugula
¼ tsp. freshly ground black pepper
½ cup raw cashews
¼ cup extra-virgin olive oil
2 peeled garlic cloves
¼ tsp. salt
½ cup fresh basil
1 pitted and peeled avocado
2 tbsps. freshly squeezed lemon juice

Instructions:

1. In a blender, combine avocado, basil, arugula, lemon juice, olive oil, garlic, cashews and seasonings.
2. Let the mixture blend for 5 minutes to form a loose paste.
3. Consume immediately or refrigerate for about 6 days.

Nutritional Info: Calories: 104, Fat: 10g, Carbs: 3g, Protein: 2g

Spicy "Cheesy" Cashew Sauce

Prep time: 5 minutes, Cook time: 0 minutes, Servings: 8

Ingredients:

2 tsps. onion flakes
1 tsp. chipotle pepper flakes
1 cup raw cashews
2 garlic cloves
1 tsp. ground turmeric
¼ cup nutritional yeast
Salt
½ cup water

Instructions:

1. In a large jar, add cashews and cover with cold water.
2. Refrigerate for 12 to 24 hours.
3. Rinse and drain the cashews.
4. Transfer the cashews into a blender and add turmeric, nutritional yeast, water, garlic, pepper flakes and onion flakes.
5. Refrigerate for up to one week.

Nutritional Info: Calories: 90, Fat: 7g, Carbs: 5g, Protein: 3g

Homemade Gravy

Prep time: 10 minutes, Cook time: 2 minutes, Servings: 1

Ingredients:

2 tbsps. cooking fat
Pepper
1 cup chicken broth
Salt
1 tbsp. whole-wheat flour

Instructions:

1. Heat the fat using medium to low heat and whisk in the flour.
2. Cook one to two minutes to make a roux.
3. Whisk the mixture well and bring to a gentle boil. Whisk to eliminate the lumps.

Nutritional Info: Calories: 25, Fat: 1g, Carbs: 4.5g, Protein: 1.0g

Conclusion

I am happy that you have read the book until the end. The next step is to decide if the Whole 30 diet plan is the best option for you to go with or not. The Whole 30 diet can be difficult. There are a lot of rules in place, and if you mess up even once during the 30 days, you have to restart and go back to the starting position. But for those who can make it through the full 30 days, it can be a life-changing experience, one that can be good for all aspects of your health.

When you are ready to work on improving your health and eating foods that are wholesome and good for you, make sure to check out this guidebook to learn more about the Whole 30 diet, and how you can find the tasty and delicious recipes you are looking for.

Thank you, and have fun!

Made in the USA
San Bernardino, CA
24 January 2020